300 CLASSIC RECIPES INDIAN

AUTHENTIC DISHES FROM KEBABS, PILAU RICE AND BIRYANI TO
KORMA, BALTI AND TANDOORI, WITH OVER 300 PHOTOGRAPHS

SHEHZAD HUSAIN AND RAFI FERNANDEZ

southwater

This edition is published by Southwater,
an imprint of Anness Publishing Ltd,
Hermes House, 88–89 Blackfriars Road,
London SE1 8HA
tel. 020 7401 2077; fax 020 7633 9499

www.southwaterbooks.com; www.annesspublishing.com

If you like the images in this book and would like to investigate
using them for publishing, promotions or advertising, please visit
our website www.practicalpictures.com for more information.

UK agent: The Manning Partnership Ltd;
tel. 01225 478444; fax 01225 478440;
sales@manning-partnership.co.uk
UK distributor: Book Trade Services; tel. 0116 2759086;
fax 0116 2759090; uksales@booktradeservices.com;
exportsales@booktradeservices.com
North American agent/distributor: National Book Network;
tel. 301 459 3366; fax 301 429 5746;
www.nbnbooks.com
Australian agent/distributor: Pan Macmillan Australia;
tel. 1300 135 113; fax 1300 135 103;
customer.service@macmillan.com.au
New Zealand agent/distributor: David Bateman Ltd;
tel. (09) 415 7664; fax (09) 415 8892

Publisher: Joanna Lorenz
Senior Editor: Felicity Forster
Additional recipes: Mridula Baljekar, Becky Johnson,
    Manisha Kanani, Sallie Morris and Deh-Ta Hsiung
Cover Design: Nigel Partridge
Production Controller: Christine Ni

© Anness Publishing Ltd 2010

Previously published as part of a larger volume,
500 Indian Recipes

Main front cover image shows Chicken Biryani with Almonds –
for recipe, see page 48.

ETHICAL TRADING POLICY
At Anness Publishing we believe that business should be
conducted in an ethical and ecologically sustainable way,
with respect for the environment and a proper regard to
the replacement of the natural resources we employ.

As a publisher, we use a lot of wood pulp to make high-quality
paper for printing, and that wood commonly comes from spruce
trees. We are therefore currently growing more than 750,000 trees
in three Scottish forest plantations: Berrymoss (130 hectares/
320 acres), West Touxhill (125 hectares/305 acres) and Deveron
Forest (75 hectares/185 acres). The forests we manage contain
more than 3.5 times the number of trees employed each year
in making paper for the books we manufacture.

Because of this ongoing ecological investment programme,
you, as our customer, can have the pleasure and reassurance of
knowing that a tree is being cultivated on your behalf to naturally
replace the materials used to make the book you are holding.

Our forestry programme is run in accordance with the UK
Woodland Assurance Scheme (UKWAS) and will be certified
by the internationally recognized Forest Stewardship Council
(FSC). The FSC is a non-government organization dedicated
to promoting responsible management of the world's forests.
Certification ensures forests are managed in an environmentally
sustainable and socially responsible way. For further information
about this scheme, go to www.annesspublishing.com/trees

PUBLISHER'S NOTES
Bracketed terms are intended for American readers. For all
recipes, quantities are given in both metric and imperial measures
and, where appropriate, in standard cups and spoons. Follow
one set, but not a mixture, because they are not interchangeable.
Standard spoon and cup measures are level.
1 tsp = 5ml, 1 tbsp = 15ml, 1 cup = 250ml/8fl oz.
Australian standard tablespoons are 20ml. Australian readers
should use 3 tsp in place of 1 tbsp for measuring small
quantities of gelatine, flour, salt etc.
Medium (US large) eggs are used unless otherwise stated.

The nutritional analysis given for each recipe is calculated
per portion (i.e. serving or item), unless otherwise stated. If the
recipe gives a range, such as Serves 4–6, then the nutritional
analysis will be for the smaller portion size, i.e. 6 servings.

Although the advice and information in this book are believed
to be accurate and true at the time of going to press, neither
the authors nor the publisher can accept any legal responsibility
or liability for any errors or omissions that may be made nor
for any inaccuracies nor for any harm or injury that comes
about from following instructions or advice in this book.

300 CLASSIC INDIAN

Please return on or before the latest date above.
You can renew online at www.kent.gov.uk/libs
or by phone 08458 247 200

CUSTOMER SERVICE EXCELLENCE   **Libraries & Archives**

Kent
County
Council

Contents

Introduction

India is home to one of the most popularly enjoyed and exciting cuisines in the world. Indian food is epitomized by brightly coloured vegetables in richly flavoured sauces, tender meat and poultry, fresh fish, nutty-flavoured beans and lentils, and, of course, the array of spices that warm the body and soothe the spirit.

Many of us live in towns and cities where restaurants that specialize in Indian food flourish, and food enthusiasts have a wealth of choice when it comes to adventurous cooking using spices and flavourings. If you enjoy creating Indian food, look no further than this volume for a wonderful selection of the most exciting eating ever. In these pages there are quick-and-easy dishes as well as an imaginative variety of recipes that involve blending aromatic spices and flavourings to achieve a truly authentic taste of the East.

The beauty of Indian cooking is in its variety. Different areas and traditions have developed their own regional specialities, and recipes have been handed down through the generations as various combinations of spices and ingredients have been explored and enjoyed. Although many Indian dishes are fiery with chillies, there are others that are mellow. Balti cuisine, which is Kashmiri cooking from the area that is now north Pakistan, is beautifully aromatic, but does not use chillies excessively, so it is not too hot. Many of the most familiar regional dishes we enjoy come from northern India. These include koftas, mild kormas and tandoori recipes. The most fiery spice blends, however, such as the famous vindaloo, come from southern India, as well as an abundance of vegetarian dishes using lentils, beans and chickpeas. Fragrant jasmine rice is another speciality of southern India. Coconuts are favourite ingredients of eastern India, and are used for making both sweet and savoury dishes, including deliciously creamy sauces. From western India there are recipes using dairy products, including yogurt and buttermilk, and the meals are also accompanied by all kinds of unusual

pickles. As many Indian people are vegetarian, there is no shortage of delectable meat-free recipes to choose from, which utilize nuts, beans, peas and lentils, making substantial and nutritious meals that are guaranteed to appeal to vegetarians and meat-eaters alike. Cook's tips throughout the book explain some of the more unusual ingredients and how they are used.

All of these fabulous types of dishes are brought together here in this collection of 300 recipes, with their diverse cooking styles and creative combinations of herbs, spices and flavourings. The book offers all the classics the enthusiast could ask for, from soups and appetizers to fish and shellfish dishes, meat, poultry, vegetable and Balti dishes. It also includes a variety

of side dishes, salads, relishes and chutneys, as well as breads, desserts and drinks – in fact everything you need to create the perfect meal, whether it be a quick evening supper or a dinner party for friends and family.

Many recipes are quick to prepare with the simplest of spice combinations, whereas others call for a more varied store of spices and flavourings, including some lesser-known ingredients, such as mango powder (amchur) and compressed tamarind. Most of these special ingredients are available from supermarkets and markets, and sometimes even health-food stores. Fresh herbs such as coriander (cilantro) are sold cheaply in large bunches in markets, so you will have plenty to use to flavour your dishes. You will also be able to buy fresh fenugreek and, occasionally, fresh curry leaves, which taste superior to the dried ones that are more readily available. It's well worth visiting a specialist store or market if you have one nearby – large bags of whole spices are often sold cheaply, and these are ideal if you enjoy preparing spicy food regularly. For the best flavour, always grind your spices just before you use them. You will immediately notice the strength of their aroma compared to spices that are bought ready ground. However, most of us want to take advantage of making quick spicy meals without a fuss and long periods of preparation, so ground spices might therefore be the best bet for busy people. Always buy ground spices in small quantities from a reputable supplier who has a quick turnover of stock, because once a spice has been ground it begins to lose its aroma and flavour. So don't be tempted to buy large quantities of ground spices, as you will lose out on taste.

To add an authentic touch to your Indian meal, try cooking and serving it in a karahi. This piece of equipment is a little like a wok but is more rounded in shape and is made of heavier metal. Traditionally the karahi is made of cast iron, although a variety of metals are now used. Karahis are available in various sizes, including small ones for cooking single portions. Before you buy a karahi, however, check whether you can use it on your particular type of stove. You can use a wok or large frying pan in place of a karahi for cooking most types of Indian dish. Another piece of equipment that is useful for cooking Indian meals is a heat diffuser. This is placed between the pan and the heat source, its function being to reduce the heat so that curries can simmer at the lowest possible temperature.

Once you have sourced your Indian ingredients and chosen your cooking vessel, you are ready to create the tantalizing dishes contained in this book. Whether it's a speedy weekday meal or a special dinner, your family and friends are in for a gastronomic treat.

Tomato & Coriander Soup

Although soups are not often eaten in India or Pakistan, tomato soup bucks the trend and is very popular. This is excellent on a cold winter's day.

Serves 4

675g/1½lb tomatoes, peeled and chopped
15ml/1 tbsp oil
1 bay leaf
4 spring onions (scallions), chopped
5ml/1 tsp salt
2.5ml/½ tsp crushed garlic
5ml/1 tsp crushed black peppercorns
30ml/2 tbsp chopped fresh coriander (cilantro)
750ml/1¼ pints/3 cups water
15ml/1 tbsp cornflour (cornstarch)
30ml/2 tbsp single (light) cream, to garnish (optional)

1 To peel the tomatoes, plunge them in very hot water, leave for 30 seconds, then take them out. The skin should now peel off easily. If not, put the tomatoes back in the water for a little longer. Once they have been peeled, roughly chop the tomatoes.

2 In a medium, heavy pan, heat the oil and fry the tomatoes, bay leaf and spring onions for a few minutes until soft.

3 Gradually add the salt, garlic, peppercorns and coriander. Pour in the water. Stir, then simmer gently over a low heat for 15–20 minutes.

4 Meanwhile, dissolve the cornflour in a little cold water to form a thick creamy paste.

5 Remove the soup from the heat and leave to cool slightly for a few minutes. Press through a sieve (strainer), or purée in a blender or food processor.

6 Return the puréed soup to the pan, add the cornflour mixture and stir over a gentle heat for about 3 minutes until thickened.

7 Pour the soup into individual serving dishes and garnish with a swirl of cream, if using. Serve hot.

Energy 76kcal/315kJ; Fat 3.4g; Saturated fat 0.43g; Carbohydrate 10.1g; Fibre 1.9g.

Curried Carrot & Apple Soup

The combination of carrot, curry powder and apple is a highly successful one. Curried fruit is delicious.

Serves 4

10ml/2 tsp sunflower oil
15ml/1 tbsp mild korma curry powder
500g/1¼lb carrots, chopped
1 large onion, chopped
1 tart cooking apple, chopped
750ml/1¼ pints/3 cups chicken stock
salt and ground black pepper
plain yogurt and carrot curls, to garnish

1 Heat the oil in a large, heavy pan. Add the curry powder and fry for 2–3 minutes.

2 Add the carrots, onion and cooking apple and stir well until coated with the curry powder. Cover the pan.

3 Cook over low heat for about 15 minutes, shaking the pan occasionally, until soft. Spoon the vegetable mixture into a food processor or blender, then add half the stock and process until the mixture is smooth.

4 Return to the pan and pour in the remaining stock. Bring the soup to the boil and adjust the seasoning before serving in bowls, garnished with a swirl of yogurt and a few curls of raw carrot.

Variations
• *Parsnips also taste great in a curried soup. Simply replace the carrots with chopped parsnips, or, if you prefer, use half the amount of carrots and half of parsnips.*
• *If you don't have any korma powder you can make up your own with 5ml/1 tsp each ground turmeric, cumin, coriander and cinnamon. Add 10ml/2 tsp grated fresh root ginger if you want to give your soup a little more kick.*

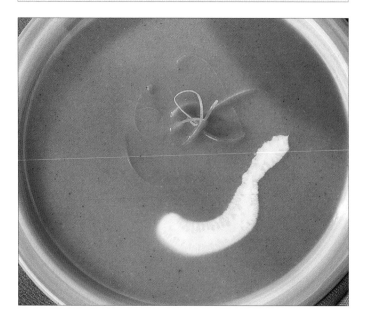

Energy 89kcal/371kJ; Fat 2g; Saturated fat 0.3g; Carbohydrate 17.2g; Fibre 4.3g.

Spiced Cauliflower Soup

Light and tasty, this creamy, mildly spicy vegetable soup is multi-purpose. It makes a wonderful warming first course, an appetizing quick meal and is delicious chilled.

Serves 4–6

I large potato, diced
I small cauliflower, chopped
I onion, chopped
15ml/I tbsp oil
I garlic clove, crushed
15ml/I tbsp grated fresh
   root ginger
10ml/2 tsp ground turmeric
5ml/I tsp cumin seeds
5ml/I tsp black mustard seeds
10ml/2 tsp ground coriander
I litre/1¾ pints/4 cups vegetable
   stock
300ml/½ pint/1¼ cups natural
   (plain) low-fat yogurt
salt and ground black pepper
fresh coriander (cilantro) or
   parsley, to garnish

I Put the potato, cauliflower and onion into a large, heavy pan with the oil and 45ml/3 tbsp water. Heat until hot and bubbling, then stir well, cover the pan and turn the heat down. Continue cooking the mixture for about 10 minutes.

2 Add the garlic, ginger and spices. Stir well, and cook for another 2 minutes, stirring occasionally. Pour in the stock and season well. Bring to the boil, then cover and simmer for about 20 minutes. Purée in a food processor and return to the pan. Stir in the yogurt, adjust the seasoning, and serve garnished with coriander or parsley.

Cook's Tip
A freshly made stock always tastes best. To make home-made vegetable stock, add to 3.5 litres/6 pints/15 cups of water: 2 sliced leeks, 3 chopped celery sticks, I chopped onion, I chopped parsnip, I seeded and chopped yellow (bell) pepper, 3 crushed garlic cloves, fresh herbs and 45ml/3 tbsp light soy sauce. Season, then slowly bring to the boil. Lower the heat and simmer for 30 minutes, stirring from time to time. Leave to cool. Strain, discard the vegetables, and use the stock as indicated in the recipe.

Energy 188kcal/789kJ; Fat 5.4g; Saturated fat 0.77g; Carbohydrate 24.6g; Fibre 3g.

Fiery Hot Yogurt & Chilli Soup

Hot chillies, cool yogurt – this is an unusual and tasty soup with a real punch.

Serves 2–3

450ml/¾ pint/scant 2 cups
   natural (plain) low-fat yogurt,
   beaten
60ml/4 tbsp gram flour
2.5ml/½ tsp chilli powder
2.5ml/½ tsp ground turmeric
2 fresh green chillies, finely
   chopped
30ml/2 tbsp vegetable oil
4 whole dried red chillies
5ml/I tsp cumin seeds
3 or 4 curry leaves
3 garlic cloves, crushed
5cm/2in piece fresh root
   ginger, crushed
salt
fresh coriander (cilantro) leaves,
   chopped, to garnish

I Mix the yogurt, gram flour, chilli powder, turmeric and salt to taste in a bowl. Press the mixture through a strainer into a pan. Add the green chillies and simmer for 10 minutes, stirring occasionally.

2 Heat the vegetable oil in a heavy pan and fry the remaining spices, crushed garlic and fresh ginger until the dried chillies turn black.

3 Pour the oil and the spices over the yogurt soup, cover the pan and leave to rest for 5 minutes off the heat. Mix well and gently reheat for a further 5 minutes. Ladle into warmed soup bowls and serve hot, garnished with the coriander leaves.

Cook's Tips
• *For a lower-fat version drain off some of the oil before adding it to the yogurt. Low-fat yogurt makes this a healthy soup.*
• *Adjust the amount of chilli according to how hot you want the soup to be.*

Energy 321kcal/1344kJ; Fat 13.7g; Saturated fat 2.5g; Carbohydrate 33.8g; Fibre 1.5g.

Lentil Soup

This is a simple, mildly spiced lentil soup, which is a good accompaniment to heavily spiced meat dishes.

Serves 4–6
50g/¹/₂oz/1 tbsp ghee
1 large onion, finely chopped
2 garlic cloves, crushed
1 fresh green chilli, chopped
2.5ml/¹/₂ tsp turmeric
75g/3oz/¹/₃ cup split red lentils (masoor dhal)
250ml/8fl oz/1 cup water
400g/14oz canned tomatoes, chopped
2.5ml/¹/₂ tsp sugar
lemon juice, to taste
200g/7oz/1³/₄ cups plain boiled rice or 2 boiled potatoes (optional)
salt
fresh coriander (cilantro), chopped, to garnish (optional)

1 Heat the ghee in a large pan and fry the onion, garlic, chilli and turmeric until the onion is translucent.

2 Add the lentils and water, and bring to the boil. Reduce the heat, cover and cook until all the water is absorbed.

3 Mash the lentils with the back of a wooden spoon until you have a smooth paste. Add salt to taste and mix well.

4 Add the tomatoes, sugar and lemon, and reheat the soup. To provide extra texture, fold in the plain boiled rice or potatoes cut into small cubes. Garnish with coriander, if you like, and serve hot.

Cook's Tips
• When using lentils, first rinse in cold water and pick over to remove any small stones or loose skins.
• Fresh coriander (cilantro) is used in so many Indian dishes it is worth growing some in a window box or in several pots on your kitchen windowsill. If you have a garden you could grow some in a raised well-drained bed, so that you have a good supply.

South Indian Pepper Water

This soothing broth is perfect for winter evenings.

Serves 4–6
30ml/2 tbsp vegetable oil
2.5ml/¹/₂ tsp black pepper
5ml/1 tsp cumin seeds
2.5ml/¹/₂ tsp mustard seeds
1.5ml/¹/₄ tsp asafoetida
2.5ml/¹/₂ tsp ground turmeric
2 dried red chillies
4–6 curry leaves
2 garlic cloves, crushed
300ml/¹/₂ pint/1¹/₄ cups tomato juice
juice of 2 lemons
120ml/4fl oz/¹/₂ cup water
salt
fresh coriander (cilantro), to garnish

Heat the oil in a large pan and fry the pepper, spices, curry leaves and garlic until the chillies are nearly black and the garlic is golden brown. Lower the heat and pour in the tomato juice, lemon juice and water. Bring to the boil then simmer for 10 minutes. Season to taste with salt. Pour into heated bowls, garnish with the chopped coriander if you like, and serve.

Indian Pea Soup

This is a delicate and tasty cream soup.

Serves 6
115g/4oz potato, chopped
75g/3oz onion, chopped
1.2 litres/2 pints/5 cups chicken stock
2cm/³/₄in piece fresh root ginger
2.5ml/¹/₂ tsp ground cumin
75ml/5 tbsp chopped fresh coriander (cilantro)
¹/₂ green chilli
275g/10oz fresh or frozen peas
15ml/1 tbsp lemon juice
150ml/¹/₄ pint/²/₃ cup double (heavy) cream
salt

Put the potato, onion, stock, ginger and cumin in a pan and bring to the boil. Simmer for 30 minutes. Remove the ginger. Add the coriander, chilli, peas and lemon juice, and add salt to taste. Simmer for 2–3 minutes. Purée in a food processor or blender, then reheat. Add the cream and heat through before serving.

Energy 123kcal/520kJ; Fat 3.4g; Saturated fat 2g; Carbohydrate 18.7g; Fibre 2.6g.

Top: Energy 76kcal/315kJ; Fat 3.4g; Saturated fat 0.43g; Carbohydrate 10.1g; Fibre 1.9g.
Above: Energy 180kcal/744kJ; Fat 14.2g; Saturated fat 8.5g; Carbohydrate 9.7g; Fibre 2.5g.

Chicken Mulligatawny

This world-famous broth hails from the days of the British Raj. It is full of flavour and makes a substantial main-course soup.

Serves 4–6

900g/2lb boneless chicken portions, skinned
600ml/1 pint/2½ cups water
6 green cardamom pods
5cm/2in piece cinnamon stick
4–6 curry leaves
15ml/1 tbsp ground coriander
5ml/1 tsp ground cumin
2.5ml/½ tsp ground turmeric
3 garlic cloves, crushed
1 onion, finely chopped
115g/4oz creamed coconut (120ml/4fl oz/½ cup coconut cream)
juice of 2 lemons
deep-fried onions, to garnish

1 Place the chicken portions in a large pan with the water. Bring to the boil, then simmer for about 1 hour, or until the chicken is tender.

2 Skim the surface, then remove the chicken pieces with a slotted spoon and keep warm.

3 Reheat the stock in the pan. Add all the remaining ingredients, except the chicken and deep-fried onions. Simmer for 10–15 minutes, then strain and return the chicken to the soup. Reheat the soup and serve garnished with the deep-fried onions.

Variation
To make a delicious Chicken Mulligatawny Soup with Lentils, cook the chicken portions as step 1. Remove from the stock and keep warm. Now cook 175g/6oz/⅔ cup red lentils in the reserved stock for 30 minutes until tender. Add 115g/4oz diced potato and cook for a further 20 minutes. Add the remaining ingredients and cook as step 3. Cut the chicken into bitesize pieces and add to the strained soup. Serve garnished as before.

Energy 444kcal/1860kJ; Fat 22.3g; Saturated fat 17.7g; Carbohydrate 5g; Fibre 0.5g.

Spicy Chicken & Mushroom Soup

This creamy chicken soup has just enough spice to make it a great winter warmer, but not so much that it overwhelms the flavour of the mushrooms.

Serves 4

225g/8oz boneless chicken, skinned
75g/3oz/6 tbsp ghee or unsalted (sweet) butter
2.5ml/½ tsp crushed garlic
5ml/1 tsp garam masala
5ml/1 tsp crushed black peppercorns
5ml/1 tsp salt
1.5ml/¼ tsp grated nutmeg
1 medium leek, sliced
75g/3oz/1 cup mushrooms, sliced
50g/2oz/⅓ cup corn
300ml/½ pint/1¼ cups water
250ml/8fl oz/1 cup single (light) cream
15ml/1 tbsp chopped fresh coriander (cilantro)
5ml/1 tsp crushed dried red chillies (optional)

1 Cut the chicken pieces into very fine strips.

2 Melt the ghee or butter in a medium pan. Lower the heat slightly and add the garlic and garam masala. Lower the heat even further and add the black peppercorns, salt and nutmeg. Finally, add the chicken pieces, sliced leek, mushrooms and corn, and cook, stirring constantly, for 5–7 minutes, or until the chicken is cooked through.

3 Remove from the heat and leave to cool slightly. Transfer three-quarters of the mixture into a food processor or blender. Add the water and process for about 1 minute.

4 Pour the resulting purée back into the pan and stir with the rest of the mixture. Bring to the boil over a medium heat. Lower the heat and stir in the cream.

5 Add the fresh coriander and taste for seasoning. Serve hot, garnished with the crushed red chillies, if you like.

Energy 342kcal/1417kJ; Fat 28.5g; Saturated fat 17.6g; Carbohydrate 4.8g; Fibre 1g.

Onion Bhajias

A favourite snack in India, bhajias consist of a savoury vegetable mixture in a crisp and spicy batter. They can be served as an appetizer or as a side dish with curries.

Makes 20–25
2 large onions
225g/8oz/2 cups gram flour
2.5ml/½ tsp chilli powder
5ml/1 tsp ground turmeric
5ml/1 tsp baking powder
1.5ml/¼ tsp asafoetida

2.5ml/½ tsp each nigella, fennel, cumin and onion seeds, coarsely crushed
2 fresh green chillies, finely chopped
50g/2oz/2 cups fresh coriander (cilantro), chopped
vegetable oil, for deep-frying
salt

1 Using a sharp knife, slice the onions into thin rounds. Separate the slices and set them aside on a plate.

2 In a bowl mix together the flour, chilli powder, ground turmeric, baking powder and asafoetida. Add salt to taste. Sift the mixture into a large mixing bowl.

3 Add the coarsely crushed seeds, onion slices, green chillies and fresh coriander and toss together well.

4 Add enough cold water to make a paste, then stir in more water to make a thick batter that coats the onions and spices.

5 Heat enough oil in a karahi or wok for deep-frying. Drop spoonfuls of the mixture into the hot oil and fry the bhajias until they are golden brown. Leave enough space to turn the bhajias. Drain well and serve hot.

> **Variation**
> This versatile batter can be used with other vegetables, including okra, cauliflower and broccoli.

Energy 157kcal/650kJ; Fat 12.7g; Saturated fat 1.5g; Carbohydrate 8.2g; Fibre 0.9g.

Vegetable Samosas

A selection of highly spiced vegetables in a pastry casing makes these samosas a delicious snack at any time of the day.

Makes 28
14 sheets of filo pastry, thawed and wrapped in a damp dish towel
oil, for brushing the pastries

For the filling
3 large potatoes, boiled and roughly mashed
75g/3oz/³⁄4 cup frozen peas, thawed
50g/2oz/1⁄3 cup canned corn, drained

5ml/1 tsp ground coriander
5ml/1 tsp ground cumin
5ml/1 tsp dry mango powder (amchur)
1 small onion, finely chopped
2 fresh green chillies, finely chopped
30ml/2 tbsp coriander (cilantro) leaves, chopped
30ml/2 tbsp chopped fresh mint leaves
juice of 1 lemon
salt

1 Preheat the oven to 200°C/400°F/Gas 6. Cut each sheet of filo pastry in half lengthways and fold each piece in half lengthways to give 28 thin strips. Lightly brush with oil.

2 Toss all the filling ingredients together in a large mixing bowl until they are well blended. Adjust the seasoning with salt and lemon juice if necessary.

3 Using one strip of the pastry at a time, place 15ml/1 tbsp of the filling mixture at one end and fold the pastry diagonally over. Continue folding to form a triangle shape. Brush the samosas with oil. Bake for 10–15 minutes, until golden brown.

> **Cook's Tip**
> Work with one or two sheets of filo pastry at a time and keep the rest covered with a damp dish towel to prevent it drying out.

Energy 50kcal/205kJ; Fat 0.78g; Saturated fat 0.1g; Carbohydrate 9.4g; Fibre 0.5g.

Cauliflower Samosas

Throughout the East, these tasty snacks are sold by street vendors, and eaten at any time of day.

Makes about 20
1 packet 25cm/10in square
    spring roll wrappers, thawed
    if frozen
30ml/2 tbsp plain (all-purpose) flour,
    mixed to a paste with water
vegetable oil, for deep-frying
coriander (cilantro) leaves, to
    garnish

For the filling
25g/1oz/2 tbsp ghee or unsalted
    (sweet) butter
1 small onion, finely chopped

1cm/½in piece fresh root ginger,
    chopped
1 garlic clove, crushed
2.5ml/½ tsp chilli powder
1 large potato, about 225g/8oz,
    cooked and finely diced
50g/2oz/½ cup cauliflower
    florets, lightly cooked and
    chopped into small pieces
50g/2oz/½ cup frozen peas,
    thawed
5–10ml/1–2 tsp garam masala
15ml/1 tbsp chopped fresh
    coriander (leaves and stems)
squeeze of lemon juice
salt

1 Heat the ghee or butter in a wok and fry the onion, ginger and garlic for 5 minutes until softened. Add the chilli powder, cook for 1 minute, then stir in the potato, cauliflower and peas. Sprinkle with garam masala and set aside to cool. Stir in the coriander, lemon juice and salt.

2 Cut the spring roll wrappers into three strips. Brush the edges with flour paste. Place a small spoonful of filling about 2cm/¾in in from the edge of one strip. Fold one corner over the filling to make a triangle and continue this folding until the entire strip has been used and a triangular pastry has been formed. Seal any open edges with more flour and water paste, adding more water if the paste is very thick.

3 Heat the oil for deep-frying to 190°C/375°F and fry the samosas until golden and crisp. Drain well on kitchen paper and serve hot garnished with coriander leaves and accompanied by cucumber, carrot and celery matchsticks, if you like.

Energy 105kcal/437kJ; Fat 6.8g; Saturated fat 1.3g; Carbohydrate 10.1g; Fibre 0.6g.

Spicy Toasts

These crunchy toasts make an ideal snack or part of a brunch. They are especially delicious served with grilled tomatoes.

Makes 4
4 eggs
300ml/½ pint/1¼ cups milk
2 fresh green chillies, finely
    chopped

30ml/2 tbsp chopped fresh
    coriander (cilantro)
75g/3oz/¾ cup grated Cheddar
    or mozzarella cheese
2.5ml/½ tsp salt
1.5ml/¼ tsp ground black
    pepper
4 slices bread
corn oil, for frying

1 Break the eggs into a medium bowl and whisk together. Slowly add the milk and whisk again. Add the chillies, coriander, cheese, salt and pepper, and mix well.

2 Cut the bread slices in half diagonally, and soak them, one at a time, in the egg mixture.

3 Heat the oil in a medium frying pan and fry the bread slices over a medium heat, turning them once or twice, until they are golden brown.

4 Drain off any excess oil as you remove the toasts from the pan, and serve immediately.

> **Variations**
> • You can also use these ingredients to make a spicy topping for toasted bread. Toast the sliced and halved bread on one side. Mix 115g/4oz cheese with the flavourings and spread on the untoasted side. Grill (broil) until bubbling and golden.
> • Try garlic and wholegrain mustard in place of the chillies for toasting.
> • Make it a creamy spread for toasting by adding 75g/3oz cubed and steamed butternut squash mashed with the cheese and flavourings.

Energy 267kcal/1118kJ; Fat 4.5g; Saturated fat 6.9g; Carbohydrate 17.8g; Fibre 0.9g

Potato Cakes with Stuffing

Only a few communities in India make these unusual potato cakes known as *petis*. They can also be served as a main meal with a fresh tomato salad.

Makes 8–10
15ml/1 tbsp vegetable oil
1 large onion, finely chopped
2 garlic cloves, finely crushed
5cm/2in piece fresh root ginger, finely crushed
5ml/1 tsp ground coriander
5ml/1 tsp ground cumin
2 fresh green chillies, finely chopped
30ml/2 tbsp each chopped fresh coriander (cilantro) and mint

225g/8oz lean minced (ground) beef or lamb
50g/2oz/⅓ cup frozen peas, thawed
juice of 1 lemon
900g/2lb potatoes, boiled and mashed
2 eggs, beaten
dry breadcrumbs, for coating
vegetable oil, for shallow-frying
salt
lemon wedges and salad leaves, to serve

1 Heat the oil and fry the onion, garlic, ginger, coriander, cumin, chillies and fresh coriander until the onion is translucent. Add the meat and peas and fry well until the meat is cooked, then season to taste with salt and lemon juice. The mixture should be very dry.

2 Divide the mashed potato into 8–10 portions, take one portion at a time and flatten into a pancake in the palm of your hand. Place a spoonful of the meat in the centre and gather the sides together to enclose the meat. Flatten it slightly to make a round.

3 Dip the cakes in beaten egg and then coat in breadcrumbs. Set aside to chill in the refrigerator for about 1 hour.

4 Heat the oil in a frying pan and shallow-fry the cakes until brown and crisp all over. Serve them hot with lemon wedges on a bed of salad leaves.

Spiced Potato Cakes with Chickpeas

Fragrant and spicy chickpeas go very well with these fiery potato cakes.

Makes 10–12
30ml/2 tbsp vegetable oil
30ml/2 tbsp ground coriander
30ml/2 tbsp ground cumin
2.5ml/½ tsp ground turmeric
2.5ml/½ tsp salt
2.5ml/½ tsp sugar
30ml/2 tbsp gram flour, mixed with a little water to make a paste
450g/1lb/3 cups cooked chickpeas, drained
2 fresh green chillies, chopped
5cm/2in piece fresh root ginger, crushed

75g/3oz/1½ cups fresh coriander (cilantro), chopped
2 firm tomatoes, chopped
fresh mint sprigs, to garnish

For the potato cakes
450g/1lb potatoes, boiled and mashed
4 fresh green chillies, finely chopped
50g/2oz/2 cups chopped fresh coriander
7.5ml/1½ tsp ground cumin
5ml/1 tsp dry mango powder (amchur)
vegetable oil, for frying
salt

1 Heat the oil in a karahi, wok or large pan. Add the coriander, cumin, turmeric, salt, sugar and gram flour paste and cook until the water has evaporated and the oil has separated.

2 Add the chickpeas to the spices in the pan, and stir in the chopped chillies, ginger, fresh coriander and tomatoes. Toss the ingredients well and simmer gently for about 5 minutes. Transfer to a serving dish and keep warm.

3 To make the potato cakes, place the mashed potato in a large bowl and add the green chillies, chopped fresh coriander, cumin, dry mango powder and salt. Mix together until all the ingredients are well blended.

4 Using your hands, shape the potato mixture into little cakes. Heat the oil in a shallow frying pan and fry the cakes on both sides until golden brown. Transfer to a serving dish, garnish with mint sprigs and serve with the spicy chickpeas.

Energy 260kcal/1086kJ; Fat 15.4g; Saturated fat 3.6g; Carbohydrate 21.3g; Fibre 1.9g.

Energy 91kcal/383kJ; Fat 3.3g; Saturated fat 0.4g; Carbohydrate 11.9g; Fibre 2.2g.

Fish Cakes

Goan fish and shellfish are skilfully prepared with spices to make cakes of all shapes and sizes, whereas the rest of India makes fish kababs. Although haddock is used in this recipe, you can use other less expensive white fish, such as coley or whiting.

Makes 20
450g/1lb skinned haddock or cod
2 potatoes, peeled, boiled and
  coarsely mashed
4 spring onions (scallions), finely
  chopped
4 fresh green chillies, finely chopped
5cm/2in piece fresh root ginger,
  crushed
a few fresh coriander (cilantro)
  and mint sprigs, chopped
2 eggs
dry breadcrumbs, for coating
vegetable oil, for shallow-frying
salt and ground black pepper
lemon wedges and chilli sauce,
  to serve

1 Place the skinned fish in a lightly greased steamer and steam gently until cooked. Remove the steamer from the heat but leave the fish on the steaming tray until cool.

2 When the fish is cool, crumble it coarsely into a large bowl, using a fork. Mix in the mashed potatoes.

3 Add the spring onions, chillies, crushed ginger, chopped coriander and mint, and one of the eggs. Mix well and season to taste with salt and pepper.

4 Shape into cakes. Beat the remaining egg and dip the cakes in it, then coat with the breadcrumbs. Heat the oil and fry the cakes until brown on all sides. Serve as an appetizer or side dish, with the lemon wedges and chilli sauce.

Cook's Tip
For a quick version, used canned tuna in brine and omit step 1. Make sure the tuna is thoroughly drained before use.

Energy 56kcal/234kJ; Fat 3.3g; Saturated fat 0.5g; Carbohydrate 1.5g; Fibre 0.1g.

Fish Cakes with Cucumber Relish

These wonderful small fish cakes are a very popular appetizer.

Makes about 12
8 kaffir lime leaves
300g/11oz cod fillet, cut into
  chunks
30ml/2 tbsp red curry paste
1 egg
30ml/2 tbsp Thai fish sauce
5ml/1 tsp sugar
30ml/2 tbsp cornflour
  (cornstarch)
15ml/1 tbsp chopped fresh
  coriander (cilantro)
50g/2oz/1/2 cup green beans,
  thinly sliced
vegetable oil, for deep-frying

For the cucumber relish
60ml/4 tbsp coconut or rice
  vinegar
50g/2oz/1/4 cup sugar
60ml/4 tbsp water
1 head pickled garlic
1cm/1/2in piece fresh root ginger,
  chopped
1 cucumber, cut into thin batons
4 shallots, thinly sliced

1 To make the cucumber relish, mix the coconut or rice vinegar, sugar and water in a pan. Heat gently, stirring constantly until the sugar has dissolved. Remove from the heat and leave to cool.

2 Place the garlic and ginger in a bowl. Add the cucumber and shallots. Mix in the vinegar and stir lightly. Cover and set aside.

3 Reserve 2 or 3 kaffir lime leaves for the garnish and thinly slice the remainder. Put the fish, curry paste and egg in a food processor and process to a smooth paste. Transfer to a bowl and stir in the fish sauce, sugar, cornflour, sliced kaffir lime leaves, coriander and green beans. Shape the mixture into thick cakes.

4 Heat the oil in a deep-frying pan or wok to 190°C/375°F or until a cube of bread, added to the oil, browns in about 45 seconds. Fry the fish cakes, a few at a time, for 4–5 minutes, until cooked and evenly brown.

5 Lift out the fish cakes and drain them on kitchen paper. Keep each batch hot while frying successive batches. Garnish with the reserved kaffir lime leaves and serve with the cucumber relish.

Energy 168kcal/696kJ; Fat 13.2g; Saturated fat 1.6g; Carbohydrate 7.4g; Fibre 0.2g.

Goan-style Mussels

Mussels make a marvellous appetizer. Serve them Goan-style, in a fragrant coconut sauce. They take only minutes to cook, and the wonderful aroma will stimulate even the most jaded appetite.

Serves 4

900g/2lb live mussels
115g/4oz creamed coconut
(120ml/4fl oz/½ cup coconut cream)
450ml/¾ pint/scant 2 cups boiling water
45ml/3 tbsp oil
1 onion, finely chopped
3 garlic cloves, crushed
2.5cm/1in piece fresh root ginger, peeled and finely chopped
2.5ml/½ tsp ground turmeric
5ml/1 tsp ground cumin
5ml/1 tsp ground coriander
1.5ml/¼ tsp salt
chopped fresh coriander (cilantro), to garnish

1 Scrub the mussels under cold water and pull off any beards that remain attached to the shells. Discard any mussels that are open and which fail to snap shut when tapped.

2 Put the creamed coconut in a measuring jug or cup and pour in the boiling water. Stir with a wooden spoon until all the coconut has dissolved, then set aside until required. Heat the oil in a karahi, wok or heavy pan. Add the onion and fry for 5 minutes, stirring frequently.

3 Add the garlic and ginger and fry for 2 minutes. Stir in the turmeric, cumin, coriander and salt and fry for 2 minutes. Pour in the coconut liquid, stir well and bring to the boil. Reduce the heat and simmer for 5 minutes.

4 Add the mussels, cover the pan and cook over medium heat for 6–8 minutes, by which time all the mussels should have opened. Spoon the mussels on to a serving platter. If any of the mussels have failed to open, discard them immediately.

5 Pour the sauce over the mussels, garnish with the chopped fresh coriander, and serve.

Ginger Chicken Wings

Many people regard chicken wings as the best part of the bird. Served this way, they are certainly delicious, and exactly the right size for an appetizer with drinks, or as a first course.

Serves 4

10–12 chicken wings, skinned
175ml/6fl oz/¾ cup natural (plain) low-fat yogurt
7.5ml/1½ tsp crushed fresh root ginger
5ml/1 tsp salt
5ml/1 tsp Tabasco sauce
15ml/1 tbsp tomato ketchup
5ml/1 tsp crushed garlic
15ml/1 tbsp lemon juice
15ml/1 tbsp fresh coriander (cilantro) leaves
15ml/1 tbsp oil
2 medium onions, sliced
15ml/1 tbsp shredded fresh root ginger

1 Place the chicken wings in a non-metallic bowl. Pour the yogurt into a separate bowl along with the ginger pulp, salt, Tabasco sauce, tomato ketchup, garlic pulp, lemon juice and half the fresh coriander leaves. Whisk everything together, then pour the mixture over the chicken wings and stir gently to coat the chicken completely.

2 Heat the oil in a wok or heavy frying pan and fry the onions until soft.

3 Pour in the chicken wings and cook over a medium heat, stirring occasionally, for 10–15 minutes.

4 Add the remaining coriander and the shredded ginger and serve hot.

Cook's Tip
You can substitute drumsticks or other chicken portions for the wings in this recipe, but remember to increase the cooking time.

Energy 339kcal/1405kJ; Fat 29.5g; Saturated fat 18.3g; Carbohydrate 5g; Fibre 0.5g.

Energy 224kcal/936kJ; Fat 9g; Saturated fat 2.23g; Carbohydrate 12.64g; Fibre 1.24g.

Chicken Tikka

This extremely popular Indian first course is quick and easy to cook. The dish can also be served as a main course for four.

Serves 6 as an appetizer
450g/1lb boneless chicken, skinned and cubed
5ml/1 tsp crushed fresh root ginger
5ml/1 tsp crushed garlic
5ml/1 tsp chilli powder
1.5ml/¼ tsp ground turmeric
5ml/1 tsp salt
150ml/¼ pint/⅔ cup natural (plain) low-fat yogurt

60ml/4 tbsp lemon juice
15ml/1 tbsp chopped fresh coriander (cilantro)
15ml/1 tbsp oil

For the garnish
mixed salad leaves
1 small onion, cut into rings
lime wedges
fresh coriander (cilantro)

1 In a medium bowl, mix together the chicken pieces, ginger, garlic, chilli powder, turmeric and salt.

2 Stir in the yogurt, lemon juice and fresh coriander and leave to marinate for at least 2 hours.

3 Place in a grill (broiler) pan or in a flameproof dish lined with foil and baste with the oil.

4 Preheat the grill to medium. Grill (broil) the chicken for 15–20 minutes until cooked, turning and basting several times. Serve on a bed of mixed salad leaves, garnished with onion rings, lime wedges and coriander.

> **Cook's Tip**
> *To make the turning and basting of the chicken easier, thread the chicken pieces on to six soaked wooden skewers before placing under the grill (broiler).*

Energy 134kcal/561kJ; Fat 5.5g; Saturated fat 1.49g; Carbohydrate 3.9g; Fibre 0.3g.

Chicken Kofta Balti with Paneer

This rather unusual appetizer looks most elegant when served in small individual karahis.

Serves 6
For the koftas
450g/1lb boneless chicken, skinned and cubed
5ml/1 tsp crushed garlic
5ml/1 tsp shredded fresh root ginger
7.5ml/1½ tsp ground coriander
7.5ml/1½ tsp chilli powder
7.5ml/1½ tsp ground fenugreek
1.5ml/¼ tsp ground turmeric

5ml/1 tsp salt
30ml/2 tbsp chopped fresh coriander (cilantro)
2 fresh green chillies, chopped
600ml/1 pint/2½ cups water
corn oil, for frying

For the paneer mixture
1 medium onion, sliced
1 red (bell) pepper, seeded and cut into strips
1 green (bell) pepper, seeded and cut into strips
175g/6oz paneer, cubed
175g/6oz/1½ cups corn
fresh mint sprigs

1 Put all the kofta ingredients, apart from the oil, into a medium pan. Bring to the boil slowly over medium heat, and cook until all the liquid has evaporated. Remove from the heat and leave to cool slightly. Put the mixture into a food processor or blender and process for 2 minutes.

2 Transfer the mixture to a large mixing bowl. Taking a little of the mixture at a time, shape it into small balls, using your hands. You should be able to make about 12 koftas. Heat the corn oil in a karahi, wok or deep pan over a high heat. Reduce the heat slightly and drop the koftas carefully into the oil. Move them around gently to ensure that they cook evenly.

3 When the koftas are lightly browned, remove them from the oil with a slotted spoon and drain on kitchen paper. Set aside.

4 Heat the oil still remaining in the karahi, and flash-fry all the ingredients for the paneer mixture. This should take about 3 minutes over high heat. Divide the paneer mixture evenly between six individual karahis. Add two koftas to each serving, and garnish with mint sprigs.

Energy 235kcal/984kJ; Fat 10.3g; Saturated fat 2.1g; Carbohydrate 12.3g; Fibre 1.9g.

Pineapple Chicken Kebabs

This chicken dish has a delicate tang and the meat is very tender. The pineapple not only tenderizes the chicken but also gives it a slight sweetness.

Serves 6

225g/8oz can pineapple
  chunks
5ml/1 tsp ground cumin
5ml/1 tsp ground coriander
5ml/1 tsp chilli powder
2.5ml/½ tsp crushed garlic
5ml/1 tsp salt

30ml/2 tbsp natural (plain)
  low-fat yogurt
15ml/1 tbsp chopped fresh
  coriander (cilantro)
few drops of orange food
  colouring, optional
275g/10oz boneless chicken,
  skinned and cubed
½ red (bell) pepper, seeded
½ yellow or green (bell) pepper,
  seeded
1 large onion
6 cherry tomatoes
15ml/1 tbsp oil
salad leaves, to serve

1 Drain the pineapple juice into a bowl. Reserve 8 large chunks of pineapple and squeeze the juice from the remaining chunks into the bowl and set aside. You should have about 120ml/4fl oz/½ cup pineapple juice.

2 In a large bowl, mix together the spices, garlic, salt, yogurt, fresh coriander and food colouring, if using. Mix in the reserved pineapple juice.

3 Add the chicken to the yogurt and spice mixture, cover and leave to marinate in a cool place for about 1–1½ hours.

4 Cut the peppers and onion into bitesize chunks.

5 Preheat the grill (broiler) to medium. Arrange the chicken pieces, vegetables and reserved pineapple chunks alternately on 6 metal skewers.

6 Brush the kebabs lightly with the oil, then place the skewers on a flameproof dish or in a grill pan, turning the chicken pieces and basting with the marinade regularly, for about 15 minutes until cooked through. Serve with salad leaves.

Energy 183kcal/768kJ; Fat 6.6g; Saturated fat 1.47g; Carbohydrate 15.4g; Fibre 1.8g.

Chicken & Pasta Balti

This is not a traditional Balti dish, as pasta is not eaten widely in India or Pakistan, however, it is included here as it is truly delicious! The crushed pomegranate seeds give this dish an unusual tangy flavour.

Serves 4–6

75g/3oz/¾ cup small pasta shells
  (the coloured ones look most
  attractive)
75ml/5 tbsp corn oil
4 curry leaves
4 whole dried red chillies
1 large onion, sliced

5ml/1 tsp garlic pulp
5ml/1 tsp chilli powder
5ml/1 tsp shredded fresh
  root ginger
5ml/1 tsp crushed pomegranate
  seeds
5ml/1 tsp salt
2 medium tomatoes, chopped
175g/6oz chicken, skinned, boned
  and cubed
225g/8oz/1½ cups canned
  chickpeas, drained
115g/4oz/1 cup corn
50g/2oz mangetouts (snow peas),
  diagonally sliced
15ml/1 tbsp chopped fresh
  coriander (cilantro)

1 Cook the pasta in boiling water, following the directions on the pack. Add 15ml/1 tbsp of the oil to the water to prevent the pasta from sticking together. When it is cooked, drain and set to one side in a sieve (strainer).

2 Heat the remaining oil in a deep round frying pan or a large karahi, and add the curry leaves, whole dried chillies and the onion. Fry for about 5 minutes.

3 Add the garlic, chilli powder, ginger, pomegranate seeds, salt and tomatoes. Stir-fry for about 3 minutes.

4 Next add the cubed chicken, chickpeas, corn and mangetouts to the onion mixture. Cook over a medium heat for about 5 minutes, stirring constantly.

5 Add the pasta and stir well. Cook for a further 7–10 minutes, until the chicken is cooked through.

6 Serve, garnished with the fresh coriander if you wish.

Energy 350kcal/1468kJ; Fat 17.6g; Saturated fat 2.7g; Carbohydrate 29.5g; Fibre 4.2g.

Stuffed Aubergines with Lamb

Lamb and aubergines go really well together. This dish uses different coloured peppers in the lightly spiced filling mixture.

Serves 4

2 medium aubergines
  (eggplants)
15ml/1 tbsp oil, plus extra for
  brushing
1 medium onion, sliced
5ml/1 tsp shredded fresh root
  ginger
5ml/1 tsp chilli powder
5ml/1 tsp crushed garlic
1.5ml/¼ tsp ground turmeric
5ml/1 tsp salt
5ml/1 tsp ground coriander
1 medium tomato, chopped
350g/12oz lean leg of lamb,
  minced (ground)
1 medium green (bell) pepper,
  seeded and roughly chopped
1 medium orange (bell) pepper,
  seeded and roughly chopped
30ml/2 tbsp chopped fresh
  coriander (cilantro)
plain rice, to serve

For the garnish

½ onion, sliced
2 cherry tomatoes, quartered
fresh coriander (cilantro)

1 Cut the aubergines in half lengthways, and scoop out and discard most of the flesh. Preheat the oven to 180°C/350°F/Gas 4. Place the aubergine shells cut side up in a lightly greased ovenproof dish.

2 In a medium heavy pan, heat the oil and fry the onion until golden brown. Gradually stir in the ginger, chilli powder, garlic, turmeric, salt and ground coriander. Add the chopped tomato, lower the heat and cook for about 5 minutes, stirring frequently.

3 Add the minced lamb and cook for 7–10 minutes more.

4 Add the chopped peppers and chopped fresh coriander to the lamb mixture and stir well.

5 Spoon the lamb mixture into the aubergine shells and brush the edge of the shells with a little oil. Bake in the oven for 1 hour or until cooked through and browned on top.

6 Serve with the garnish ingredients, on a bed of plain rice.

Energy 238kcal/997kJ; Fat 11.7g; Saturated fat 4.08g; Carbohydrate 12.6g; Fibre 5.9g.

Koftas in a Spicy Sauce

Little meatballs are called koftas in Indian cooking and are usually served in a spicy curry sauce. This curry is popular in most Indian homes.

Serves 4

225g/8oz/1 cup lean minced
  (ground) lamb
10ml/2 tsp poppy seeds
1 medium onion, chopped
5ml/1 tsp shredded fresh root
  ginger
5ml/1 tsp crushed garlic
5ml/1 tsp salt
5ml/1 tsp chilli powder
7.5ml/1½ tsp ground coriander
30ml/2 tbsp fresh coriander
  (cilantro) leaves
1 small egg, beaten

For the sauce

75ml/2fl oz/⅓ cup natural (plain)
  low-fat yogurt
30ml/2 tbsp tomato purée
  (paste)
5ml/1 tsp chilli powder
5ml/1 tsp salt
5ml/1 tsp crushed garlic
5ml/1 tsp crushed fresh root
  ginger
5ml/1 tsp garam masala
10ml/2 tsp oil
1 cinnamon stick
400ml/14fl oz/1⅔ cups water

1 Place the lamb in a food processor and mince (grind) it further for about 1 minute. Scrape the meat into a bowl, sprinkle the poppy seeds on top and set aside.

2 Place the onion in the food processor with the next 5 ingredients and half the fresh coriander. Grind for about 30 seconds, then add it to the lamb. Add the egg and mix well. Leave to stand for about 1 hour.

3 To make the sauce, whisk together the yogurt, tomato purée, chilli powder, salt, crushed garlic, ginger and garam masala. Heat the oil with the cinnamon stick in a pan for about 1 minute, then pour in the sauce. Lower the heat and cook for 1 minute. Remove from the heat and set aside.

4 Roll small balls of the meat mixture using your hands. Return the sauce to the heat and stir in the water. Drop in the koftas one by one. Add the remaining coriander, cover with a lid and cook for 7–10 minutes, stirring occasionally. Serve hot.

Energy 155kcal/647kJ; Fat 9.24g; Saturated fat 2.79g; Carbohydrate 7.56g; Fibre 1.16g.

Curried Lamb Samosas

Filo pastry is perfect for making samosas. Once you've mastered folding them, you'll be amazed at how quick they are to make. These lamb samosas have a simple filling that is tasty and quick to make – perfect for party fare.

Makes 12
25g/1oz/2 tbsp butter
225g/8oz/1 cup minced (ground) lamb
30ml/2 tbsp mild curry paste
12 sheets of filo pastry, thawed and wrapped in a damp dish towel
salt and ground black pepper

1 Heat a little of the butter in a large pan and add the lamb. Fry for 5–6 minutes, stirring occasionally until browned. Stir in the curry paste and cook for 1–2 minutes. Season and set aside. Preheat the oven to 200°C/400°F/Gas 6.

2 Melt the remaining butter in a pan. Cut the pastry sheets in half lengthways. Brush one strip of pastry with butter, then lay another strip on top and brush with more butter.

3 Place a spoonful of lamb in the corner of the strip and fold over to form a triangle at one end. Keep folding over in the same way to form a triangular shape.

4 Brush with butter and place on a baking sheet. Repeat using the remaining pastry and filling. Bake for 10–15 minutes until golden. Serve hot.

> **Variation**
> For Cashew Nut Samosas, mix together 225g/8oz cooked and mashed potato, 15ml/1 tbsp chopped cashew nuts, 5ml/1 tsp coconut milk powder, ½ chopped green chilli, 5ml/ 1 tsp mustard seeds, 5ml/1 tsp cumin seeds, 15ml/1 tbsp chopped fresh coriander (cilantro) and 5ml/1 tsp soft light brown sugar. Use to fill the samosas in place of the lamb filling. If you like, the mustard and cumin seeds can be dry-roasted first.

Energy 81kcal/341kJ; Fat 5.2g; Saturated fat 2.4g; Carbohydrate 4.9g; Fibre 0.2g.

Tandoori Masala Spring Lamb Chops

These spicy, lean and trimmed lamb chops are marinated for three hours and then cooked in the oven using very little oil. They make a tasty appetizer, served with a salad garnish, and would also serve three as a main course if served with rice.

Serves 6 as an appetizer
6 small lean spring lamb chops
30ml/2 tbsp natural (plain) low-fat yogurt
15ml/1 tbsp tomato purée (paste)
10ml/2 tsp ground coriander
5ml/1 tsp crushed fresh root ginger
5ml/1 tsp crushed garlic
5ml/1 tsp chilli powder
a few drops of red food colouring (optional)
5ml/1 tsp salt
15ml/1 tbsp oil, plus extra for basting
45ml/3 tbsp lemon juice

For the salad garnish
lettuce leaves (optional)
lime wedges
1 small onion, sliced
fresh coriander (cilantro)

1 Rinse the chops and pat dry. Trim off all excess fat.

2 In a medium bowl, mix together the yogurt, tomato purée, ground coriander, ginger and garlic, chilli powder, food colouring (if using), salt, oil and lemon juice.

3 Rub this spice mixture over the lamb chops, using your hands, and leave the chops to marinate in a cool place for at least 3 hours.

4 Preheat the oven to 240°C/475°F/Gas 9. Place the marinated chops in an ovenproof dish.

5 Using a brush, baste the chops with about 5ml/1 tsp oil and cook in the oven for 15 minutes. Lower the heat to 180°C/350°F/Gas 4 and cook for a further 10–15 minutes.

6 Check that the chops are cooked and serve immediately on a bed of lettuce leaves, if you like, garnished with lime wedges, sliced onion and fresh coriander.

Energy 117kcal/488kJ; Fat 6.6g; Saturated fat 2.42g; Carbohydrate 3.1g; Fibre 0.3g.

Lamb Kebabs

First introduced by the Muslims, kebabs have now become a favourite Indian dish and are often sold at open stalls; the wonderful aroma of the spicy meat is guaranteed to stop passers-by in their tracks to buy one.

Serves 8

For the kebabs
900g/2lb lean minced
   (ground) lamb
1 large onion, roughly chopped
5cm/2in piece fresh root ginger,
   chopped
2 garlic cloves, crushed
1 fresh green chilli,
   finely chopped
5ml/1 tsp chilli powder
30ml/2 tbsp chopped fresh
   coriander (cilantro)
5ml/1 tsp garam masala
10ml/2 tsp ground coriander
5ml/1 tsp ground cumin
5ml/1 tsp salt
1 egg
15ml/1 tbsp natural (plain)
   low-fat yogurt
15ml/1 tbsp oil
mixed salad, to serve

For the raita
250ml/8fl oz/1 cup natural
   (plain) low-fat yogurt
½ cucumber, finely chopped
30ml/2 tbsp chopped fresh mint
1.5ml/¼ tsp salt

1 Put all the ingredients for the kebabs, except the yogurt and oil, into a food processor or blender and process until the mixture binds together. Spoon into a bowl, cover and leave to marinate for 1 hour.

2 To make the raita, mix together all the ingredients and chill for at least 15 minutes in a refrigerator.

3 Preheat the grill (broiler). Divide the lamb mixture into eight equal portions with lightly floured hands and mould into long sausage shapes. Thread on to skewers and chill.

4 Brush the kebabs lightly with the yogurt and oil and cook under a hot grill for 8–10 minutes, turning occasionally, until brown all over. Serve the kebabs on a bed of mixed salad, accompanied by the raita.

Energy 249kcal/1045kJ; Fat 12.75g; Saturated fat 5.3g; Carbohydrate 7g; Fibre 0.6g.

Shammi Kebabs

These Indian treats are derived from the kebabs of the Middle East. They can be served either as appetizers or side dishes with a raita or chutney.

Serves 5–6
2 onions, finely chopped
250g/9oz lean lamb, boned
   and cubed
50g/2oz/¼ cup chana dhal or
   yellow split peas
5ml/1 tsp cumin seeds
5ml/1 tsp garam masala
4–6 fresh green chillies
5cm/2in piece fresh root
   ginger, grated
175ml/6fl oz/¾ cup water
juice of 1 lemon
a few fresh coriander (cilantro)
   and mint leaves, chopped, plus
   extra coriander sprigs
   to garnish
15ml/1 tbsp gram flour
2 eggs, beaten
vegetable oil, for shallow-frying
salt

1 Put the first seven ingredients and the water into a large pan with salt, and bring to the boil. Simmer, covered, until the meat and dhal are cooked. Remove the lid and continue to cook for a few more minutes, to reduce the excess liquid. Set aside to cool.

2 Transfer the cooled meat mixture to a food processor or blender and process well until the mixture becomes a rough, gritty paste.

3 Put the paste into a large mixing bowl and add the chopped coriander and mint leaves, lemon juice and gram flour. Knead well with your fingers for a good couple of minutes, to ensure that all ingredients are evenly distributed through the mixture, and any excess liquid has been thoroughly absorbed. When the colour appears even throughout, and the mixture has taken on a semi-solid, sticky rather than powdery consistency, the kebabs are ready for shaping into portions.

4 Divide the mixture into 10–12 equal portions and use your hands to roll each into a ball, then flatten slightly. Chill for 1 hour. Dip the kebabs in the beaten egg and shallow-fry each side until golden brown. Pat dry on kitchen paper.

Energy 179kcal/750kJ; Fat 8.5g; Saturated fat 3.4g; Carbohydrate 10.4g; Fibre 1.3g.

Fish with Mango Sauce

This salad is best served during the summer months, preferably out of doors. The dressing combines the flavour of rich mango with hot chilli, ginger and lime.

Serves 4

1 French loaf
4 redfish, black bream or porgy, about 275g/10oz each
15ml/1 tbsp vegetable oil
1 mango
1cm/½in piece fresh root ginger
1 fresh red chilli, seeded and finely chopped
30ml/2 tbsp lime juice
30ml/2 tbsp chopped fresh coriander (cilantro)
175g/6oz young spinach
150g/5oz pak choi (bok choy)
175g/6oz cherry tomatoes, halved

1 Preheat the oven to 180°C/350°F/Gas 4. Cut the French loaf into 20cm/8in lengths. Slice lengthways, then cut the bread into thick fingers.

2 Place the bread on a baking sheet and leave to dry in the oven for 15 minutes.

3 Preheat the grill (broiler) or light the barbecue and allow the embers to settle. Slash the fish deeply on both sides and moisten with oil. Cook the fish on the barbecue for 6 minutes, turning once.

4 Peel the mango and cut in half, discarding the stone (pit). Thinly slice one half and set aside. Place the other half in a food processor or blender.

5 Peel the ginger, grate finely, then add to the mango with the chilli, lime juice and fresh coriander. Process until smooth. Adjust to a pouring consistency with 30–45ml/2–3 tbsp water.

6 Wash the spinach and pak choi leaves and spin dry, then distribute them among four serving plates.

7 Place the fish on the leaves. Spoon on the mango dressing and finish with the reserved slices of mango and the tomato halves. Serve with the fingers of crisp French bread.

Energy 512kcal/2164kJ; Fat 12.3g; Saturated fat 0.8g; Carbohydrate 50g; Fibre 4.9g.

Braised Whole Fish in Chilli & Garlic Sauce

In India there are an increasing number of unusual dishes that borrow from other cultures. The vinegar in the sauce for this fish dish is typical of Goa, but the rice wine and bean sauce reveal a distinct Sichuan influence.

Serves 4–6

1 carp, bream, sea bass, trout, grouper or grey mullet, about 675g/1½lb, gutted
15ml/1 tbsp light soy sauce
15ml/1 tbsp rice wine or dry sherry
vegetable oil, for deep-frying

For the sauce

2 garlic cloves, finely chopped
2 or 3 spring onions (scallions), finely chopped, the white and green parts separated
5ml/1 tsp finely chopped fresh root ginger
30ml/2 tbsp chilli bean sauce
15ml/1 tbsp tomato purée (paste)
10ml/2 tsp light brown sugar
15ml/1 tbsp rice vinegar
120ml/4fl oz/½ cup chicken stock
15ml/1 tbsp cornflour (cornstarch), mixed to a paste with 10ml/2 tsp water
a few drops of sesame oil

1 Rinse and dry the fish well. Using a sharp knife, score both sides of the fish down to the bone with diagonal cuts about 2.5cm/1in apart. Rub both sides of the fish with the soy sauce and rice wine or sherry. Set aside for 10–15 minutes to marinate.

2 Heat sufficient oil for deep-frying in a wok. When it is hot, carefully add the fish and fry for 3–4 minutes on both sides, until golden brown.

3 To make the sauce pour away all but about 15ml/1 tbsp of the oil. Push the fish to one side of the wok and add the garlic, the white part of the spring onions, the ginger, chilli bean sauce, tomato purée, sugar, vinegar and chicken stock. Bring to the boil and braise the fish in the sauce for 4–5 minutes, turning it over once. Add the green of the spring onions. Stir in the cornflour paste to thicken the sauce. Sprinkle over a little sesame oil and serve immediately.

Energy 292kcal/1222kJ; Fat 16.1g; Saturated fat 2.5g; Carbohydrate 10.7g; Fibre 0.4g.

Hot & Fragrant Trout

This wickedly hot spice paste could be used as a marinade for any fish or meat. It also makes a wonderful spicy dip for grilled meat.

Serves 4

2 large fresh green chillies, seeded and coarsely chopped
5 shallots, peeled
5 garlic cloves, peeled
30ml/2 tbsp fresh lime juice
30ml/2 tbsp Thai fish sauce
15ml/1 tbsp palm sugar or light muscovado (brown) sugar
4 kaffir lime leaves, rolled into cylinders and thinly sliced
2 trout or similar firm-fleshed fish, about 350g/12oz each, cleaned
fresh garlic chives, to garnish
boiled rice, to serve

1 Wrap the chillies, shallots and garlic in a foil package. Place under a hot grill (broiler) for 10 minutes, until softened.

2 When the package is cool enough to handle, tip the contents into a mortar or food processor and pound with a pestle or process to a paste.

3 Add the lime juice, fish sauce, sugar and lime leaves and mix well. With a teaspoon, stuff this paste inside the fish. Smear a little on the skin too. Grill (broil) the fish for about 5 minutes on each side, until just cooked through. Lift the fish on to a platter, garnish with garlic chives and serve with rice.

> **Cook's Tip**
> *Farmed rainbow trout is available all year. The better-flavoured wild brown trout, however, is rarely available and more expensive. Salmon trout is also suitable for this dish; as it is a large fish, one will probably be sufficient for four people. For an economical dish, try mackerel. You can use one for each person or buy two larger fish; the larger fish will be easier to stuff.*

Marinated Fried Fish with Ginger & Chilli

Fish and shellfish are a strong feature of the cuisine in the coastal region of southern India. Kerala, in the southernmost part of the country, produces some of the finest fish and shellfish dishes. These are flavoured with local spices, grown in the fabulous spice plantations that are the pride and joy of the state.

Serves 4–6

1 small onion, coarsely chopped
4 garlic cloves, crushed
5cm/2in piece fresh root ginger, chopped
5ml/1 tsp ground turmeric
10ml/2 tsp chilli powder
4 red mullet or snapper
vegetable oil, for shallow-frying
5ml/1 tsp cumin seeds
3 fresh green chillies, finely sliced
salt
lemon or lime wedges, to serve

1 In a food processor, grind the first five ingredients with salt to a smooth paste.

2 Make several slashes on both sides of the fish and rub them with the paste. Leave to rest for 1 hour. Excess fluid will be released as the salt dissolves, so lightly pat the fish dry with kitchen paper, without removing the paste.

3 Heat the vegetable oil and fry the cumin seeds and sliced chillies for 1 minute.

4 Add the fish, in batches if necessary, and fry on one side. When the first side is sealed, turn them over very gently to ensure they do not break. Fry until golden brown on both sides and fully cooked. Drain and serve hot, with lemon or lime wedges.

> **Variation**
> *To enhance the flavour, add 15ml/1 tbsp chopped fresh coriander (cilantro) leaves to the spice paste in step 1.*

Energy 171kcal/719kJ; Fat 5.3g; Saturated fat 1.2g; Carbohydrate 3.9g; Fibre 0g.

Energy 336kcal/1403kJ; Fat 20.1g; Saturated fat 1.5g; Carbohydrate 1.2g; Fibre 0.2g.

Green Fish Curry with Coconut

This dish combines all the delicious flavours of the East. A subtle blend of spices and a hint of coconut complement the flavour of the cod perfectly.

Serves 4

1.5ml/¼ tsp ground turmeric
30ml/2 tbsp lime juice
pinch of salt
4 cod fillets, skinned and cut into 5cm/2in chunks
1 onion, chopped
1 fresh green chilli, sliced
1 garlic clove, crushed
25g/1oz/¼ cup cashew nuts
2.5ml/½ tsp fennel seeds

30ml/2 tbsp desiccated (dry unsweetened shredded) coconut
30ml/2 tbsp oil
1.5ml/¼ tsp cumin seeds
1.5ml/¼ tsp ground coriander
1.5ml/¼ tsp ground cumin
1.5ml/¼ tsp salt
150ml/¼ pint/⅔ cup water
175ml/6fl oz/¾ cup natural (plain) low-fat yogurt
45ml/3 tbsp finely chopped fresh coriander (cilantro), plus extra to garnish

1 Mix together the turmeric, lime juice and salt, and rub over the fish. Cover and marinate for 15 minutes.

2 Meanwhile, grind the onion, chilli, garlic, cashew nuts, fennel seeds and coconut to a paste. Spoon the paste into a bowl and set aside.

3 Heat the oil in a large, heavy pan and fry the cumin seeds for 2 minutes or until they begin to splutter. Add the paste and fry for 5 minutes, then stir in the ground coriander, cumin, salt and water and cook for 2–3 minutes.

4 Stir in the yogurt and chopped fresh coriander. Simmer gently for 5 minutes. Gently stir in the fish pieces. Cover and cook gently for 10 minutes until the fish is tender. Garnish with more coriander. This curry is particularly good served with a vegetable pilau.

Energy 244kcal/1016kJ; Fat 14.3g; Saturated fat 5.21g; Carbohydrate 5.4g; Fibre 1.7g.

Cod in a Tomato Sauce

Dusting cod with spices before cooking gives it a delectable coating.

Serves 4

30ml/2 tbsp cornflour (cornstarch)
5ml/1 tsp salt
5ml/1 tsp garlic powder
5ml/1 tsp chilli powder
5ml/1 tsp ground ginger
5ml/1 tsp ground fennel seeds
5ml/1 tsp ground coriander
2 medium cod fillets, each cut into 2 pieces
15ml/1 tbsp oil
mashed potatoes, to serve

For the sauce

30ml/2 tbsp tomato purée (paste)
5ml/1 tsp garam masala
5ml/1 tsp chilli powder
5ml/1 tsp crushed garlic
5ml/1 tsp grated fresh root ginger
2.5ml/½ tsp salt
175ml/6fl oz/¾ cup water
15ml/1 tbsp oil
1 bay leaf
3 or 4 black peppercorns
1cm/½in piece cinnamon stick
15ml/1 tbsp chopped fresh coriander (cilantro)
15ml/1 tbsp chopped fresh mint

1 Mix together the cornflour, salt, garlic powder, chilli powder, ground ginger, ground fennel seeds and ground coriander. Use to coat the four cod pieces.

2 Preheat the grill (broiler) to very hot, then reduce the heat slightly and place the cod under the heat. After about 5 minutes spoon the oil over the cod. Turn the cod over and repeat the process. Cook for a further 5 minutes, check that the fish is cooked through and set aside.

3 Make the sauce by mixing together the tomato purée, garam masala, chilli powder, garlic, ginger, salt and water. Set aside.

4 Heat the oil in a karahi or wok and add the bay leaf, peppercorns and cinnamon. Pour the sauce into the pan and reduce the heat to low. Bring slowly to the boil, stirring occasionally, then simmer for about 5 minutes. Gently slide the pieces of fish into this mixture and cook for a further 2 minutes. Add the chopped fresh coriander and mint and serve the dish with mashed potatoes.

Energy 122kcal/509kJ; Fat 6.65g; Saturated fat 0.89g; Carbohydrate 4.73g; Fibre 0.48g.

Fish Fillets with a Chilli Sauce

For this recipe, the fish fillets are first marinated with fresh coriander and lemon juice, then cooked quickly before being served with a chilli sauce.

Serves 4

4 flat-fish fillets, such as plaice, sole or flounder, about 115g/4oz each
30ml/2 tbsp lemon juice
15ml/1 tbsp finely chopped fresh coriander (cilantro)
15ml/1 tbsp oil

lime wedges and a fresh coriander sprig, to garnish
yellow rice, to serve

For the sauce

5ml/1 tsp grated fresh root ginger
30ml/2 tbsp tomato purée (paste)
5ml/1 tsp sugar
5ml/1 tsp salt
15ml/1 tbsp chilli sauce
15ml/1 tbsp malt vinegar
300ml/½ pint/1¼ cups water

1 Rinse and pat dry the fish fillets and place in a medium bowl. Add the lemon juice, coriander and oil and rub into the fish. Leave to marinate for at least 1 hour.

2 Make the sauce. Mix the grated ginger, tomato purée, sugar, salt and chilli sauce in a bowl. Stir in the vinegar and water.

3 Pour into a small pan and simmer gently over a low heat for about 6 minutes, stirring occasionally.

4 Meanwhile, preheat the grill (broiler) to medium. Lift the fish fillets out of the marinade and place them in a grill pan. Grill (broil) for about 5–7 minutes.

5 When the fish is cooked, arrange it on a warmed serving dish.

6 The chilli sauce should now be fairly thick – about the consistency of a thick chicken soup. Spoon the sauce over the fish fillets, garnish with the lime wedges and coriander sprig and serve immediately with yellow rice.

Cod with a Spicy Mushroom Sauce

Grilling fish before adding it to a sauce helps to prevent it from breaking up during the cooking process.

Serves 4

4 cod fillets
15ml/1 tbsp lemon juice
15ml/1 tbsp oil
1 medium onion, chopped
1 bay leaf
4 black peppercorns, crushed

115g/4oz/1 cup mushrooms
175ml/6fl oz/¾ cup natural (plain) low-fat yogurt
5ml/1 tsp grated fresh root ginger
5ml/1 tsp crushed garlic
2.5ml/½ tsp garam masala
2.5ml/½ tsp chilli powder
5ml/1 tsp salt
15ml/1 tbsp fresh coriander (cilantro) leaves, to garnish
lightly cooked green beans, to serve

1 Preheat the grill (broiler). Remove the skin and any bones from the cod fillets. Sprinkle with lemon juice, then par-cook under the grill for 5 minutes on each side. Remove the fillets from the heat and set aside.

2 Heat the oil in a karahi or wok and fry the chopped onion with the bay leaf and peppercorns for 2–3 minutes. Lower the heat, add the whole mushrooms and stir-fry for a further 4–5 minutes.

3 In a bowl mix together the natural yogurt, crushed ginger and grated garlic, garam masala, chilli powder and salt. Pour this over the onions and stir-fry for 3 minutes.

4 Add the cod fillets to the sauce and cook for a further 2 minutes. Serve garnished with the fresh coriander and accompanied by lightly cooked green beans.

Cook's Tip
If you can find tiny button (white) mushrooms they look particularly attractive in this fish dish. Alternatively, choose from the many other pretty coloured varieties, such as ceps and oyster mushrooms.

Energy 149kcal/627kJ; Fat 5.4g; Saturated fat 0.81g; Carbohydrate 3.9g; Fibre 0.2g.

Energy 170kcal/715kJ; Fat 4.32g; Saturated fat 0.79g; Carbohydrate 7.67g; Fibre 1g.

Fish Stew with Potatoes & Chilli

Cooking fish with vegetables is a tradition in eastern regions of India. This hearty dish with potatoes, peppers and tomatoes is perfect served with breads such as chapatis or parathas. You can try other combinations, such as green beans and spinach, but you do need a starchy vegetable in order to thicken the sauce.

Serves 4
30ml/2 tbsp vegetable oil
5ml/1 tsp cumin seeds
1 onion, chopped
1 red (bell) pepper,
    thinly sliced
1 garlic clove, crushed

2 fresh red chillies,
    finely chopped
2 bay leaves
2.5ml/½ tsp salt
5ml/1 tsp ground cumin
5ml/1 tsp ground coriander
5ml/1 tsp chilli powder
400g/14oz can chopped
    tomatoes
2 large potatoes, cut into
    2.5cm/1in chunks
300ml/½ pint/1¼ cups
    fish stock
4 cod fillets
chapatis, to serve

1 Heat the oil in a karahi, wok or large pan over a medium heat and fry the cumin seeds for 30–40 seconds until they begin to splutter. Add the chopped onion, red pepper, garlic, chillies and bay leaves, and fry for 5–7 minutes more until the onions have softened and browned.

2 Add the salt, ground cumin, ground coriander and chilli powder to the onion and red pepper mixture. Cook for 1–2 minutes, stirring occasionally.

3 Stir in the tomatoes, potatoes and fish stock. Bring to the boil, then lower the heat and simmer for a further 10 minutes, or until the potatoes are almost tender.

4 Add the fish fillets, then cover the pan and leave to simmer for 5–6 minutes until the fish is just cooked. Serve the fish piping hot, with chapatis.

Energy 251kcal/1053kJ; Fat 7.2g; Saturated fat 0.9g; Carbohydrate 8.4g; Fibre 1.8g.

Fish in a Tomato & Onion Sauce

It is difficult to imagine the cuisine of eastern India without fish. Bengal is as well known for its fish and shellfish dishes as Goa on the west coast. In both regions, coconut is used extensively, and the difference in the taste, as always, lies in the spicing. This onion-rich dish is known as *kalia* in Bengal, and a firm-fleshed fish such as monkfish is essential.

Serves 4
675g/1½lb firm-textured fish
    steaks, such as tuna or
    monkfish, skinned
30ml/2 tbsp lemon juice
5ml/1 tsp salt
5ml/1 tsp ground turmeric
vegetable oil, for shallow-frying

40g/1½oz/⅓ cup plain
    (all-purpose) flour
2.5ml/¼ tsp ground black pepper
60ml/4 tbsp vegetable oil
10ml/2 tsp sugar
1 large onion, finely chopped
15ml/1 tbsp grated fresh
    root ginger
15ml/1 tbsp crushed garlic
5ml/1 tsp ground coriander
2.5–5ml/½–1 tsp hot chilli
    powder
175g/6oz canned chopped
    tomatoes, including the juice
300ml/½ pint/1¼ cups
    warm water
30ml/2 tbsp chopped fresh
    coriander (cilantro) leaves,
    to garnish
plain boiled rice, to serve

1 Cut the fish into 7.5cm/3in pieces and put it in a large bowl. Add the lemon juice and sprinkle with half the salt and half the turmeric. Mix gently with your fingertips, then cover and set aside for 15 minutes.

2 Pour enough oil into a 23cm/9in frying pan to cover the base to a depth of 1cm/½in and heat over a medium setting. Mix the flour and pepper and dust the fish in the seasoned flour. Add to the oil in a single layer and fry until browned on both sides and a light crust has formed. Drain on kitchen paper.

3 In a karahi, wok or large pan, heat 60ml/4 tbsp oil. When the oil is hot, but not smoking, add the sugar and let it caramelize. As soon as the sugar is brown, add the finely chopped onion, ginger and garlic and fry for 7–8 minutes, until just beginning to colour. Stir regularly.

4 Add the ground coriander, chilli powder and the remaining turmeric. Stir-fry for about 30 seconds and add the tomatoes. Cook until the tomatoes are mushy and the oil separates from the spice paste, stirring regularly.

5 Pour the warm water and remaining salt into the pan, and bring to the boil. Carefully add the fried fish, reduce the heat to low and simmer, uncovered, for 5–6 minutes.

6 Transfer to a serving dish and garnish with the coriander leaves. Serve with plain boiled rice.

> **Cook's Tip**
> *Choose fresh rather than frozen fish for the best flavour.*

Energy 435kcal/1811kJ; Fat 30.7g; Saturated fat 3.8g; Carbohydrate 12.5g; Fibre 1.2g.

Monkfish & Okra Curry

Okra, when cut into short lengths, releases a liquid that helps to thicken this tasty sauce surrounding tender morsels of monkfish.

Serves 4

450g/1lb monkfish
5ml/1 tsp ground turmeric
2.5ml/½ tsp chilli powder
2.5ml/½ tsp salt
5ml/1 tsp cumin seeds

2.5ml/½ tsp fennel seeds
2 dried red chillies
30ml/2 tbsp oil
1 onion, finely chopped
2 garlic cloves, crushed
4 tomatoes, peeled and finely chopped
150ml/¼ pint/⅔ cup water
225g/8oz okra, trimmed and cut into 2.5cm/1in lengths
5ml/1 tsp garam masala
plain rice, to serve

1 Remove the membrane and bones from the monkfish, cut into 2.5cm/1in cubes and place in a dish. Mix together the ground turmeric, chilli powder and 1.5ml/¼ tsp of the salt, and rub the mixture all over the fish. Cover and marinate for 15 minutes.

2 Put the cumin seeds, fennel seeds and chillies in a large, heavy pan and dry-roast the spice mixture for 3–4 minutes. Put the spices into a blender or use a pestle and mortar to grind to a coarse powder.

3 Heat 15ml/1 tbsp of the oil in the frying pan and fry the monkfish cubes for about 4–5 minutes. Remove with a slotted spoon and drain on kitchen paper.

4 Add the remaining oil to the pan and fry the onion and garlic for about 5 minutes. Add the roasted spice powder and the remaining salt and fry for 2–3 minutes. Stir in the tomatoes and water and simmer for 5 minutes.

5 Add the prepared okra and cook for about 5–7 minutes.

6 Return the fish to the pan together with the garam masala. Cover and simmer for 5–6 minutes or until the fish is tender. Serve immediately with plain rice.

Energy 193kcal/805kJ; Fat 8.8g; Saturated fat 1.31g; Carbohydrate 9.4g; Fibre 3.6g.

Tuna Curry

This not-very-authentic fish curry can be made in minutes. It's the ideal dish for a wannabe Bollywood star on a tight schedule.

Serves 4

1 onion
1 red (bell) pepper
1 green (bell) pepper
30ml/2 tbsp oil
1.5ml/¼ tsp cumin seeds
2.5ml/½ tsp ground cumin
2.5ml/½ tsp ground coriander
2.5ml/½ tsp chilli powder

1.5ml/¼ tsp salt
2 garlic cloves, crushed
400g/14oz can tuna in brine, drained and flaked
1 fresh green chilli, finely chopped
2.5cm/1in piece fresh root ginger, grated
1.5ml/¼ tsp garam masala
5ml/1 tsp lemon juice
30ml/2 tbsp chopped fresh coriander (cilantro)
fresh coriander sprig, to garnish
pitta bread and cucumber raita, to serve

1 Thinly slice the onion and the red and green peppers, discarding the seeds from the peppers.

2 Heat the oil in a karahi, wok or heavy pan and stir-fry the cumin seeds for 2–3 minutes until they begin to spit and splutter.

3 Add the ground cumin, coriander, chilli powder and salt and cook for 2–3 minutes. Then add the garlic, onion and peppers.

4 Fry the vegetables, stirring from time to time, for 5–7 minutes until the onion has browned. Stir in the tuna, chopped green chilli and grated ginger and cook for 5 minutes.

5 Add the garam masala, lemon juice and chopped fresh coriander and continue to cook the curry for a further 3–4 minutes.

6 Meanwhile, place the pitta breads on a grill (broiler) rack and grill (broil) until they just puff up. Split with a sharp knife. Serve the curry in the pitta breads with the cucumber raita, garnished with a coriander sprig.

Energy 165kcal/690kJ; Fat 6.8g; Saturated fat 0.97g; Carbohydrate 8.7g; Fibre 1.8g.

Stir-fried Monkfish with Vegetables

Monkfish is fabulous stir-fried, as it holds its shape well during cooking. Here it is partnered with tomatoes and courgette in a mildly spiced sauce that complements the sweet flavour of the monkfish perfectly.

Serves 4
30ml/2 tbsp oil
2 medium onions, sliced

5ml/1 tsp crushed garlic
5ml/1 tsp ground cumin
5ml/1 tsp ground coriander
5ml/1 tsp chilli powder
900g/2lb monkfish, filleted and
    cut into cubes
30ml/2 tbsp fresh fenugreek
    leaves
2 tomatoes, seeded and sliced
1 courgette (zucchini), sliced
salt
15ml/1 tbsp lime juice

1 Heat the oil in a karahi, wok or heavy pan and fry the onions over a low heat until soft.

2 Meanwhile mix together the garlic, cumin, coriander and chilli powder. Add this spice mixture to the onions and stir-fry for about 1 minute.

3 Add the fish and continue to stir-fry for 3–5 minutes until the fish is well cooked throughout.

4 Add the fenugreek, tomatoes and courgette, followed by salt to taste, and stir-fry for a further 2 minutes. Sprinkle with lime juice before serving.

Cook's Tip
Monkfish is ideal here as it has firm flesh that does not disintegrate during cooking. It can be quite expensive, but is well worth using for this dish. As it has only one central bone, there are no fiddly bones to worry about. However, the dish would also work with cubed cod or uncooked, peeled prawns (shrimp). Watch the cooking times for both cod and prawns as overcooked cod will disintegrate and overcooked prawns will be tough. The prawns are cooked as soon as they turn pink.

Goan Fish Casserole

The cooking of Goa is a mixture of Portuguese and Indian; the addition of tamarind gives a slightly sour note to the spicy coconut sauce.

Serves 4
7.5ml/1½ tsp ground turmeric
5ml/1 tsp salt
450g/1lb monkfish fillet, cut
    into pieces
15ml/1 tbsp lemon juice
5ml/1 tsp cumin seeds
5ml/1 tsp coriander seeds
5ml/1 tsp black peppercorns
1 garlic clove, chopped

5cm/2in piece fresh root ginger,
    finely chopped
25g/1oz tamarind paste
150ml/¼ pint/⅔ cup hot water
30ml/2 tbsp vegetable oil
2 onions, halved and sliced
    lengthways
400ml/14fl oz/1⅔ cups coconut
    milk
4 mild fresh green chillies,
    seeded and cut into thin
    strips
16 large raw prawns (shrimp),
    peeled
30ml/2 tbsp chopped fresh
    coriander (cilantro) leaves,
    to garnish

1 Mix together the ground turmeric and salt in a small bowl. Place the monkfish in a shallow dish and sprinkle over the lemon juice, then rub the turmeric and salt mixture over the fish fillets to coat them completely. Cover and chill until you are ready to cook them.

2 Put the cumin seeds, coriander seeds and black peppercorns in a blender or small food processor and grind to a powder. Add the chopped garlic and ginger and process together for a few seconds more.

3 Preheat the oven to 200°C/400°F/Gas 6. Mix the tamarind paste with the hot water and set aside.

4 Heat the oil in a frying pan, add the onions and cook for 5–6 minutes, until softened and golden. Transfer the onions to a shallow earthenware dish.

5 Add the monkfish fillets to the oil remaining in the frying pan, and fry briefly over a high heat, turning them to seal on all sides. Remove the monkfish from the pan and place on top of the fried onions.

6 Add the ground spice mixture to the frying pan and cook over a medium heat, stirring constantly, for 1–2 minutes. Stir in the tamarind liquid, coconut milk and chilli strips and bring to the boil.

7 Pour the sauce into the earthenware dish to coat the fish completely.

8 Cover the earthenware dish and cook the fish casserole in the preheated oven for about 10 minutes.

9 Add the prawns, pushing them down so that they are completely immersed in the liquid, then cover the dish again and return it to the oven for 5 minutes, or until the prawns turn pink. Be careful not to overcook them or they will toughen. Check the seasoning and add more salt if necessary, then sprinkle with chopped coriander leaves and serve.

Energy 86kcal/360kJ; Fat 2.38g; Saturated fat 0.35g; Carbohydrate 8.32g; Fibre 1.87g.

Energy 211kcal/889kJ; Fat 6.7g; Saturated fat 1g; Carbohydrate 10.8g; Fibre 1.1g.

Mackerel in Tamarind

Coconut cream makes a heavenly sauce flavoured with ginger, chillies, coriander and turmeric in this delicious dish originating from Western India. Mackerel has a superbly rich flesh and yet it is a surprisingly inexpensive fish.

Serves 6–8

1kg/2¼ lb fresh mackerel fillets, skinned
30ml/2 tbsp tamarind pulp, soaked in 200ml/7fl oz/ scant 1 cup water
1 onion
1cm/½in piece fresh root ginger

2 garlic cloves
1 or 2 fresh red chillies, seeded, or 5ml/1 tsp chilli powder
5ml/1 tsp ground coriander
5ml/1 tsp ground turmeric
2.5ml/½ tsp ground fennel seeds
15ml/1 tbsp dark brown sugar
90–105ml/6–7 tbsp oil
200ml/7fl oz/scant 1 cup coconut cream
fresh chilli shreds, to garnish

1 Rinse the fish fillets in cold water and dry them well on kitchen paper. Put into a shallow dish and sprinkle with a little salt. Strain the tamarind and pour the juice over the fish fillets. Leave for 30 minutes.

2 Quarter the onion, peel and slice the ginger and peel the garlic. Grind the onion, ginger, garlic and chillies or chilli powder to a paste in a food processor or with a pestle and mortar. Add the ground coriander, turmeric, fennel seeds and sugar.

3 Heat half the oil in a frying pan. Drain the fish fillets and fry for 5 minutes, or until cooked. Set aside.

4 Wipe out the pan and heat the remaining oil. Fry the spice paste, stirring all the time, until it gives off a spicy aroma. Do not let it brown. Add the coconut cream and simmer gently for a few minutes. Add the fish fillets and gently heat through.

5 Taste for seasoning and serve sprinkled with shredded chilli.

Energy 482kcal/1999kJ; Fat 38g; Saturated fat 6.9g; Carbohydrate 3.6g; Fibre 0.4g.

Fish & Prawns in Herb Sauce

Bengalis are famous for their seafood dishes and like to use mustard oil in recipes because it imparts a unique taste, flavour and aroma. No feast in Bengal is complete without one of these celebrated fish dishes.

Serves 4–6

3 garlic cloves
5cm/2in piece fresh root ginger
1 large leek, roughly chopped
4 fresh green chillies
60ml/4 tbsp mustard oil or vegetable oil
15ml/1 tbsp ground coriander
2.5ml/½ tsp fennel seeds

15ml/1 tbsp crushed yellow mustard seeds, or 5ml/1 tsp mustard powder
175ml/6fl oz/¾ cup thick coconut milk
225g/8oz huss or monkfish fillets, cut into thick chunks
225g/8oz king prawns (jumbo shrimp), peeled and deveined, with tails intact
salt
115g/4oz/4 cups fresh coriander (cilantro), chopped
2 fresh green chillies, to garnish

1 In a food processor, grind the garlic, ginger, leek and chillies to a coarse paste. Add a little vegetable oil if the mixture is too dry and process the mixture again.

2 In a large frying pan, heat the mustard or vegetable oil with the paste until it is well blended. Keep the window open and take care not to overheat the mixture as any smoke from the mustard oil will sting the eyes.

3 Stir the ground coriander, fennel seeds, mustard and coconut milk into the pan. Gently bring the mixture to the boil and then lower the heat and simmer, uncovered, for about 5 minutes.

4 Add the fish chunks. Simmer for 2 minutes, then fold in the king prawns and cook until the prawns turn a bright orange/pink colour. Season with salt, fold in the chopped fresh coriander and serve immediately, garnished with the fresh green chillies.

Energy 204kcal/852kJ; Fat 12.1g; Saturated fat 1.6g; Carbohydrate 3.7g; Fibre 1.4g.

Prawns with Chayote in Turmeric Sauce

This delicious, attractively coloured dish contains the squash chayote, but courgette also works well.

Serves 4

1 or 2 chayotes or 2 or 3
    courgettes (zucchini)
2 fresh red chillies, seeded
1 onion, quartered
5ml/1 tsp grated fresh root ginger
1 lemon grass stalk, lower
    5cm/2in sliced, top bruised

2.5cm/1in fresh turmeric, peeled
200ml/7fl oz/scant 1 cup water
lemon juice
400ml/14fl oz can coconut milk
450g/1lb cooked, peeled prawns
    (shrimp)
salt
fresh red chilli shreds, to garnish
boiled rice, to serve

1 Peel the chayotes, remove the seeds and cut into strips. If using courgettes, cut into 5cm/2in strips.

2 Grind the fresh red chillies, onion, ginger, sliced lemon grass and the fresh turmeric to a paste in a food processor or with a pestle and mortar. Add the water to the paste mixture, with a squeeze of lemon juice and salt to taste.

3 Pour into a pan. Add the top of the lemon grass stem. Bring to the boil and cook for 1–2 minutes. Add the chayote or courgette pieces and cook for 2 minutes. Stir in the coconut milk. Taste and adjust the seasoning.

4 Stir in the prawns and cook gently for 2–3 minutes. Remove the lemon grass stalk. Garnish with shreds of chilli and serve with rice.

Cook's Tip
The chayote is a small, green pear-shaped squash, whose mild taste is rather like a cross between a cucumber and an apple.

Pineapple Curry with Prawns & Mussels

The delicate sweet-and-sour flavour of this curry comes from the pineapple and although it seems an odd combination, it is rather delicious. Use the freshest shellfish that you can find.

Serves 4–6

600ml/1 pint/2½ cups
    coconut milk
30ml/2 tbsp curry paste
15ml/1 tbsp sugar

225g/8oz king prawns (jumbo
    shrimp), peeled and deveined
450g/1lb mussels, cleaned
    (see Cook's Tip)
175g/6oz fresh pineapple, finely
    crushed or chopped
2 bay leaves
2 fresh red chillies, chopped,
    and coriander (cilantro) leaves,
    to garnish

1 In a large pan, bring half the coconut milk to the boil and heat, stirring, until it separates.

2 Add the curry paste and cook until fragrant. Add the sugar and continue to cook for 1 minute.

3 Stir in the remainder of the coconut milk and bring back to the boil. Add the king prawns, mussels, chopped pineapple and bay leaves.

4 Reheat until boiling and then simmer for 3–5 minutes, until the prawns are cooked and the mussels have opened. Remove any mussels that have not opened and throw them away. Discard the bay leaves if you like. Serve the curry garnished with chopped red chillies and coriander leaves.

Cook's Tip
To clean mussels, scrub the shells with a stiff brush and rinse them under cold running water. Scrape off any barnacles and remove the "beards" with a small knife. Rinse well.

Energy 132kcal/559kJ; Fat 1.3g; Saturated fat 0.4g; Carbohydrate 9g; Fibre 1.1g.

Energy 125kcal/534kJ; Fat 1.7g; Saturated fat 0.5g; Carbohydrate 12.8; Fibre 0.5g.

Curried Prawns in Coconut Milk

This is a curry-like dish where the prawns are cooked in a spicy coconut gravy. It is a simple but flavoursome dish that is quick to prepare.

Serves 4–6
600ml/1 pint/2½ cups coconut milk
30ml/2 tbsp yellow curry paste
2.5ml/½ tsp salt
5ml/1 tsp sugar
450g/1lb king prawns
   (jumbo shrimp), peeled,
   tails left intact, deveined
225g/8oz cherry tomatoes
juice of ½ lime, to serve
red chilli strips and coriander
   (cilantro) leaves, to garnish

1 Put half the coconut milk into a pan or wok and bring to the boil.

2 Add the curry paste to the coconut milk, stir until it disperses, then simmer for about 10 minutes.

3 Add the salt, sugar and remaining coconut milk. Simmer for another 5 minutes.

4 Add the prawns and cherry tomatoes. Simmer very gently for about 5 minutes until the prawns are pink and tender.

5 Serve sprinkled with lime juice and garnished with chillies and fresh coriander.

Cook's Tip
Curry paste is a useful standby, but if you prefer a more authentic flavour you can make your own curry powder and mix 30ml/2 tbsp of it with a little water to form a paste. Dry roast 75g/3oz/1 cup coriander seeds, 15ml/1 tbsp cumin seeds, 8 dried red chillies, 12 cardamom pods and 12 cloves gently for 10 minutes. Cool and add 5ml/1 tsp turmeric and 15ml/ 1 tbsp ground cinnamon. Grind to a fine powder and store in an airtight jar.

Energy 129kcal/547kJ; Fat 1.4g; Saturated fat 0.5g; Carbohydrate 9g; Fibre 0.6g.

Prawns with Okra

This dish has a sweet taste with a strong chilli flavour. It should be cooked fast to prevent the okra from breaking up and releasing its distinctive, sticky juice.

Serves 4–6
4–6 tbsp oil
225g/8oz okra, washed, dried and
   left whole
4 cloves garlic, crushed
1 piece fresh ginger, 5cm/2in long,
   crushed
4–6 fresh green chillies,
   cut diagonally
2.5ml/½ tsp turmeric
4–6 curry leaves
5ml/1 tsp cumin seeds
450g/1lb fresh king prawns
   (jumbo shrimp), peeled
   and deveined
10ml/2 tsp brown sugar
juice of 2 lemons
salt

1 Heat the oil in a frying pan and fry the okra over a fairly high heat until they are slightly crisp and browned on all sides. Remove from the oil and put to one side on a piece of kitchen paper.

2 In the same oil, gently fry the garlic, ginger, chillies, turmeric, curry leaves and cumin seeds for 2–3 minutes. Add the prawns and mix well. Cook until the prawns are tender.

3 Add the salt, sugar, lemon juice and fried okra. Increase the heat and quickly fry for a further 5 minutes, stirring gently to prevent the okra from breaking. Adjust the seasoning, if necessary. Serve hot.

Cook's Tip
Okra, sometimes known as "lady's fingers" is a small, long seed pod that exudes a sticky liquid when the pod is cut. This liquid is useful for dishes that require a thick sauce, but for other dishes, such as this one, the pod must be left whole. Remove the stalk using a sharp knife but do not cut into the pod itself.

Energy 215kcal/895kJ; Fat 12.3g; Saturated fat 1.6g; Carbohydrate 4.6g; Fibre 2.5g.

King Prawn Korma

This korma has a light, mild, creamy texture, and makes a good introduction to Indian cuisine for people who claim not to like spicy food.

Serves 4

12–16 cooked king prawns (jumbo shrimp), peeled and deveined
45ml/3 tbsp natural (plain) low-fat yogurt
45ml/3 tbsp low-fat fromage frais or ricotta cheese
5ml/1 tsp ground paprika
5ml/1 tsp garam masala
15ml/1 tbsp tomato purée (paste)
45ml/3 tbsp coconut milk
5ml/1 tsp chilli powder
150ml/¼ pint/⅔ cup water
15ml/1 tbsp oil
5ml/1 tsp crushed garlic
5ml/1 tsp grated fresh root ginger
½ cinnamon stick
2 green cardamom pods
salt
15ml/1 tbsp chopped fresh coriander (cilantro), to garnish

1 Rinse the prawns and drain them thoroughly to ensure that all excess liquid is removed.

2 Place the yogurt, fromage frais or ricotta, paprika, garam masala, tomato purée, coconut milk, chilli powder and water in a bowl.

3 Stir the yogurt and coconut mixture together well and set aside.

4 Heat the oil in a karahi, wok or heavy pan, add the crushed garlic, ginger, cinnamon stick, cardamoms and salt to taste and fry over low heat.

5 Increase the heat and pour in the yogurt and coconut mixture. Bring to the boil, stirring occasionally.

6 Add the drained king prawns to the spices and continue to stir-fry until the prawns are thoroughly heated through and the sauce is quite thick. Serve the korma garnished with the chopped fresh coriander.

Goan Prawn Curry

Cardamom, cloves and cinnamon are the essential flavourings for this dish.

Serves 4

15g/½oz/1 tbsp ghee or butter
2 garlic cloves, crushed
450g/1lb small raw prawns (shrimp), peeled and deveined
15ml/1 tbsp groundnut (peanut) oil
4 cardamom pods
4 cloves
5cm/2in piece cinnamon stick
15ml/1 tbsp mustard seeds
1 large onion, finely chopped
½–1 fresh red chilli, seeded and sliced
4 tomatoes, peeled, seeded and chopped
175ml/6fl oz/¾ cup fish stock or water
350ml/12fl oz/1½ cups coconut milk
45ml/3 tbsp Fragrant Spice Mix (see Cook's Tip)
10–20ml/2–4 tsp chilli powder
salt
turmeric-coloured basmati rice, to serve

1 Melt the ghee or butter in a wok, karahi or large pan, add the garlic and stir over a low heat for a few seconds. Add the prawns and stir-fry briskly to coat. Transfer to a plate. In the same pan, heat the oil and fry the cardamom, cloves and cinnamon for 2 minutes. Add the mustard seeds and fry for 1 minute. Add the onion and chilli and fry for 7–8 minutes or until softened and lightly browned.

2 Add the remaining ingredients except the prawns and bring to a slow simmer. Cook gently for 6–8 minutes and add the prawns. Simmer for 5–8 minutes until the prawns are cooked through. Serve the curry with basmati rice cooked with turmeric so that it is tinted a pale yellow colour, and lightly flavoured with the spice.

Cook's Tip
To make a Fragrant Spice Mix, dry-fry 25ml/1½ tbsp coriander seeds, 15ml/1 tbsp mixed peppercorns, 5ml/1 tsp cumin seeds, 1.5ml/¼ tsp fenugreek seeds and 1.5ml/¼ tsp fennel seeds until aromatic, then grind finely in a spice mill.

Energy 93kcal/391kJ; Fat 4.1g; Saturated fat 0.57g; Carbohydrate 7.2g; Fibre 0.4g.

Energy 187kcal/784kJ; Fat 7g; Saturated fat 2.8g; Carbohydrate 10.5g; Fibre 1.3g.

Cod & Prawn Green Coconut Curry

This quick curry involves very little preparation, and takes just minutes to cook, so it's ideal if friends spring a surprise visit. If you can't find green masala curry paste at your local grocer or supermarket, simply substitute another variety – the curry will taste just as good.

Serves 4
675g/1½lb cod fillets, skinned
90ml/6 tbsp green masala
   curry paste
175ml/6fl oz/¾ cup canned
   coconut milk
175g/6oz raw or cooked, peeled
   prawns (shrimp)
fresh coriander (cilantro),
   to garnish
basmati rice, to serve

1 Using a sharp knife, cut the skinned cod fillets into 4cm/1½in pieces.

2 Put the green masala curry paste and coconut milk in a frying pan. Heat to simmering and simmer gently for 5 minutes, stirring occasionally.

3 Add the cod pieces and prawns (if raw) to the cream mixture and cook gently for 5 minutes. If using ready-cooked prawns rather than raw shellfish, add them to the pan after this time has elapsed, and heat through.

4 Spoon into a serving dish, garnish the curry with fresh coriander and serve immediately with basmati rice.

> **Variation**
> Any firm fish, such as monkfish, can be used instead of cod. Whole fish steaks can be cooked in the sauce, but allow an extra 5 minutes' cooking time and baste them with the sauce from time to time.

Rich Prawn Curry

A rich, flavoursome curry made with tiger prawns and a delicious blend of aromatic spices.

Serves 4
675g/1½lb tiger prawns (shrimp)
4 dried red chillies
25g/1oz/⅓ cup desiccated
   (dry unsweetened shredded)
   coconut
5ml/1 tsp black mustard seeds
1 large onion, chopped
30ml/2 tbsp oil
4 bay leaves
2.5cm/1in piece fresh root ginger,
   finely chopped
2 garlic cloves, crushed
15ml/1 tbsp ground coriander
5ml/1 tsp chilli powder
5ml/1 tsp salt
4 tomatoes, finely chopped
plain rice, to serve

1 Peel the prawns and discard the shells. Run a sharp knife along the centre back of each prawn to make a shallow cut and carefully remove the thin black intestinal vein. Set aside.

2 Put the dried red chillies, coconut, mustard seeds and onion in a large, heavy frying pan and dry-fry for 8–10 minutes or until the spices begin to brown. The onion should turn a deep golden brown but do not let it burn or it will taste bitter.

3 Tip the mixture into a food processor or blender and process to a coarse paste.

4 Heat the oil in the frying pan and fry the bay leaves for 1 minute. Add the chopped ginger and the garlic and fry for 2–3 minutes. Add the coriander, chilli powder, salt and the coconut paste and fry gently for 5 minutes.

5 Stir in the chopped tomatoes and about 175ml/6fl oz/¾ cup water and simmer gently for 5–6 minutes or until the sauce has thickened.

6 Add the prawns and cook for about 4–5 minutes or until they turn pink and the edges are curling slightly. Serve with plain boiled rice.

Energy 227kcal/954kJ; Fat 7.1g; Saturated fat 1g; Carbohydrate 2.2g; Fibre 0g.

Energy 289kcal/1212kJ; Fat 12.13g; Saturated fat 4.18g; Carbohydrate 12.77g; Fibre 2.65g.

Classic Tandoori Chicken

This is probably the most famous of all the Indian dishes. Marinate the chicken well and cook in an extremely hot oven for a clay-oven-baked taste. If you want authentic "burnt" spots on the chicken, place the dish under a hot grill for a few minutes after baking.

Serves 4–6
1.5kg/3lb oven-ready chicken
250ml/8fl oz/1 cup natural
  (plain) yogurt, beaten
60ml/4 tbsp tandoori
  masala paste
75g/3oz/6 tbsp ghee
salt
salad leaves, to serve
lemon twist and onion slices,
  to garnish

1 Using a sharp knife or scissors, remove the skin from the chicken and trim off any excess fat. Using a fork, beat the flesh at random.

2 Cut the chicken in half down the centre and through the breast. Cut each piece in half again. Make a few deep gashes diagonally into the flesh. Mix the yogurt with the masala paste and salt. Spread the chicken evenly with the yogurt mixture, spreading some into the gashes. Leave for at least 2 hours, but preferably overnight.

3 Preheat the oven to maximum heat. Place the chicken quarters on a wire rack in a deep baking tray. Spread the chicken with any excess marinade, reserve a little for basting halfway through cooking time.

4 Melt the ghee and pour over the chicken to seal the surface. This helps to keep the centre moist during the roasting period. Cook in the preheated oven for 10 minutes, then remove, leaving the oven on.

5 Baste the chicken pieces with the remaining marinade. Return to the oven and switch off the heat. Leave the chicken in the oven for about 15–20 minutes without opening the door. Serve on a bed of salad leaves and garnish with the lemon twist and onion slices.

Energy 610kcal/2530kJ; Fat 44.6g; Saturated fat 12.2g; Carbohydrate 3.8g; Fibre 0g.

Spicy Tandoori Chicken

A delicious and popular Indian–Pakistani chicken dish which is traditionally cooked in a clay oven called a tandoor, this is extremely popular in the West and appears on the majority of restaurant menus.

Serves 4
4 chicken quarters, skinned
175ml/6fl oz/3/4 cup natural
  (plain) low-fat yogurt

5ml/1 tsp garam masala
5ml/1 tsp grated fresh root ginger
5ml/1 tsp crushed garlic
7.5ml/11/2 tsp chilli powder
1.5ml/1/4 tsp ground turmeric
5ml/1 tsp ground coriander
15ml/1 tbsp lemon juice
5ml/1 tsp salt
few drops of red food
  colouring
15ml/1 tbsp oil
mixed salad leaves, to serve
lime wedges, to garnish

1 Rinse and pat dry the chicken quarters. Make two deep slits in the flesh of each piece, place in a dish and set aside.

2 Mix together the yogurt, garam masala, ginger, garlic, chilli powder, turmeric, coriander, lemon juice, salt, red food colouring and oil, and beat so that all the ingredients are well combined.

3 Cover the chicken quarters with the spice mixture, cover and leave to marinate for about 3 hours.

4 Preheat the oven to 240°C/475°F/Gas 9. Transfer the chicken pieces to an ovenproof dish.

5 Bake the chicken in the oven for 20–25 minutes or until the chicken is cooked right through and evenly browned on top.

6 Remove from the oven, arrange on salad leaves on a serving dish and garnish with lime wedges.

> **Cook's Tip**
> *The traditional bright red colour is derived from food colouring. This is only optional and may be omitted if you prefer.*

Energy 300kcal/1256kJ; Fat 12g; Saturated fat 3.39g; Carbohydrate 5.9g; Fibre 0.2g.

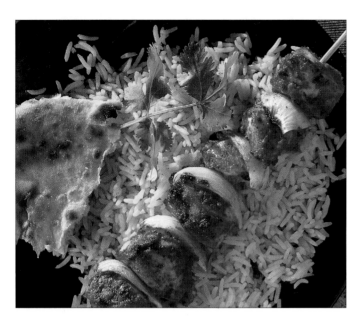

Tandoori Chicken Kebabs

This dish originates from the plains of the Punjab at the foot of the Himalayas. Allow the chicken to marinate for about three hours to absorb the tandoori flavourings.

Serves 4

4 skinned chicken breast fillets, about 175g/6oz each
15ml/1 tbsp lemon juice
45ml/3 tbsp tandoori paste
45ml/3 tbsp natural (plain) low-fat yogurt
1 garlic clove, crushed
30ml/2 tbsp chopped fresh coriander (cilantro)
salt and ground black pepper
1 small onion, cut into wedges and separated into layers
a little oil, for brushing
fresh coriander sprigs, to garnish
pilau rice and naan bread, to serve

1 Chop the chicken breast fillets into 2.5cm/1in cubes, place in a mixing bowl and add the lemon juice, tandoori paste, yogurt, garlic, chopped coriander and seasoning. Cover and leave the chicken to marinate in the refrigerator for 2–3 hours.

2 Preheat the grill (broiler) to high. Thread alternate pieces of marinated chicken and onion on to four skewers.

3 Brush the onions with a little oil, place on a grill rack and cook under a high heat for 10–12 minutes, or until the chicken is cooked through, turning once midway through. Garnish the kebabs with fresh coriander sprigs and serve with pilau rice and naan bread.

Cook's Tip
Use chopped, boned and skinned chicken thighs, or turkey breasts, for a tasty and less expensive alternative.

Energy 257kcal/1078kJ; Fat 9.4g; Saturated fat 2.31g; Carbohydrate 3.5g; Fibre 2.9g.

Stuffed Roast Chicken

At one time this dish was cooked only in royal palaces and the ingredients varied according to individual chefs. The saffron and the rich stuffing make it a truly royal dish.

Serves 4–6
1 sachet saffron powder
2.5ml/½ tsp ground nutmeg
15ml/1 tbsp warm milk
1.3kg/3lb whole chicken
75g/3oz/6 tbsp ghee
75ml/5 tbsp hot water

For the stuffing
3 medium onions, finely chopped
2 fresh green chillies, chopped
50g/2oz/⅓ cup sultanas (golden raisins)

50g/2oz/½ cup ground almonds
50g/2oz dried apricots, soaked until soft
3 hard-boiled eggs, coarsely chopped
salt

For the masala
4 spring onions (scallions), chopped
2 cloves garlic, crushed
5ml/1 tsp five-spice powder
4–6 green cardamom pods
2.5ml/½ tsp turmeric
5ml/1 tsp ground black pepper
30ml/2 tbsp natural (plain) yogurt
50g/2oz/1 cup desiccated (dry unsweetened shredded) coconut, toasted

1 Mix together the saffron, nutmeg and milk. Use to brush the inside of the chicken and over the skin. Heat 50g/2oz/4 tbsp of the ghee in a large frying pan and fry the chicken on all sides to seal it. Remove and keep warm.

2 To make the stuffing, in the same ghee, fry the onions, chillies, and sultanas for 2–3 minutes. Allow to cool and add the ground almonds, apricots, chopped eggs and salt. Use to stuff the chicken.

3 Heat the remaining ghee in a large, heavy pan and gently fry all the masala ingredients except the coconut for 2–3 minutes. Add the water. Place the chicken on the bed of masala, cover the pan and cook until the chicken is tender. Remove the chicken from the pan. Cook the liquid to reduce excess fluids in the masala. When the mixture thickens, pour over the chicken. Sprinkle with toasted coconut and serve hot.

Energy 823kcal/3420kJ; Fat 57.9g; Saturated fat 19.7g; Carbohydrate 21.1g; Fibre 4.9g.

Jeera Chicken

An aromatic dish with a delicious, distinctive taste of cumin. Serve simply with a cooling cucumber raita.

Serves 4

45ml/3 tbsp cumin seeds
15ml/1 tbsp oil
2.5ml/½ tsp black peppercorns
4 green cardamom pods
2 fresh green chillies,
    finely chopped
2 garlic cloves, crushed
2.5cm/1in piece fresh root
    ginger, grated
5ml/1 tsp ground coriander
10ml/2 tsp ground cumin
2.5ml/½ tsp salt
8 chicken pieces, skinned
5ml/1 tsp garam masala
fresh coriander (cilantro)
    and chilli powder,
    to garnish
cucumber raita, to serve

1 Dry-roast 15ml/1 tbsp of the cumin seeds for 5 minutes and then set aside.

2 Heat the oil in a large, heavy pan or wok and fry the remaining cumin seeds, black peppercorns and cardamoms for about 2–3 minutes.

3 Add the chillies, garlic and ginger and fry for about 2 minutes.

4 Add the ground coriander, ground cumin and salt. Stir well, then cook for a further 2–3 minutes.

5 Add the chicken and stir to coat the pieces in the sauce. Cover with a lid and simmer for 20–25 minutes.

6 Add the garam masala and reserved toasted cumin seeds and cook for a further 5 minutes. Garnish with fresh coriander and chilli powder and serve with cucumber raita.

Cook's Tip
Dry-roast the cumin seeds in a small, heavy frying pan over a medium heat, stirring them until they turn a few shades darker and give off a wonderful roasted aroma.

Chicken Naan Pockets

This easy dish is ideal for a light snack lunch or supper. For speed, use the ready-baked naans available in most of today's supermarkets and Asian stores, but beware that as they are larger than typical home-cooked naan they will contain more fat.

Serves 4

4 small naan, about 90g/3½oz
    each
45ml/3 tbsp natural (plain)
    low-fat yogurt
7.5ml/1½ tsp garam masala
5ml/1 tsp chilli powder
5ml/1 tsp salt
45ml/3 tbsp lemon juice
15ml/1 tbsp chopped fresh
    coriander (cilantro)
1 fresh green chilli, chopped
450g/1lb skinned boneless
    chicken, cubed
8 onion rings
2 tomatoes, quartered
½ white cabbage, shredded

For the garnish
mixed salad leaves
2 small tomatoes, halved
lemon wedges
fresh coriander (cilantro)

1 Cut into the middle of each naan to make a pocket, then set them aside.

2 Mix together the yogurt, garam masala, chilli powder, salt, lemon juice, fresh coriander and chopped green chilli.

3 Pour the marinade over the chicken, cover and leave to marinate for about 1 hour.

4 Preheat the grill (broiler) to very hot, then lower the heat to medium. Put the chicken pieces in a pan or flameproof dish lined with foil.

5 Grill (broil) for 15–20 minutes until tender and fully cooked, turning the chicken twice.

6 Remove from the heat and fill each naan with the chicken and then with the onion rings, tomatoes and cabbage. Serve garnished with mixed salad leaves, tomato halves, lemon wedges and coriander.

Energy 286kcal/1198kJ; Fat 14.1g; Saturated fat 3.19g; Carbohydrate 7.6g; Fibre 0.1g.

Energy 472kcal/1986kJ; Fat 15.3g; Saturated fat 6.46g; Carbohydrate 53.4g; Fibre 4.2g.

Goan Chicken Curry

Coconut in all its forms is widely used to enrich Goan cuisine.

Serves 4
75g/3oz/1 cup desiccated (dry unsweetened shredded) coconut
30ml/2 tbsp vegetable oil
2.5ml/½ tsp cumin seeds
4 black peppercorns
15ml/1 tbsp fennel seeds
15ml/1 tbsp coriander seeds
2 onions, finely chopped
2.5ml/½ tsp salt
8 small chicken pieces, such as thighs and drumsticks, skinned
fresh coriander (cilantro) sprigs and lemon wedges, to garnish

1 Put the desiccated coconut in a bowl with 45ml/3 tbsp water. Leave to soak for 15 minutes.

2 Heat 15ml/1 tbsp of the oil in a karahi, wok or large pan and fry the cumin seeds, peppercorns, fennel and coriander seeds over a low heat for 3–4 minutes until they begin to splutter.

3 Add the finely chopped onions and fry for about 5 minutes without browning, stirring occasionally, until the onion has softened and turned opaque.

4 Stir in the coconut, along with the soaking water and salt, and continue to fry for a further 5 minutes, stirring occasionally to prevent the mixture from sticking to the pan.

5 Put the coconut mixture into a food processor or blender and process to form a coarse paste. Spoon into a bowl and set aside until required.

6 Heat the remaining oil and fry the chicken for 10 minutes. Add the coconut paste and cook over a low heat for 15–20 minutes, or until the coconut mixture is golden brown and the chicken is tender.

7 Transfer the curry to a warmed serving plate, and garnish with sprigs of fresh coriander and lemon wedges. Mint and Coconut Chutney, rice or lentils make good accompaniments.

Energy 305kcal/1271kJ; Fat 21.4g; Saturated fat 12.1g; Carbohydrate 1.2g; Fibre 2.6g.

Chicken Dopiaza

Dopiaza translates literally as "two onions" and describes this chicken dish in which two types of onion – large and small – are used at different stages.

Serves 4
30ml/2 tbsp oil
8 small onions, halved
2 bay leaves
8 green cardamom pods
4 cloves
3 dried red chillies
8 black peppercorns
2 medium onions, finely chopped
2 garlic cloves, crushed
2.5cm/1in piece fresh root ginger, finely chopped
5ml/1 tsp ground coriander
5ml/1 tsp ground cumin
2.5ml/½ tsp ground turmeric
5ml/1 tsp chilli powder
2.5ml/½ tsp salt
4 tomatoes, peeled and finely chopped
120ml/4fl oz/½ cup water
8 chicken pieces, such as thighs and drumsticks, skinned
plain rice, to serve

1 Heat half the oil in a wok or large heavy pan and fry the small onions for 10 minutes, or until golden brown. Remove and set aside.

2 Add the remaining oil and fry the bay leaves, cardamoms, cloves, chillies and peppercorns for 2 minutes. Add the medium onions, garlic and ginger and fry for 5 minutes. Stir in the ground spices and salt and cook for 2 minutes.

3 Add the tomatoes and water and simmer for 5 minutes until the sauce thickens. Add the chicken and cook for 15 minutes.

4 Add the reserved small onions, then cover and cook for a further 10 minutes, or until the chicken is cooked through. Spoon the mixture on to a serving dish or individual plates. Serve with plain boiled rice.

Cook's Tip
Soak the small onions in boiling water for 2–3 minutes to make them easier to peel.

Energy 352kcal/1469kJ; Fat 15.1g; Saturated fat 3.67g; Carbohydrate 22.6g; Fibre 3.9g.

Chicken Dhansak

Dhansak curries originally came from Iran with the Parsee community. The curries traditionally include lentils, which make the dish substantial and flavoursome.

Serves 4

75g/3oz/⅓ cup green lentils
475ml/16fl oz/2 cups chicken
   stock
15ml/1 tbsp oil
5ml/1 tsp cumin seeds
2 curry leaves
1 onion, finely chopped
2.5cm/1in piece fresh root
   ginger, chopped
1 fresh green chilli, finely chopped
5ml/1 tsp ground cumin
5ml/1 tsp ground coriander
1.5ml/¼ tsp salt
1.5ml/¼ tsp chilli powder
400g/14oz can chopped
   tomatoes
8 chicken pieces, skinned
90ml/6 tbsp chopped fresh
   coriander (cilantro)
5ml/1 tsp garam masala
boiled plain and yellow rice,
   to serve

1 Rinse the lentils under cold running water. Put into a pan with the stock. Bring to the boil, cover and simmer for about 15–20 minutes. Put the lentils and stock to one side.

2 Heat the oil in a large, heavy pan and fry the cumin seeds and curry leaves for 2 minutes. Add the onion, ginger and chilli and fry for about 5 minutes. Stir in the cumin, ground coriander, salt and chilli powder with 30ml/2 tbsp water.

3 Add the tomatoes and the chicken pieces to the spices. Cover and cook for 10–15 minutes.

4 Add the lentils and stock, half the chopped fresh coriander and the garam masala. Cook for a further 10 minutes or until the chicken is tender. Garnish with the remaining fresh coriander and serve with spiced plain and yellow rice.

> **Cook's Tip**
> *Before cooking green lentils, always pick them over and remove any small sticks or stones that might be hidden.*

Energy 328kcal/1376kJ; Fat 10.8g; Saturated fat 2.54g; Carbohydrate 19.7g; Fibre 3.5g.

Hot Chilli Chicken

Not for the faint-hearted, this fiery hot curry is made with a spicy chilli masala paste.

Serves 4

30ml/2 tbsp tomato purée
   (paste)
2 garlic cloves, roughly chopped
2 fresh green chillies, roughly
   chopped
5 dried red chillies
2.5ml/½ tsp salt
1.5ml/¼ tsp sugar
5ml/1 tsp chilli powder
2.5ml/½ tsp paprika
15ml/1 tbsp curry paste
15ml/1 tbsp oil
2.5ml/½ tsp cumin seeds
1 onion, finely chopped
2 bay leaves
5ml/1 tsp ground coriander
5ml/1 tsp ground cumin
1.5ml/¼ tsp ground turmeric
400g/14oz can chopped
   tomatoes
150ml/¼ pint/⅔ cup water
8 chicken thighs, skinned
5ml/1 tsp garam masala
sliced fresh green chillies,
   to garnish
chapatis and natural (plain)
   low-fat yogurt, to serve

1 Put the tomato purée, chopped garlic cloves, fresh green chillies and the dried red chillies into a food processor or blender.

2 Add the salt, sugar, chilli powder, paprika and curry paste. Process all the ingredients to a smooth paste, stopping once or twice to scrape down any of the mixture that has stuck to the sides of the bowl.

3 Heat the oil in a large, heavy pan and fry the cumin seeds for 2 minutes. Add the onion and bay leaves and fry for about 5 minutes.

4 Add the chilli paste and fry the mixture for 2–3 minutes. Add the ground coriander, cumin and turmeric and cook for 2 minutes. Add the tomatoes.

5 Pour in the water and stir to mix. Bring to the boil and simmer for 5 minutes until the sauce thickens. Add the chicken and garam masala. Cover and simmer for 25–30 minutes, until the chicken is tender. Garnish with sliced green chillies and serve with chapatis and natural low-fat yogurt.

Energy 290kcal/1212kJ; Fat 13g; Saturated fat 3.5g; Carbohydrate 11.6g; Fibre 1.4g.

Chicken in Cashew Nut Sauce

This strongly flavoured chicken dish has a deliciously thick and nutty sauce, and is best served with plain boiled rice.

Serves 4

2 medium onions
30ml/2 tbsp tomato purée (paste)
50g/2oz/½ cup cashew nuts
7.5ml/1½ tsp garam masala
5ml/1 tsp crushed garlic
5ml/1 tsp chilli powder
15ml/1 tbsp lemon juice
1.5ml/¼ tsp ground turmeric
5ml/1 tsp salt
15ml/1 tbsp natural (plain) low-fat yogurt
30ml/2 tbsp oil
30ml/2 tbsp chopped fresh coriander (cilantro)
15ml/1 tbsp sultanas (golden raisins)
450g/1lb boneless chicken, skinned and cubed
175g/6oz/2½ cups button (white) mushrooms
300ml/½ pint/1¼ cups water

1 Cut the onions into quarters, place in a food processor or blender and process for about 1 minute. Add the tomato purée, cashew nuts, garam masala, garlic, chilli powder, lemon juice, turmeric, salt and yogurt. Process the spiced onion mixture in the food processor for a further 1–1½ minutes.

2 In a heavy pan or karahi, heat the oil, lower the heat to medium and pour in the spice mixture from the food processor. Fry the mixture for 2 minutes, lowering the heat a little more if necessary.

3 When the spice mixture is lightly cooked, add half the chopped fresh coriander, the sultanas and the chicken cubes and continue to stir-fry for a further 1 minute.

4 Add the mushrooms, pour in the water and simmer. Cover the pan and cook over a low heat for about 10 minutes.

5 After this time, check that the chicken is cooked through and the sauce is thick. Cook for a little longer if necessary, then spoon into a serving bowl. Garnish with the remaining fresh coriander and serve.

Chicken Saag

A mildly spiced dish using a popular combination of spinach and chicken. This recipe is best made using fresh spinach.

Serves 4

225g/8oz fresh spinach leaves, washed but not dried
2.5cm/1in piece fresh root ginger, grated
2 garlic cloves, crushed
1 fresh green chilli, roughly chopped
200ml/7fl oz/scant 1 cup water
15ml/1 tbsp oil
2 bay leaves
1.5ml/¼ tsp black peppercorns
1 onion, finely chopped
4 tomatoes, peeled and finely chopped
10ml/2 tsp curry powder
5ml/1 tsp salt
5ml/1 tsp chilli powder
45ml/3 tbsp natural (plain) low-fat yogurt
8 chicken thighs, skinned
naan bread, to serve
natural low-fat yogurt and chilli powder, to garnish

1 Cook the spinach leaves, without extra water, in a tightly covered pan for 5 minutes. Put the cooked spinach, ginger, garlic and chilli with 50ml/2fl oz/¼ cup of the measured water into a food processor or blender and process to a thick purée. Set aside.

2 Heat the oil in a large, heavy pan, add the bay leaves and black peppercorns and fry for 2 minutes. Stir in the onion and fry for a further 6–8 minutes or until the onion has browned.

3 Add the tomatoes and simmer for about 5 minutes.

4 Stir in the curry powder, salt and chilli powder. Cook for 2 minutes over medium heat, stirring once or twice. Stir in the spinach purée and the remaining measured water, then simmer for 5 minutes. Add the yogurt, 15ml/1 tbsp at a time, and simmer for 5 minutes.

5 Add the chicken thighs and stir to coat them in the sauce. Cover and cook for 25–30 minutes until the chicken is tender. Serve on naan bread, drizzle over some natural yogurt and dust with chilli powder.

Energy 283kcal/1182kJ; Fat 12.70g; Saturated fat 3.48g; Carbohydrate 9.70g; Fibre 3.10g.

Energy 283kcal/1182kJ; Fat 12.7g; Saturated fat 3.48g; Carbohydrate 9.7g; Fibre 3.1g.

Chicken Tikka Masala

This is said to be the UK's favourite chicken dish. In this version, tender chicken pieces are cooked in a creamy, spicy tomato sauce and served on naan bread.

Serves 4
675g/1½lb skinned chicken
  breast portions
90ml/6 tbsp tikka paste
120ml/4fl oz/½ cup natural
  (plain) low-fat yogurt
15ml/1 tbsp oil
1 onion, chopped

1 garlic clove, crushed
1 fresh green chilli, seeded
  and chopped
2.5cm/1in piece fresh root
  ginger, grated
15ml/1 tbsp tomato purée
  (paste)
250ml/8fl oz/1 cup water
a little melted ghee or butter
15ml/1 tbsp lemon juice
fresh coriander (cilantro) sprigs,
  natural (plain) low-fat yogurt
  and toasted cumin seeds,
  to garnish
naan bread, to serve

1 Cut the chicken into 2.5cm/1in cubes. Mix 45ml/3 tbsp of the tikka paste and 60ml/4 tbsp of the yogurt into a bowl. Add the chicken and leave to marinate for 20 minutes.

2 Heat the oil in a heavy pan and fry the onion, garlic, chilli and ginger for 5 minutes. Add the remaining tikka paste and fry for 2 minutes. Stir in the tomato purée and water, bring to the boil and simmer for 15 minutes.

3 Meanwhile, thread the chicken pieces on to wooden kebab skewers. Preheat the grill (broiler).

4 Brush the chicken pieces with melted ghee or butter and cook under a medium heat for 15 minutes, turning occasionally.

5 Put the tikka sauce into a food processor or blender and process until smooth. Return to the pan.

6 Add the remaining yogurt and the lemon juice, remove the chicken from the skewers and add to the pan, then simmer for 5 minutes. Garnish with the fresh coriander, yogurt and toasted cumin seeds and serve on naan bread.

Chicken with Green Mango

Green, unripe mango is used for making various dishes on the Indian subcontinent, including pickles, chutneys and some meat, chicken and vegetable dishes. This is a fairly simple chicken dish to prepare and is good served with rice and dhal.

Serves 4
1 medium green mango
450g/1lb skinned boneless
  chicken, cubed
1.5ml/¼ tsp onion seeds

5ml/1 tsp grated fresh root
  ginger
2.5ml/½ tsp crushed garlic
5ml/1 tsp chilli powder
1.5ml/¼ tsp ground turmeric
5ml/1 tsp salt
5ml/1 tsp ground coriander
30ml/2 tbsp oil
2 medium onions, sliced
4 curry leaves
300ml/½ pint/1¼ cups water
2 medium tomatoes, quartered
2 fresh green chillies, chopped
30ml/2 tbsp chopped fresh
  coriander (cilantro)

1 To prepare the mango, peel off the skin and slice the flesh thickly. Discard the stone (pit) from the middle. Place the mango slices in a small bowl, cover and set aside.

2 Place the chicken cubes in a bowl and add the onion seeds, ginger, garlic, chilli powder, turmeric, salt and ground coriander. Mix to coat the chicken with the spices, then add half the mango slices.

3 In a medium, heavy pan, heat the oil and fry the sliced onions until golden brown. Add the curry leaves and stir lightly.

4 Gradually add the chicken pieces and mango to the onions in the pan, stirring all the time.

5 Pour in the water, lower the heat and cook for about 12–15 minutes, stirring occasionally, until the chicken is cooked through and the water has been absorbed.

6 Add the remaining mango slices, the quartered tomatoes, chopped green chillies and fresh coriander. Serve the curry piping hot.

Energy 315kcal/1321kJ; Fat 12.5g; Saturated fat 4g; Carbohydrate 7.5g; Fibre 0.6g.

Energy 281kcal/1172kJ; Fat 11.2g; Saturated fat 2.44g; Carbohydrate 20.6g; Fibre 3.6g.

Chicken in Orange & Black Pepper Sauce

This is a low-fat version of a favourite Indian dish which is very creamy and full of flavour.

Serves 4

225g/8oz low-fat fromage frais
  or ricotta cheese
50ml/2fl oz/¼ cup natural
  (plain) low-fat yogurt
120ml/4fl oz/½ cup orange juice
7.5ml/1½ tsp grated fresh
  root ginger

5ml/1 tsp crushed garlic
5ml/1 tsp ground black pepper
5ml/1 tsp salt
5ml/1 tsp ground coriander
1 small chicken, about
  675g/1½lb, skinned and cut
  into 8 pieces
15ml/1 tbsp oil
1 bay leaf
1 large onion, chopped
15ml/1 tbsp fresh mint leaves
1 fresh green chilli, seeded
  and chopped

1 In a small mixing bowl whisk the fromage frais or ricotta cheese with the yogurt, orange juice, ginger, garlic, pepper, salt and coriander.

2 Pour the fromage frais and orange mixture over the chicken, cover, and set aside for 3–4 hours.

3 Heat the oil with the bay leaf in a wok or heavy frying pan and fry the chopped onion for about 5 minutes or until just beginning to become soft.

4 Pour the chicken mixture into the pan with the onions and bay leaf and stir-fry for 3–5 minutes over a medium heat. Lower the heat, cover and cook for 7–10 minutes, adding a little water if the sauce is too thick. Add the fresh mint and chilli and serve.

> **Cook's Tip**
> If you prefer the spicy taste of curry leaves, you can use them instead of the bay leaf, but you will need to double the quantity.

Spicy Masala Chicken

These tender chicken pieces have a sweet-and-sour taste. Serve cold with a salad and rice or hot with potatoes.

Serves 6

12 chicken thighs, skinned
90ml/6 tbsp lemon juice
5ml/1 tsp grated fresh root
  ginger
5ml/1 tsp crushed garlic
5ml/1 tsp crushed dried
  red chillies
5ml/1 tsp salt
5ml/1 tsp soft brown sugar

30ml/2 tbsp clear honey
30ml/2 tbsp chopped fresh
  coriander (cilantro)
1 fresh green chilli, finely
  chopped
30ml/2 tbsp vegetable oil
fresh coriander, to garnish
yellow rice and salad,
  to serve

1 Prick the chicken thighs with a fork, rinse them, pat dry with kitchen paper and set aside in a bowl.

2 In a large mixing bowl, mix together the lemon juice, grated ginger, garlic, crushed dried red chillies, salt, sugar and honey.

3 Transfer the chicken thighs to the spice mixture and coat well. Cover and set aside for about 45 minutes.

4 Preheat the grill (broiler) to medium. Add the fresh coriander and chopped chilli to the chicken thighs and place them in a flameproof dish.

5 Pour any remaining marinade over the chicken and brush with the oil.

6 Grill (broil) the chicken thighs for 15–20 minutes, turning and basting with the marinade occasionally, until cooked through and browned.

7 Serve cold, garnished with fresh coriander and accompanied by yellow rice and salad.

Energy 199kcal/836kJ; Fat 5.11g; Saturated fat 1.06g; Carbohydrate 14.4g; Fibre 1.02g.

Energy 243kcal/1017kJ; Fat 12g; Saturated fat 3.18g; Carbohydrate 5.3g; Fibre 0g.

Mild Chicken Curry with Lentils

In this low-fat dish, the mildly spiced sauce is thickened using low-fat lentils rather than the traditional onions fried in ghee. The resulting dish is delicious and filling as well as healthy.

Serves 4–6
75g/3oz/⅓ cup red lentils
30ml/2 tbsp mild curry
   powder
10ml/2 tsp ground coriander
5ml/1 tsp cumin seeds
475ml/16fl oz/2 cups
   vegetable stock
8 chicken thighs, skinned
225g/8oz fresh spinach, shredded,
   or frozen spinach, thawed and
   well drained
15ml/1 tbsp chopped fresh
   coriander (cilantro), plus extra
   to garnish
salt and ground black pepper
white or brown basmati rice and
   grilled (broiled) poppadums,
   to serve

1 Put the red lentils in a large, heavy pan and add the mild curry powder, ground coriander, cumin seeds and vegetable stock.

2 Bring the mixture to the boil, then lower the heat. Cover and simmer for 10 minutes, stirring often.

3 Add the chicken thighs and spinach. Replace the cover and simmer gently for a further 40 minutes, or until the chicken is cooked through.

4 Stir in the chopped coriander and season with salt and ground black pepper to taste. Serve garnished with fresh coriander sprigs and accompanied by white or brown basmati rice and poppadums.

> **Cook's Tip**
> *Nourishing lentils are an excellent low-fat source of vitamins, protein and fibre. Yellow and red lentils, in particular, are very popular in Indian cooking, adding subtle colour and texture to dishes.*

Chicken Korma

Although kormas are traditionally rich and high in fat, this recipe uses low-fat yogurt instead of cream, which gives the sauce a delicious creamy flavour while keeping down the fat content.

Serves 4
675g/1½lb skinned chicken
   breast portions
2 garlic cloves, crushed
2.5cm/1in piece fresh root ginger,
   roughly chopped
15ml/1 tbsp oil
3 green cardamom pods
1 onion, finely chopped
10ml/2 tsp ground cumin
1.5ml/¼ tsp salt
300ml/½ pint/1¼ cups natural
   (plain) low-fat yogurt
toasted flaked or sliced almonds
   (optional) and a fresh coriander
   (cilantro) sprig, to garnish
plain rice, to serve

1 Using a sharp knife, remove any visible fat from the chicken and cut the meat into 2.5cm/1in cubes.

2 Put the crushed garlic and ginger into a food processor or blender with 30ml/2 tbsp water and process to a smooth, creamy paste.

3 Heat the oil in a large, heavy pan and cook the chicken cubes for 8–10 minutes until browned on all sides. Remove the chicken cubes with a slotted spoon and set aside.

4 Add the cardamom pods and fry for 2 minutes. Add the finely chopped onion and fry for a further 5 minutes. Stir in the garlic and ginger paste, cumin and salt and cook, stirring, for a further 5 minutes. Add half the yogurt, stirring in a spoonful at a time, and cook over a low heat until it has all been absorbed.

5 Return the chicken to the pan. Cover and simmer over a low heat for 5–6 minutes or until the chicken is tender.

6 Add the remaining yogurt and simmer for a further 5 minutes. Garnish with toasted almonds and coriander and serve with rice.

Energy 288kcal/1211kJ; Fat 9.3g; Saturated fat 2.54g; Carbohydrate 9.8g; Fibre 0.5g.

Energy 296kcal/1244kJ; Fat 10.2g; Saturated fat 2.83g; Carbohydrate 15.1g; Fibre 3.8g.

Chicken Jalfrezi

A jalfrezi is a stir-fried curry which features onions, ginger and garlic in a rich pepper sauce.

Serves 4

675g/1½lb chicken breast portions
15ml/1 tbsp oil
5ml/1 tsp cumin seeds
1 onion, finely chopped
1 green (bell) pepper, seeded and finely chopped
1 red (bell) pepper, seeded and finely chopped

1 garlic clove, crushed
2cm/¾in piece fresh root ginger, finely chopped
15ml/1 tbsp curry paste
1.5ml/¼ tsp chilli powder
5ml/1 tsp ground coriander
5ml/1 tsp ground cumin
2.5ml/½ tsp salt
400g/14oz can chopped tomatoes
30ml/2 tbsp chopped fresh coriander (cilantro), plus extra to garnish
plain rice, to serve

1 Skin the chicken breast portions and remove any visible fat. Cut the meat into 2.5cm/1in cubes.

2 Heat the oil in a karahi, wok or heavy pan and fry the cumin seeds for 2 minutes until they splutter. Add the onion, peppers, garlic and ginger and fry for 6–8 minutes.

3 Add the curry paste and fry for about 2 minutes. Stir in the chilli powder, ground coriander, cumin and salt and add 15ml/1 tbsp water; fry for a further 2 minutes.

4 Add the chicken cubes and fry for about 5 minutes. Add the canned tomatoes and chopped fresh coriander. Cover the pan tightly with a lid and cook for about 15 minutes or until the chicken cubes are tender. Garnish with sprigs of fresh coriander and serve with rice.

Cook's Tip
Removing the skin and any visible fat from the chicken makes a healthier dish which is low in fat.

Energy 291kcal/1224kJ; Fat 9.8g; Saturated fat 2.24g; Carbohydrate 11.7g; Fibre 3.5g.

Karahi Chicken with Fresh Fenugreek

Fresh fenugreek is a flavour that many people are unfamiliar with and this recipe is a good introduction to this delicious herb. The chicken is boiled before being quickly stir-fried, to make sure that it is cooked all the way through.

Serves 4

115g/4oz boneless chicken thigh meat, skinned and cut into strips
115g/4oz chicken breast fillet, skinned and cut into strips

2.5ml/½ tsp crushed garlic
5ml/1 tsp chilli powder
2.5ml/½ tsp salt
10ml/2 tsp tomato purée (paste)
30ml/2 tbsp oil
1 bunch fresh fenugreek leaves
15ml/1 tbsp chopped fresh coriander (cilantro)
300ml/½ pint/1¼ cups water
pilau rice and wholemeal (whole-wheat) chapatis, to serve (optional)

1 Bring a pan of water to the boil, add the chicken strips and cook for about 5–7 minutes. Drain the chicken and set aside.

2 In a mixing bowl, combine the garlic, chilli powder and salt with the tomato purée.

3 Heat the oil in a large, heavy pan. Lower the heat and stir in the tomato purée and spice mixture.

4 Add the chicken pieces to the spices and stir-fry for 5 7 minutes, then lower the heat further.

5 Add the fenugreek leaves and chopped fresh coriander. Continue to stir-fry for 5–7 minutes until all the ingredients are well mixed.

6 Pour in the water, cover and cook for about 5 minutes, stirring several times, until the dish is simmering. Serve hot with pilau rice and warm wholemeal chapatis, if you like.

Energy 127kcal/528kJ; Fat 7.9g; Saturated fat 1.51g; Carbohydrate 1.2g; Fibre 0.1g.

Karahi Chicken & Tomatoes with Mint

A traditional herb that goes deliciously well with spicy chicken is mint, which has cooling qualities to counter the heat of ginger and chillies. This is mildly spiced recipe is perfect for children or those who like a piquant flavour without heat.

Serves 4

275g/10oz skinned chicken
    breast fillets, cut into strips
300ml/½ pint/1¼ cups
    water
30ml/2 tbsp oil
2 small bunches spring onions
    (scallions), roughly chopped
5ml/1 tsp shredded fresh
    root ginger
5ml/1 tsp crushed dried
    red chillies
30ml/2 tbsp lemon juice
15ml/1 tbsp chopped fresh
    coriander (cilantro)
15ml/1 tbsp chopped
    fresh mint
3 tomatoes, peeled, seeded
    and roughly chopped
5ml/1 tsp salt
fresh mint and coriander sprigs,
    to garnish

1 Put the strips of chicken breast and water into a pan, bring to the boil and lower the heat to medium. Cook for about 10 minutes, uncovered, or until the water has evaporated and the chicken is cooked. Remove the pan from the heat and set aside.

2 Heat the oil in a heavy pan and stir-fry the spring onions for 2 minutes until soft but not browned.

3 Add the cooked chicken strips and stir-fry for about 3 minutes over a medium heat.

4 Gradually add the shredded ginger, dried red chillies, lemon juice, chopped coriander and mint, tomatoes and salt and gently stir to blend all the flavours.

5 Transfer the spicy chicken mixture to a serving dish and garnish with a few sprigs of fresh mint and coriander before serving piping hot.

Energy 157kcal/655kJ; Fat 8.2g; Saturated fat 1.5g; Carbohydrate 4.2g; Fibre 1.4g.

Red Hot Chicken Curry

This curry has a satisfyingly thick sauce, and uses sweet red and green peppers for extra colour and flavour.

Serves 4

2 medium onions
½ red (bell) pepper
½ green (bell) pepper
30ml/2 tbsp oil
1.5ml/¼ tsp fenugreek seeds
1.5ml/¼ tsp onion seeds
2.5ml/½ tsp crushed garlic
2.5ml/½ tsp grated fresh
    root ginger
5ml/1 tsp ground coriander
5ml/1 tsp chilli powder
5ml/1 tsp salt
400g/14oz can tomatoes
30ml/2 tbsp lemon juice
350g/12oz chicken, skinned
    and cubed
30ml/2 tbsp chopped fresh
    coriander (cilantro)
3 fresh green chillies, chopped
fresh coriander, to garnish

1 Using a sharp knife, dice the onions. Seed the peppers and cut them into chunks.

2 In a medium, heavy pan, heat the oil and fry the fenugreek and onion seeds until they turn a shade darker. Add the chopped onions, crushed garlic and fresh ginger. Fry for about 5 minutes until the onions turn golden brown. Reduce the heat to very low.

3 In a bowl, mix together the ground coriander, chilli powder, salt, canned tomatoes and lemon juice. Stir well.

4 Pour this mixture into the pan and increase the heat to medium. Stir-fry for about 3 minutes.

5 Add the chicken cubes and stir-fry for 5–7 minutes.

6 Add the chopped fresh coriander and green chillies and the red and green pepper chunks.

7 Lower the heat, cover the pan and allow to simmer for about 10 minutes, until the chicken cubes are cooked.

8 Serve the curry hot, garnished with fresh coriander.

Energy 214kcal/895kJ; Fat 10g; Saturated fat 2.08g; Carbohydrate 11g; Fibre 2.2g.

Kashmiri Chicken Curry

Surrounded by the snow-capped Himalayas, Kashmir is popularly known as the "Switzerland of the East". The state is also renowned for its rich culinary heritage, and this aromatic dish is one of the simplest among the region's repertoire.

Serves 4–6

20ml/4 tsp Kashmiri masala paste
60ml/4 tbsp tomato ketchup
5ml/1 tsp Worcestershire sauce
5ml/1 tsp five-spice powder
5ml/1 tsp sugar
8 chicken joints, skinned
5cm/2in piece fresh
    root ginger
45ml/3 tbsp vegetable oil
4 garlic cloves, crushed
juice of 1 lemon
15ml/1 tbsp coriander (cilantro)
    leaves, finely chopped
salt

1 To make the marinade, mix the masala paste, tomato ketchup, Worcestershire sauce and five-spice powder with the sugar and a little salt. Leave the mixture to rest in a warm place until the sugar has dissolved.

2 Rub the chicken pieces with the marinade and set aside in a cool place for at least 2 hours, or preferably in the refrigerator overnight. Bring the chicken to room temperature before cooking.

3 Thinly peel the ginger, using a sharp knife or vegetable peeler. Grate the peeled root finely.

4 Heat the oil in a karahi, wok or large pan and fry half the ginger and all the garlic until golden.

5 Add the chicken and fry until both sides are sealed. Cover and cook until the chicken is tender, and the oil has separated from the sauce.

6 Sprinkle the chicken with the lemon juice, remaining grated ginger and chopped coriander leaves, and mix in well. Serve the chicken piping hot. Plain boiled rice would make a good accompaniment.

Energy 483kcal/2009kJ; Fat 34.9g; Saturated fat 8.2g; Carbohydrate 5.7g; Fibre 0.2g.

Mughlai-style Chicken

The cuisine of Andhra Pradesh is renowned for its pungency because the hottest variety of chilli is grown there. In contrast, however, the region is also home to the subtle flavours of a style of cooking known as *nizami*, which has a distinct Mughal influence. This recipe, with the heady aroma of saffron and the captivating flavour of a silky almond sauce, is a good example.

Serves 4–6

1 large onion
2 eggs
4 skinned chicken breast fillets
15–30ml/1–2 tbsp garam masala
90ml/6 tbsp ghee or vegetable oil
5cm/2in piece fresh root ginger,
    finely crushed
4 garlic cloves, finely crushed
4 cloves
4 green cardamom pods
5cm/2in piece cinnamon stick
2 bay leaves
15–20 saffron threads
150ml/¼ pint/⅔ cup natural
    (plain) yogurt, beaten with
    5ml/1 tsp cornflour
    (cornstarch)
75ml/2½fl oz/⅓ cup double
    (heavy) cream
50g/2oz/½ cup ground almonds
salt and ground black pepper

1 Chop the onion finely. Break the eggs into a bowl and season with salt and pepper.

2 Rub the chicken fillets with the garam masala, then brush with the beaten egg. In a karahi, wok, or large pan, heat the ghee or vegetable oil and fry the chicken until cooked through and browned on both sides. Remove from the pan and keep warm.

3 In the same pan, fry the chopped onion, ginger, garlic, cloves, cardamom pods, cinnamon and bay leaves. When the onion turns golden, remove the pan from the heat, allow the contents to cool a little and add the saffron and yogurt mixture. Stir well to prevent the yogurt from curdling.

4 Return the chicken to the pan, along with any juices, and gently cook until the chicken is tender. Adjust the seasoning. Just before serving, pour in the cream. Fold it in then repeat the process with the ground almonds. Serve when piping hot.

Energy 514kcal/2141kJ; Fat 32.3g; Saturated fat 9.9g; Carbohydrate 7.9g; Fibre 0.9g.

Chicken Curry with Sliced Apples

This mild yet flavoursome dish is pleasantly flavoured with a warming combination of spices and chilli. Yogurt and almonds make a creamy sauce, which is given an additional lift by the use of sliced apples.

Serves 4

10ml/2 tsp oil
2 medium onions, diced
1 bay leaf
2 cloves
2.5cm/1in piece cinnamon stick
4 black peppercorns
1 baby chicken, about 675g/1½lb, skinned and cut into 8 pieces
5ml/1 tsp garam masala
5ml/1 tsp grated fresh root ginger
5ml/1 tsp crushed garlic
5ml/1 tsp salt
5ml/1 tsp chilli powder
15ml/1 tbsp ground almonds
150ml/¼ pint/⅔ cup natural (plain) low-fat yogurt
2 green eating apples, peeled, cored and roughly sliced
15ml/1 tbsp chopped fresh coriander (cilantro)
15g/½oz flaked (sliced) almonds, lightly toasted, and fresh coriander leaves, to garnish

1 Heat the oil in a karahi, wok or heavy pan and fry the onions with the bay leaf, cloves, cinnamon and peppercorns for about 3–5 minutes until the onions are beginning to soften but have not yet begun to brown.

2 Add the chicken pieces to the onions and continue to stir-fry for at least another 3 minutes.

3 Lower the heat and add the garam masala, ginger, garlic, salt, chilli powder and ground almonds and cook, stirring constantly, for 2–3 minutes.

4 Pour in the yogurt and stir for a couple more minutes.

5 Add the apples and chopped coriander, cover and cook for about 10–15 minutes.

6 Check that the chicken is cooked through and serve immediately, garnished with the flaked almonds and whole coriander leaves.

Energy 237kcal/994kJ; Fat 8.25g; Saturated fat 1.31g; Carbohydrate 17.21g; Fibre 2.88g.

Chicken & Potatoes with Rice

This dish, *Murgh Biryani*, is mainly prepared for important occasions in India, and is truly fit for royalty. Every cook in India has a subtle variation which is kept a closely guarded secret.

Serves 4–6

1.3kg/3lb skinned chicken breast portions, cut into large pieces
60ml/4 tbsp biryani masala paste
2 fresh green chillies, chopped
15ml/1 tbsp grated fresh root ginger
15ml/1 tbsp crushed garlic
50g/2oz/2 cups fresh coriander (cilantro), chopped
6–8 fresh mint leaves, chopped
150ml/¼ pint/⅔ cup natural (plain) yogurt, beaten
30ml/2 tbsp tomato purée (paste)
4 onions, finely sliced, deep-fried and crushed
450g/1lb/2¼ cups basmati rice, washed and drained
5ml/1 tsp black cumin seeds
5cm/2in piece cinnamon stick
4 green cardamom pods
2 black cardamom pods
vegetable oil, for shallow-frying
4 large potatoes, peeled and quartered
175ml/6fl oz/¾ cup milk, mixed with 90ml/6 tbsp water
1 sachet saffron powder, mixed with 90ml/6 tbsp milk
25g/1oz/2 tbsp ghee or unsalted (sweet) butter
1 tomato, sliced
salt

For the garnish

ghee or unsalted (sweet) butter, for shallow-frying
50g/2oz/½ cup cashew nuts
50g/2oz/⅓ cup sultanas (golden raisins)

1 Mix the chicken pieces with the next 9 ingredients and salt in a large bowl and marinate, covered, in a cool place for about 2 hours. Place in a large heavy pan and cook over a low heat for about 10 minutes. Set aside.

2 Boil a large pan of water and soak the rice with the cumin seeds, cinnamon stick and green and black cardamom pods for about 5 minutes. Drain well. If you prefer, some of the whole spices may be removed and discarded at this stage.

3 Heat the oil for shallow-frying and fry the quartered potatoes until they are evenly browned on all sides. Drain the potatoes and set them aside.

4 Place half the rice on top of the chicken in the pan in an even layer. Then make an even layer with the potatoes. Put the remaining rice on top of the potatoes and spread to make an even layer.

5 Sprinkle the water mixed with milk all over the rice. Make random holes through the rice with the handle of a spoon and pour into each a little saffron milk. Place a few knobs (pats) of ghee or butter on the surface, cover the pan and cook over a low heat for 35–45 minutes.

6 While the biryani is cooking, make the garnish. Heat a little ghee or butter and fry the cashew nuts and sultanas until they swell. Drain and set aside. When the biryani is ready, gently toss the rice, chicken and potatoes together, garnish with the nut mixture and serve hot.

Energy 1032kcal/4349kJ; Fat 9.8g; Saturated fat 2.4g; Carbohydrate 131.1g; Fibre 2.9g.

Chicken Biryani

Biryanis originated in Persia and are traditionally made with a combination of meat and rice. They are often served at dinner parties and on festive occasions.

Serves 4

275g/10oz/1½ cups basmati rice
30ml/2 tbsp oil
1 onion, thinly sliced
2 garlic cloves, crushed
1 green chilli, finely chopped
2.5cm/1in piece fresh root ginger, finely chopped
675g/1½lb skinned chicken breast fillets, cut into 2.5cm/1in cubes
45ml/3 tbsp curry paste
1.5ml/¼ tsp salt
1.5ml/¼ tsp garam masala
3 tomatoes, cut into thin wedges
1.5ml/¼ tsp ground turmeric
2 bay leaves
4 green cardamom pods
4 cloves
1.5ml/¼ tsp saffron strands
Tomato and Fresh Chilli Chutney, to serve

1 Wash the rice in several changes of cold water. Put into a bowl, cover with water and leave to soak for 30 minutes.

2 Meanwhile, heat the oil in a large heavy frying pan and fry the onion for about 5–7 minutes until lightly browned. Add the garlic, chilli and ginger and fry for about 2 minutes. Add the chicken and fry for 5 minutes, stirring occasionally.

3 Add the curry paste, salt and garam masala and cook for 5 minutes. Stir in the tomato wedges and continue cooking for another 3–4 minutes, then remove from the heat and set aside.

4 Preheat the oven to 190°C/375°F/Gas 5. Bring a pan of water to the boil. Drain the rice and add it to the pan with the turmeric. Cook for about 10 minutes, or until the rice is almost tender. Drain the rice and toss together with the bay leaves, cardamoms, cloves and saffron.

5 Layer the rice and chicken in a shallow, ovenproof dish until all the mixture has been used, finishing off with a layer of rice. Cover and bake in the oven for 15–20 minutes or until the chicken is tender. Serve with Tomato and Fresh Chilli Chutney.

Chicken Pilau

Like biryanis, pilaus that include cooked meat and poultry make a convenient one-pot meal. A vegetable curry makes a good accompaniment, although for a simpler meal, such as supper, you could serve the pilau with a simple raita.

Serves 4

400g/14oz/2 cups basmati rice
75g/3oz/6 tbsp ghee or unsalted (sweet) butter
1 onion, sliced
1.5ml/¼ tsp mixed onion seeds and mustard seeds
3 curry leaves
5ml/1 tsp grated fresh root ginger
5ml/1 tsp crushed garlic
5ml/1 tsp ground coriander
5ml/1 tsp chilli powder
7.5ml/1½ tsp salt
2 tomatoes, sliced
1 potato, cubed
50g/2oz/½ cup frozen peas, thawed
175g/6oz skinned chicken breast fillets, cubed
60ml/4 tbsp chopped fresh coriander (cilantro)
2 fresh green chillies, chopped
750ml/1¼ pints/3 cups water

1 Wash the rice thoroughly under running water, then leave to soak for 30 minutes. Drain in a strainer or colander and set aside.

2 In a pan, melt the ghee or butter and fry the sliced onion until golden.

3 Add the onion and mustard seeds, the curry leaves, ginger, garlic, ground coriander, chilli powder and salt. Stir-fry for about 2 minutes over a low heat.

4 Add the sliced tomatoes, cubed potato, peas and chicken cubes and mix everything together well.

5 Add the rice and stir to combine with the other ingredients.

6 Add the coriander and chillies. Mix and stir-fry for 1 minute. Pour in the water, bring to the boil and then lower the heat. Cover tightly and cook for 20 minutes. Remove from the heat, leaving the lid in place, and leave the pilau to stand for 6–8 minutes. Serve hot.

Energy 531kcal/2224kJ; Fat 14.1g; Saturated fat 2.77g; Carbohydrate 61.3g; Fibre 3.7g.

Energy 603kcal/2515kJ; Fat 16.8g; Saturated fat 10g; Carbohydrate 91.9g; Fibre 2.1g.

Chicken Biryani with Almonds

Biryani is a meal in itself and needs no accompaniment.

Serves 4
275g/10oz/1½ cups basmati rice
10 whole green cardamom pods
2.5ml/½ tsp salt
2 or 3 whole cloves
5cm/2in piece cinnamon stick
45ml/3 tbsp vegetable oil
3 onions, sliced
4 skinned chicken breast fillets,
   about 175g/6oz each, cubed
1.5ml/¼ tsp ground cloves
1.5ml/¼ tsp hot chilli powder
5ml/1 tsp ground cumin
5ml/1 tsp ground coriander

2.5ml/½ tsp ground black pepper
3 garlic cloves, chopped
5ml/1 tsp finely chopped fresh
   root ginger
juice of 1 lemon
4 tomatoes, sliced
30ml/2 tbsp chopped fresh
   coriander (cilantro)
150ml/¼ pint/⅔ cup natural
   (plain) yogurt, plus extra
   to serve
4–5 saffron threads, soaked in
   10ml/2 tsp warm milk
150ml/¼ pint/⅔ cup water
toasted flaked (sliced) almonds
   and fresh coriander sprigs,
   to garnish

1 Wash the rice well and leave to soak in water for 30 minutes. Drain. Preheat the oven to 190°C/375°F/Gas 5. Remove the seeds from half the cardamom pods and grind them finely, using a mortar and pestle. Set aside the ground seeds.

2 Bring a pan of water to the boil. Add the rice with the salt, cardamoms, cloves and cinnamon stick. Boil for 2 minutes, then drain. Keep the rice hot in a covered pan.

3 Heat the oil in another pan, and fry the onions for 8 minutes, until browned. Add the chicken and the ground spices, including the ground cardamom. Mix well, then add the garlic, ginger and lemon juice. Stir-fry for 5 minutes. Transfer to a casserole and arrange the tomatoes on top. Sprinkle on the coriander, spoon the yogurt on top and cover with the rice.

4 Drizzle the saffron milk over the rice and pour over the water. Cover, then bake in the oven for 1 hour. Transfer to a serving platter and discard the whole spices. Garnish with almonds and coriander and serve immediately.

Energy 548kcal/2298kJ; Fat 11.1g; Saturated fat 1.7g; Carbohydrate 67.5g; Fibre 2.2g.

Chicken with Spicy Onions

Chunky onion slices infused with toasted cumin seeds and shredded ginger add a delicious contrast to the flavour of the chicken.

Serves 4–6
1.3kg/3lb chicken, jointed
   and skinned
17.5ml/½ tsp turmeric
2.5ml/½ tsp chilli powder
60ml/4 tbsp oil
4 small onions, finely chopped
175g/6oz/6 cups fresh coriander
   (cilantro), coarsely chopped

5cm/2in piece fresh root ginger,
   finely shredded
2 fresh green chillies,
   finely chopped
10ml/2 tsp cumin seeds,
   dry-roasted
75ml/5 tbsp natural
   (plain) yogurt
75ml/5 tbsp double
   (heavy) cream
2.5ml/½ tsp cornflour
   (cornstarch)
salt

1 With a sharp knife, make a few slashes in the chicken joints and then rub the meat with the turmeric, chilli powder and salt to taste. Heat the oil in a large frying pan and fry the chicken pieces in batches until both sides are sealed. Remove to a plate and keep hot.

2 Reheat the oil remaining in the pan and add three-quarters of the chopped onions, most of the fresh coriander, half the ginger, the green chillies and the cumin seeds and fry until the onions are translucent.

3 Return the chicken to the pan with any juices and mix well. Cover and cook gently for 15 minutes.

4 Remove the pan from the heat and leave to cool a little. Mix the yogurt, cream and cornflour in a bowl and gradually fold into the chicken, mixing well.

5 Return the pan to the heat and cook gently until the chicken is tender. Just before serving, stir in the reserved chopped onion, coriander and ginger. Spoon into a serving bowl and serve hot.

Energy 819kcal/3391kJ; Fat 65.4g; Saturated fat 23.4g; Carbohydrate 8.2g; Fibre 0.9g.

Fragrant Chicken Curry

This dish is perfect for a party as the chicken and sauce can be prepared in advance and combined and heated at the last minute.

Serves 4

45ml/3 tbsp oil
1 onion, coarsely chopped
2 garlic cloves, crushed
15ml/1 tbsp Thai red curry paste
1 litre/1¾ pints/4 cups coconut milk
2 lemon grass stalks, coarsely chopped
6 kaffir lime leaves, chopped
150ml/¼ pint/⅔ cup Greek (US strained plain) yogurt
30ml/2 tbsp apricot jam
1 cooked chicken, about 1.6kg/3–3½lb
30ml/2 tbsp chopped fresh coriander (cilantro)
salt and ground black pepper
kaffir lime leaves, shredded, toasted coconut and fresh coriander, to garnish
boiled rice, to serve

1 Heat the oil in a large pan. Add the onion and garlic and cook over a low heat for 5–10 minutes until soft. Stir in the red curry paste. Cook, stirring constantly, for 2–3 minutes.

2 Stir in the coconut milk, then add the lemon grass, lime leaves, yogurt and apricot jam. Stir well. Cover and simmer for 30 minutes.

3 Remove the pan from the heat and leave to cool slightly. Transfer the sauce to a food processor or blender and process to a smooth purée, then strain it back into the rinsed-out pan, pressing as much of the puréed mixture as possible through the sieve (strainer) with the back of a wooden spoon. Set aside while you prepare the chicken.

4 Remove the skin from the chicken, slice the meat off the bones and cut it into bitesize pieces. Add to the sauce.

5 Bring the sauce back to simmering point. Stir in the fresh coriander and season with salt and pepper. Garnish with extra lime leaves, shredded coconut and coriander. Serve with rice.

Green Chicken Curry

Use fresh green chillies in this dish, if you like your curry hot. The mild aromatic flavour of the rice is a good foil for the spicy chicken.

Serves 3–4

4 spring onions (scallions), trimmed and coarsely chopped
1 or 2 fresh green chillies, seeded and coarsely chopped
2cm/¾in piece fresh root ginger, peeled
2 garlic cloves
5ml/1 tsp Thai fish sauce
large bunch fresh coriander (cilantro)
small handful of fresh parsley
30–45ml/2–3 tbsp water
30ml/2 tbsp sunflower oil
4 boneless chicken breast portions, skinned and diced
1 green (bell) pepper, seeded and thinly sliced
600ml/1 pint/2½ cups coconut milk
salt and ground black pepper
hot coconut rice, to serve

1 Put the spring onions, green chillies, ginger, garlic, fish sauce, coriander and parsley in a food processor or blender. Pour in 30ml/2 tbsp of the water and process to a smooth paste, adding a further 15ml/1 tbsp water if required.

2 Heat half the oil in a large frying pan. Cook the diced chicken until evenly browned. Transfer to a plate. Heat the remaining oil in the pan. Add the green pepper and stir-fry for 3–4 minutes, then add the chilli and ginger paste. Stir-fry for a further 3–4 minutes, until the mixture becomes fairly thick.

3 Return the chicken to the pan and add the coconut milk. Season with salt and pepper and bring to the boil, then reduce the heat, half-cover the pan and simmer for 8–10 minutes. When the chicken is cooked, transfer it, with the green pepper, to a plate. Boil the cooking liquid remaining in the pan for 10–12 minutes, until it is well reduced and fairly thick.

4 Return the chicken and pepper to the green curry sauce, stir well and cook gently for 2–3 minutes to heat through. Spoon the curry over the coconut rice, and serve immediately.

Energy 387kcal/1632kJ; Fat 11.1g; Saturated fat 2g; Carbohydrate 14.5g; Fibre 2.3g.

Energy 531kcal/2216kJ; Fat 34.3g; Saturated fat 20.6g; Carbohydrate 4.3g; Fibre 0.8g.

Spicy Lamb Tikka

One of the best ways of tenderizing meat is to marinate it in papaya, which must be unripe or it will lend its sweetness to what should be a savoury dish.

Serves 4
675g/1½lb lean lamb, cubed
1 unripe papaya
45ml/3 tbsp natural (plain) yogurt
5ml/1 tsp grated fresh root ginger
5ml/1 tsp chilli powder
5ml/1 tsp crushed garlic
1.5ml/¼ tsp turmeric
10ml/2 tsp ground coriander
5ml/1 tsp ground cumin
5ml/1 tsp salt
30ml/2 tbsp lemon juice
15ml/1 tbsp chopped fresh coriander (cilantro), plus extra to garnish
1.5ml/¼ tsp red food colouring
300ml/½ pint/1¼ cups corn oil
lemon wedges and onion rings, to garnish

1 Place the lamb in a large bowl. Peel the papaya, cut it in half and scoop out the seeds. Cut the flesh into cubes and place in a food processor or blender. Process in bursts until the papaya forms a purée, adding about 15ml/1 tbsp water if necessary.

2 Pour 30ml/2 tbsp of the papaya over the lamb and rub it in well with your fingers. Cover and set aside for at least 3 hours.

3 Meanwhile, mix the yogurt, ginger, chilli powder, garlic, turmeric, ground coriander, ground cumin, salt and lemon juice in a bowl. Add the fresh coriander, red food colouring and 30ml/2 tbsp of the oil and mix well. Pour the spicy yogurt mixture over the lamb and mix well.

4 Heat the remaining oil in a karahi, wok or deep pan. Lower the heat slightly and add the lamb cubes, a few at a time.

5 Deep-fry each batch for 5–7 minutes or until the lamb is thoroughly cooked and tender. Keep the cooked pieces warm while frying the remainder.

6 Transfer to a serving dish and garnish with lemon wedges, onion rings and fresh coriander. Serve with raita and freshly baked naan bread.

Energy 438kcal/1820kJ; Fat 32.7g; Saturated fat 10.4g; Carbohydrate 2.4g; Fibre 0.7g.

Indian Lamb Burgers

Serve this spicy Indian burger in a bun with chilli sauce and a salad of tomatoes, onion and lettuce, or unaccompanied as an appetizer.

Serves 4–6
50g/2oz/⅓ cup chickpeas, soaked overnight in water
2 onions, finely chopped
250g/9oz lean lamb, cut into small cubes
5ml/1 tsp cumin seeds
5ml/1 tsp garam masala
4–6 fresh green chillies, roughly chopped
5cm/2in piece fresh ginger, crushed
175ml/6fl oz/¾ cup water
a few fresh coriander (cilantro) and mint leaves, chopped
juice of 1 lemon
15ml/1 tbsp gram flour
2 eggs, beaten
vegetable oil, for shallow-frying
½ lime
salt

1 Drain the chickpeas and cook them in a pan of boiling water for 1 hour. Drain again, return to the pan and add the onions, lamb, cumin seeds, garam masala, chillies, ginger and water, and salt to taste. Bring to the boil. Simmer, covered, until the meat and chickpeas are cooked.

2 Remove the lid and cook uncovered to reduce the excess liquid. Cool, and grind to a paste in a food processor.

3 Scrape the mixture into a mixing bowl and add the fresh coriander (cilantro) and mint, lemon juice and flour. Knead well. Divide into 10–12 portions and roll each into a ball, then flatten slightly. Chill for 1 hour.

4 Dip the burgers in the beaten egg and shallow-fry each side until golden brown. Serve hot, with the lime.

Variation
Chicken or lean pork would work well instead of the lamb in this recipe.

Energy 357kcal/1485kJ; Fat 25.1g; Saturated fat 6g; Carbohydrate 15.6g; Fibre 1.5g.

Lamb Chops Kashmiri-style

These chops are cooked in a unique way, being boiled in milk and then fried.

Serves 4

8–12 lamb chops, about
  50–75g/2–3oz each
1 piece cinnamon bark
1 bay leaf
2.5ml/½ tsp fennel seeds
2.5ml/½ tsp black peppercorns
3 green cardamom pods
5ml/1 tsp salt
600ml/1 pint/2½ cups milk
150ml/¼ pint/⅔ cup
  evaporated milk
150ml/¼ pint/⅔ cup natural
  (plain) yogurt
30ml/2 tbsp plain (all-purpose)
  flour
5ml/1 tsp chilli powder
5ml/1 tsp grated fresh root ginger
2.5ml/½ tsp garam masala
2.5ml/½ tsp crushed garlic
pinch of salt
300ml/½ pint/1¼ cups corn oil
fresh mint sprigs and lime
  quarters, to garnish

1 Trim the lamb chops to remove any excess fat, and place them in a large pan. Add the cinnamon bark, bay leaf, fennel seeds, peppercorns, cardamoms and salt. Pour in the milk. Bring to the boil over a high heat.

2 Lower the heat and cook for 12–15 minutes, or until the milk has reduced to about half its original volume. At this stage, pour in the evaporated milk and lower the heat further. Simmer until the chops are cooked through and all the milk has evaporated.

3 While the chops are cooking, blend together the yogurt, flour, chilli powder, ginger, garam masala, crushed garlic and a pinch of salt in a mixing bowl.

4 Remove the chops from the pan and discard the whole spices. Add the chops to the spicy yogurt mixture.

5 Heat the oil in a deep pan, wok or medium karahi. Lower the heat slightly and add the chops. Fry until they are golden brown, turning them once or twice as they cook.

6 Transfer the chops to a serving dish, and garnish with mint sprigs and lime quarters. Serve immediately.

Lamb Meatballs in a Spicy Sauce

The word "meatballs" conjures up something quite humdrum, but these spicy little patties, with their delectable sauce, are exciting and full of flavour.

Serves 6

For the meatballs

675g/1½lb lean minced
  (ground) lamb
1 fresh green chilli, roughly
  chopped
1 garlic clove, chopped
2.5cm/1in piece fresh root
  ginger, chopped
1.5ml/¼ tsp garam masala
1.5ml/¼ tsp salt
45ml/3 tbsp chopped fresh
  coriander (cilantro), plus extra
  to garnish
pilau rice, to serve

For the sauce

15ml/1 tbsp oil
1.5ml/¼ tsp mustard seeds
2.5ml/½ tsp cumin seeds
1 onion, chopped
1 garlic clove, chopped
2.5cm/1in piece fresh root ginger,
  finely chopped
5ml/1 tsp ground cumin
5ml/1 tsp ground coriander
2.5ml/½ tsp salt
2.5ml/½ tsp chilli powder
15ml/1 tbsp tomato purée
  (paste)
400g/14oz can chopped
  tomatoes

1 To make the meatballs, put all the ingredients into a food processor or blender and process until the mixture binds together. Shape the mixture into 18 balls. Cover and chill in the refrigerator for 10 minutes.

2 To make the sauce, heat the oil in a heavy pan and fry the mustard and cumin seeds until they splutter.

3 Add the onion, garlic and ginger and fry for 5 minutes. Stir in the remaining sauce ingredients and simmer for 5 minutes.

4 Add the meatballs to the spicy sauce. Bring to the boil, cover and simmer for 25–30 minutes, or until the meatballs are cooked through. Serve on a bed of pilau rice and garnish with chopped fresh coriander.

Energy 231kcal/968kJ; Fat 12.3g; Saturated fat 5g; Carbohydrate 5.4g; Fibre 0.9g.

Energy 484kcal/2022kJ; Fat 29g; Saturated fat 9.3g; Carbohydrate 17.6g; Fibre 0.2g.

Lamb Korma with Mint

This superb dish of lamb cooked in a creamy sauce flavoured with mint, coconut, chillies and a subtle blend of spices is quick to cook because the lamb is sliced into thin strips.

Serves 4
2 fresh green chillies
120ml/4fl oz/½ cup natural (plain) low-fat yogurt
50ml/2fl oz/¼ cup coconut milk
15ml/1 tbsp ground almonds
5ml/1 tsp salt
5ml/1 tsp crushed garlic
5ml/1 tsp grated fresh root ginger
5ml/1 tsp garam masala
1.5ml/¼ tsp ground cardamom
large pinch of ground cinnamon
15ml/1 tbsp chopped fresh mint
15ml/1 tbsp oil
2 medium onions, diced
1 bay leaf
4 black peppercorns
225g/8oz lean lamb, cut into strips
150ml/¼ pint/⅔ cup water
fresh mint leaves, to garnish

1 Finely chop the chillies. Whisk the yogurt with the chillies, coconut milk, ground almonds, salt, garlic, ginger, garam masala, cardamom, cinnamon and mint.

2 Heat the oil in a karahi, wok or heavy pan and fry the onions with the bay leaf and peppercorns for about 5 minutes.

3 When the onions are soft and golden brown, add the lamb and stir-fry for about 2 minutes.

4 Pour in the yogurt and coconut mixture and the water, lower the heat, cover and cook for about 15 minutes or until the lamb is cooked through, stirring occasionally. Using two spoons, toss the mixture over the heat for a further 2 minutes. Serve garnished with fresh mint leaves.

Cook's Tip
Rice with peas and curry leaves goes very well with this korma.

Energy 193kcal/803kJ; Fat 10.14g; Saturated fat 2.91g; Carbohydrate 11.5g; Fibre 1.6g.

Spiced Lamb with Tomatoes & Peppers

Select lean tender lamb from the leg for this lightly spiced curry with juicy peppers and wedges of onion. Serve warm naan bread to mop up the tomato-rich juices.

Serves 6
2.5cm/1in piece fresh root ginger
1.5kg/3¼lb lean boneless lamb, cubed
250ml/8fl oz/1 cup natural (plain) yogurt
30ml/2 tbsp sunflower oil
3 onions
2 red (bell) peppers, seeded and cut into chunks
3 garlic cloves, finely chopped
1 fresh red chilli, seeded and chopped
30ml/2 tbsp mild curry paste
2 × 400g/14oz cans chopped tomatoes
large pinch of saffron threads
800g/1¾lb plum tomatoes, halved, seeded and cut into chunks
salt and ground black pepper
chopped fresh coriander (cilantro), to garnish

1 Thinly peel the fresh root ginger, using a sharp knife or a vegetable peeler, then grate the peeled root finely. Set the grated ginger aside.

2 Mix the lamb with the yogurt in a bowl. Cover and chill for about 1 hour.

3 Heat the oil in a large pan. Drain the lamb and reserve the yogurt, then cook the lamb in batches until it is golden on all sides – this will take about 15 minutes in total. Remove the lamb from the pan using a slotted spoon and set aside.

4 Cut two of the onions into wedges (six from each onion) and add to the oil remaining in the pan. Fry the onions over a medium heat for 10 minutes, or until they soften and are beginning to colour.

5 Add the peppers and cook for 5 minutes. Use a slotted spoon to remove the vegetables from the pan and set aside.

6 Meanwhile, chop the remaining onion. Add it to the rest of the oil in the pan with the chopped garlic, chilli and grated ginger, and cook for 4–5 minutes, stirring frequently, until the onion has softened.

7 Stir in the curry paste and canned chopped tomatoes with the reserved yogurt. Return the lamb to the pan, season and stir well. Bring to the boil, then reduce the heat and simmer for 30 minutes.

8 Pound the saffron to a powder in a mortar, then stir in a little boiling water to dissolve the saffron. Add this liquid to the curry and stir well.

9 Return the onion and pepper mixture to the pan, then stir in the fresh tomatoes. Bring the curry back to simmering point and cook for 15 minutes. Garnish with chopped fresh coriander and serve hot.

Energy 594kcal/2445kJ; Fat 32.8g; Saturated fat 13.8g; Carbohydrate 19.7g; Fibre 4.3g.

Lamb with Spinach

Serve this Punjabi dish with plain boiled rice, naan bread or parathas.

Serves 4–6

5ml/1 tsp grated fresh root ginger
5ml/1 tsp crushed garlic
7.5ml/1½ tsp chilli powder
5ml/1 tsp salt
5ml/1 tsp garam masala
90ml/6 tbsp corn oil
2 medium onions, sliced

675g/1½lb lean lamb, cut into
   5cm/2in cubes
600–900ml/1–1½
   pints/2½–3¾ cups water
400g/14oz fresh spinach
1 large red (bell) pepper, seeded
   and chopped
3 fresh green chillies, chopped
45ml/3 tbsp chopped fresh
   coriander (cilantro)
15ml/1 tbsp lemon juice
   (optional)

1 Mix together the ginger, garlic, chilli powder, salt and garam masala in a bowl. Set to one side.

2 Heat the oil in a medium pan. Add the onions and fry for 10–12 minutes or until well browned. Add the cubed lamb to the sizzling onion slices and fry for about 2 minutes, stirring frequently. Add the spice mixture and stir thoroughly until the meat pieces are well coated.

3 Pour in the water and bring to the boil. As soon as it is boiling, cover the pan and lower the heat. Cook gently for 25–35 minutes without letting the contents of the pan burn. If there is still a lot of water in the pan when the meat has become tender, remove the lid and boil briskly to evaporate any excess.

4 Meanwhile, wash and chop the spinach roughly, then blanch it for about 1 minute in a pan of boiling water. Drain well. Add the spinach to the lamb as soon as the water has evaporated. Fry over a medium heat for 7–10 minutes, using a wooden spoon in a semi-circular motion.

5 Add the red pepper, green chillies and fresh coriander to the pan and stir over a medium heat for 2 minutes. Sprinkle over the lemon juice (if using) and serve immediately.

Spring Lamb Chops

Tender spring lamb has the best flavour. Here, quick-cooking chops are finely spiced to enhance the flavour without masking the sweetness of the lamb.

Serves 4

8 small lean spring lamb chops
1 large fresh red chilli, seeded
30ml/2 tbsp chopped fresh
   coriander (cilantro)

15ml/1 tbsp chopped fresh mint
5ml/1 tsp salt
5ml/1 tsp soft brown sugar
5ml/1 tsp garam masala
5ml/1 tsp crushed garlic
5ml/1 tsp grated fresh root ginger
175ml/6fl oz/¾ cup low-fat
   natural (plain) yogurt
10ml/2 tsp oil
mixed salad, to serve

1 Trim any excess fat from each of the lamb chops. Place them in a large bowl.

2 Finely chop the chilli, then place in a bowl and mix with the chopped fresh coriander, mint, salt, brown sugar, garam masala, crushed garlic and ginger.

3 Pour the yogurt into the chilli mixture and, using a small whisk or a fork, mix together thoroughly.

4 Pour this mixture over the top of the chops and turn them with your fingers to make sure that they are completely covered. Cover and marinate overnight in the refrigerator.

5 Heat the oil in a karahi, wok or heavy pan and add the chops. Cook over a medium heat for about 20 minutes or until cooked right through, turning the chops from time to time. Alternatively, grill (broil) the chops, basting often with oil. Serve with the mixed salad.

> **Cook's Tip**
> You can freeze peeled fresh root ginger and grate it from frozen as you need it.

Energy 500kcal/2079kJ; Fat 36.4g; Saturated fat 11.3g; Carbohydrate 6.8g; Fibre 3.2g.

Energy 207kcal/864kJ; Fat 10.29g; Saturated fat 4.26g; Carbohydrate 6.63g; Fibre 0.27g.

Lamb with Courgettes

For this simple supper dish, lamb is cooked first with yogurt and then the sliced courgettes, which have already been browned, are added to the mixture.

Serves 4

15ml/1 tbsp oil
2 medium onions, chopped
225g/8oz lean lamb steaks, cut into strips
120ml/4fl oz/½ cup natural (plain) low-fat yogurt
5ml/1 tsp garam masala
5ml/1 tsp chilli powder
5ml/1 tsp crushed garlic
5ml/1 tsp grated fresh root ginger
2.5ml/½ tsp ground coriander
2 medium courgettes (zucchini), sliced
15ml/1 tbsp chopped fresh coriander (cilantro), to garnish

1 Heat the oil in a karahi, wok or heavy pan and fry the onions until golden brown (see Cook's Tip).

2 Add the lamb strips and stir-fry with the onions for 1 minute to seal the meat.

3 Put the yogurt, garam masala, chilli powder, garlic, ginger and ground coriander into a bowl. Whisk the mixture together.

4 Pour the yogurt mixture over the lamb and stir-fry for 2 minutes. Cover and cook over medium to low heat for 12–15 minutes.

5 Preheat the grill (broiler). Put the courgettes in a flameproof dish and brown lightly under the heat for about 3 minutes, turning once.

6 Check that the lamb is cooked through and the sauce is quite thick, then add the courgettes and serve garnished with the fresh coriander.

> **Cook's Tip**
> *Stir the onions only occasionally so that their moisture will be retained.*

Stir-fried Lamb with Baby Onions

The baby onions are stir-fried whole before being added to the lamb and pepper mixture in this recipe. Serve this dish with rice, lentils or naan bread.

Serves 4

15ml/1 tbsp oil
8 baby onions
225g/8oz boned lean lamb, cut into strips
5ml/1 tsp ground cumin
5ml/1 tsp ground coriander
15ml/1 tbsp tomato purée (paste)
5ml/1 tsp chilli powder
5ml/1 tsp salt
15ml/1 tbsp lemon juice
2.5ml/½ tsp onion seeds
4 curry leaves
300ml/½ pint/1¼ cups water
1 small red (bell) pepper, seeded and roughly sliced
1 small green (bell) pepper, seeded and roughly sliced
15ml/1 tbsp chopped fresh coriander (cilantro)
15ml/1 tbsp chopped fresh mint

1 Heat the oil in a karahi, wok or heavy pan and stir-fry the whole baby onions for about 3 minutes. Using a slotted spoon, remove the onions from the pan and set aside to drain. Set the pan aside, with the oil remaining in it.

2 Mix together the lamb strips, cumin, ground coriander, tomato purée, chilli powder, salt and lemon juice in a bowl until the lamb is well coated. Set aside.

3 Reheat the oil and briskly stir-fry the onion seeds and curry leaves for 2–3 minutes.

4 Add the lamb and spice mixture, and stir-fry for about 5 minutes, then pour in the measured water. Lower the heat and cook the lamb mixture gently for about 10 minutes, until the lamb is cooked through.

5 Add the peppers and half the fresh coriander and mint. Stir-fry for a further 2 minutes.

6 Finally, add the baby onions and the remaining chopped fresh coriander and mint, and serve immediately.

Energy 178kcal/742kJ; Fat 8.36g; Saturated fat 2.78g; Carbohydrate 10.83g; Fibre 1.99g.

Energy 155kcal/644kJ; Fat 9.48g; Saturated fat 2.82g; Carbohydrate 5.74g; Fibre 1.49g.

Spiced Lamb with Chillies

This is a fairly hot stir-fry dish, although you can, of course, make it less so by either discarding the seeds from the chillies, or using just one of each colour.

Serves 4

225g/8oz lean lamb fillet
120ml/4fl oz/½ cup natural (plain) low-fat yogurt
1.5ml/¼ tsp ground cardamom
5ml/1 tsp grated fresh root ginger
5ml/1 tsp crushed garlic
5ml/1 tsp chilli powder
5ml/1 tsp garam masala

5ml/1 tsp salt
15ml/1 tbsp oil
2 medium onions, chopped
1 bay leaf
300ml/½ pint/1¼ cups water
2 fresh green chillies, sliced lengthways
2 fresh red chillies, sliced lengthways
30ml/2 tbsp fresh coriander (cilantro) leaves

1 Using a sharp knife, remove any excess fat from the lamb and cut the meat into even strips.

2 In a bowl, mix the yogurt, cardamom, ginger, garlic, chilli powder and garam masala. Stir in the salt. Add the lamb strips. Mix well in the spicy yogurt to coat evenly. Leave for about 1 hour to marinate.

3 Heat the oil in a karahi, wok or heavy pan and fry the onions for 3–5 minutes until golden.

4 Add the bay leaf, then add the lamb with the yogurt and spice mixture. Stir-fry for 2–3 minutes.

5 Pour the water over the spicy lamb mixture, cover and cook for 15–20 minutes over a low heat, checking and stirring occasionally. Once the water has evaporated, stir-fry the mixture for 1 further minute.

6 Stir in the red and green chillies and the fresh coriander. Spoon into a serving dish and serve hot.

Khara Masala Lamb

This is a dish which involves a cooking technique called bhooning – stirring with a semi-circular motion.

Serves 4

15ml/1 tbsp oil
3 small onions, chopped
5ml/1 tsp shredded fresh root ginger
5ml/1 tsp sliced garlic
6 dried red chillies
3 cardamom pods

2 cinnamon sticks
6 black peppercorns
3 cloves
2.5ml/½ tsp salt
450g/1lb boned lean leg of lamb, cubed
600ml/1 pint/2½ cups water
2 fresh green chillies, sliced
30ml/2 tbsp chopped fresh coriander (cilantro)

1 Heat the oil in a large pan and add the onions. Lower the heat and fry the onions until they are lightly browned, stirring occasionally.

2 Add half the ginger and half the garlic, and stir well. Drop in half the red chillies, the cardamom pods, cinnamon, peppercorns, cloves and salt.

3 Add the lamb and fry over a medium heat. Stir continuously with a semi-circular movement, using a wooden spoon to scrape the bottom of the pan and prevent the meat from burning. Cook for about 5 minutes.

4 Stir in the water, cover with a lid and cook slowly over a medium-low heat for 35–40 minutes, or until the water has evaporated and the meat is tender, stirring from time to time to prevent the mixture from burning on the bottom of the pan.

5 Add the remaining ginger, garlic and dried red chillies, with the fresh green chillies and the chopped coriander. Continue to stir the mixture over the heat until some free oil is visible on the sides of the pan. Transfer the curry to a serving dish and serve immediately.

Energy 169kcal/706kJ; Fat 8.13g; Saturated fat 2.71g; Carbohydrate 10.01g; Fibre 1.32g.

Energy 242kcal/1012kJ; Fat 13.2g; Saturated fat 5.19g; Carbohydrate 6.7g; Fibre 0.9g.

Spicy Lamb & Potato Stew

Indian spices transform a simple lamb and potato stew into a mouthwatering dish fit for princes.

Serves 6
675g/1½lb lean lamb fillet (tenderloin)
15ml/1 tbsp oil
1 onion, finely chopped
2 bay leaves
1 fresh green chilli, seeded and finely chopped
2 garlic cloves, finely chopped
10ml/2 tsp ground coriander
5ml/1 tsp ground cumin
2.5ml/½ tsp ground turmeric
2.5ml/½ tsp chilli powder
2.5ml/½ tsp salt
2 tomatoes, peeled and chopped
600ml/1 pint/2½ cups chicken stock
2 large potatoes, cut in large chunks
chopped fresh coriander (cilantro), to garnish

1 Remove any visible fat from the lamb and cut the meat into neat 2.5cm/1in cubes.

2 Heat the oil in a large, heavy pan and fry the onion, bay leaves, chilli and garlic for 5 minutes.

3 Add the cubed meat and cook for about 6–8 minutes until lightly browned.

4 Add the ground coriander, ground cumin, ground turmeric, chilli powder and salt and cook the spices for 3–4 minutes, stirring all the time to prevent the spices from sticking to the bottom of the pan.

5 Add the tomatoes and stock and simmer for 5 minutes. Bring to the boil, cover and simmer for 1 hour.

6 Add the bitesize chunks of potato to the simmering mixture, stir in, and cook for a further 30–40 minutes, or until the meat is tender and much of the excess juices have been absorbed, leaving a thick but minimal sauce. Garnish with chopped fresh coriander and serve piping hot.

Energy 283kcal/1187kJ; Fat 12.4g; Saturated fat 5.02g; Carbohydrate 17.2g; Fibre 1.7g.

Lamb Dhansak

This is time-consuming to make, but the excellent flavour is just reward.

Serves 4–6
90ml/6 tbsp vegetable oil
5 fresh green chillies, chopped
2.5cm/1in piece fresh root ginger, grated
3 garlic cloves, crushed, plus 1 garlic clove, sliced
2 bay leaves
5cm/2in piece cinnamon stick
900g/2lb lean lamb, cut into pieces
600ml/1 pint/2½ cups water
175g/6oz/¾ cup whole red lentils, washed and drained
50g/2oz/¼ cup each chana dhal or yellow split peas, husked moong dhal and split red lentils, washed and drained
2 potatoes, diced, soaked in water
1 aubergine (eggplant), chopped, soaked in water
4 onions, finely sliced, deep-fried and drained
50g/2oz fresh spinach, trimmed, washed and chopped
25g/1oz fresh or dried fenugreek leaves
2 carrots, sliced
115g/4oz fresh coriander (cilantro), chopped
50g/2oz fresh mint, chopped
30ml/2 tbsp dhansak masala
30ml/2 tbsp sambhar masala
5ml/1 tsp salt
10ml/2 tsp soft brown sugar
60ml/4 tbsp tamarind juice

1 Heat 45ml/3 tbsp of the oil in a wok, karahi or large pan, and gently fry the fresh chillies, ginger, crushed garlic, bay leaves and cinnamon for 2 minutes. Add the lamb pieces and the measured water. Bring to the boil, then simmer, covered, until the lamb is half cooked.

2 Drain the meat stock into another pan and put the lamb aside. Add the whole red lentils, chana dhal or split peas, moong dhal and split red lentils to the stock and cook gently for 25–30 minutes at a low temperature until they are tender. Mash the lentils with the back of a spoon.

3 Drain the potatoes and aubergine and add to the lentils. Reserve a little of the deep-fried onions and stir the remainder into the pan, along with the spinach, fenugreek and carrot. Add some hot water to the pan if the mixture seems too thick. Cook until the vegetables are tender, then mash again with a spoon, keeping the vegetables a little coarse.

4 Heat 15ml/1 tbsp of the remaining oil in a large frying pan. Reserve a few coriander and mint leaves to use as a garnish, and gently fry the remaining leaves with the dhansak and sambhar masala, salt and sugar. Add the lamb pieces and fry gently for 5 minutes.

5 Add the lamb and spices to the lentil mixture and stir. Cover, reduce the heat to low and cook until the lamb is tender. The lentils will absorb liquid, so add more water if needed. Mix in the tamarind juice.

6 Heat the remaining vegetable oil in a small pan and fry the sliced garlic until golden brown. Sprinkle the fried garlic slices over the dhansak. Garnish with the remaining deep-fried onion and the reserved fresh coriander and mint leaves. Serve the dish hot, with Caramelized Basmati Rice if you like.

Energy 720kcal/3017kJ; Fat 34.8g; Saturated fat 10g; Carbohydrate 58.6g; Fibre 7.6g.

Lahore-style Lamb Curry

This hearty dish of braised lamb with chana dhal has a wonderfully aromatic flavour imparted by the winter spices.

Serves 4

60ml/4 tbsp vegetable oil
1 bay leaf
2 cloves
4 black peppercorns
1 onion, sliced
450g/1lb lean boneless lamb, cubed

1.5ml/¼ tsp ground turmeric
7.5ml/1½ tsp chilli powder
5ml/1 tsp crushed coriander seeds
2.5cm/1in piece cinnamon stick
5ml/1 tsp crushed garlic
7.5ml/1½ tsp salt
1.5 litres/2½ pints/6 cups water
50g/2oz/⅓ cup chana dhal (yellow split peas)
2 tomatoes, quartered
2 fresh green chillies, chopped
15ml/1 tbsp chopped fresh coriander (cilantro)

1 Heat the oil in a karahi, wok or large pan. Lower the heat slightly and add the bay leaf, cloves, peppercorns and onion. Fry for about 5 minutes, or until the onion is golden brown.

2 Add the cubed lamb, turmeric, chilli powder, coriander seeds, cinnamon stick, garlic and most of the salt, and stir-fry for about 5 minutes over a medium heat. Pour in 900ml/1½ pints/3¾ cups of the water and cover the pan with a lid or foil, making sure the foil does not come into contact with the food. Simmer for 35–40 minutes or until the lamb is tender.

3 Put the chana dhal into a large pan with the remaining measured water and a good pinch of salt and boil for 12–15 minutes, or until the water has almost evaporated and the dhal is soft enough to be mashed. If the mixture is too thick, add up to 150ml/¼ pint/⅔ cup water.

4 When the lamb is tender, remove the lid or foil and stir-fry the mixture using a wooden spoon, until some free oil begins to appear on the sides of the pan.

5 Add the cooked lentils to the lamb and mix together well. Stir in the tomatoes, chillies and chopped coriander and serve.

Energy 362kcal/1508kJ; Fat 24g; Saturated fat 7.3g; Carbohydrate 11.5g; Fibre 1.6g.

Glazed Lamb

Lemon and honey make a classic stir-fry combination in sweet dishes, and this lamb recipe shows how well they work together in savoury dishes, too. Serve with a fresh mixed salad to complete this delicious dish.

Serves 4

450g/1lb boneless lean lamb
15ml/1 tbsp grapeseed oil
175g/6oz mangetouts (snow peas), trimmed
3 spring onions (scallions), sliced
30ml/2 tbsp clear honey
juice of ½ lemon
30ml/2 tbsp chopped fresh coriander (cilantro)
15ml/1 tbsp sesame seeds
salt and ground black pepper

1 Using a cleaver, cut the lamb into thin strips.

2 Heat the wok, then add the oil. When the oil is hot, stir-fry the lamb until browned all over. Remove and keep warm.

3 Add the mangetouts and spring onions to the hot wok and stir-fry for 30 seconds.

4 Return the lamb to the wok and add the honey, lemon juice, chopped coriander and sesame seeds and season well. Stir thoroughly to mix. Bring to the boil, then allow to bubble vigorously for 1 minute until the lamb is completely coated in the honey mixture. Serve immediately.

Cook's Tip
Use a tender cut of lamb such as leg for this recipe.

Variations
This recipe would work just as well made with pork or chicken instead of lamb. You could substitute chopped fresh basil for the coriander if using chicken.

Energy 268kcal/1119kJ; Fat 17.8g; Saturated fat 6.5g; Carbohydrate 2.4g; Fibre 2g.

Creamy Lamb Korma

A heritage of the talented cooks who served the Mughal emperors, this is a rich and luxurious dish. Mild in flavour, it is ideal for serving when you are unsure about how hot your guests like their curries to be.

Serves 4–6

15ml/1 tbsp white sesame seeds
15ml/1 tbsp white poppy seeds
50g/2oz/½ cup blanched almonds
2 fresh green chillies, seeded
6 garlic cloves, sliced
5cm/2in piece fresh root ginger, sliced
1 onion, finely chopped
45ml/3 tbsp ghee or vegetable oil
6 green cardamom pods
5cm/2in piece cinnamon stick
4 cloves
900g/2lb lean lamb, boned and cubed
5ml/1 tsp ground cumin
5ml/1 tsp ground coriander
300ml/½ pint/1¼ cups double (heavy) cream mixed with 2.5ml/½ tsp cornflour (cornstarch)
salt
roasted sesame seeds, to garnish

1 Preheat a karahi, wok or large pan over a medium heat without any fat, and add the first seven ingredients. Stir until they begin to change colour. They should go just a shade darker.

2 Leave the mixture to cool, then grind to a fine paste using a pestle and mortar or in a food processor. Heat the ghee or oil in the pan over a low heat.

3 Fry the cardamoms, cinnamon and cloves until the cloves swell. Add the lamb, ground cumin and coriander and the prepared paste, and season with salt to taste. Increase the heat to medium and stir well. Reduce the heat to low, then cover the pan and cook until the lamb is almost done.

4 Remove from the heat, leave to cool a little and gradually fold in the cream, reserving 5ml/1 tsp to garnish.

5 When ready to serve, gently reheat the lamb, uncovered. Spoon into a dish and garnish with the sesame seeds and the reserved cream. This korma is very good served with pilau rice.

Energy 939kcal/3892kJ; Fat 80.8g; Saturated fat 38.3g; Carbohydrate 5.1g; Fibre 1.5g.

Lamb Curry with Cardamom Rice

This Indian-style lamb biryani, with the meat and rice cooked together in a clay pot, is a delicious meal in itself.

Serves 4

1 large onion, quartered
2 garlic cloves
1 fresh green chilli, halved and seeded
5cm/2in piece fresh root ginger
15ml/1 tbsp ghee
15ml/1 tbsp vegetable oil
675g/1½lb boned shoulder or leg of lamb, cut into chunks
15ml/1 tbsp ground coriander
10ml/2 tsp ground cumin
1 cinnamon stick, broken into 3 pieces
150ml/¼ pint/⅔ cup thick natural (plain) yogurt
150ml/¼ pint/⅔ cup water
75g/3oz/⅓ cup ready-to-eat dried apricots, cut into chunks
salt and ground black pepper

For the rice
250g/9oz/1⅓ cups basmati rice
6 cardamom pods, split open
25g/1oz/2 tbsp butter, cut into small pieces
45ml/3 tbsp toasted cashew nuts or flaked (sliced) almonds

For the garnish
1 onion, sliced and fried until golden
a few sprigs of fresh coriander (cilantro)

1 Soak a large clay pot or chicken brick in cold water for 20 minutes, then drain. Place the onion, garlic, chilli and ginger in a food processor or blender and process with 15ml/1 tbsp water to a smooth paste.

2 Heat the ghee and vegetable oil in a heavy frying pan. Fry the lamb chunks in batches over a high heat until golden brown. Remove from the pan using a slotted spoon and set aside. Scrape the onion paste into the remaining oil left in the frying pan, stir in the ground coriander and cumin, add the cinnamon stick pieces and fry for 1–2 minutes, stirring constantly with a wooden spoon.

3 Return the meat to the frying pan, then gradually add the yogurt, a spoonful at a time, stirring well between each addition with a wooden spoon. Season the meat well with plenty of salt and pepper and stir in the water.

4 Transfer the contents of the frying pan to the prepared clay pot, cover with the lid and place in an unheated oven. Set the oven to 180°C/350°F/Gas 4 and cook for 45 minutes.

5 Meanwhile, prepare the basmati rice. Place it in a bowl, cover with cold water and leave to soak for 20 minutes. Drain the rice and place it in a large pan of boiling salted water, bring back to the boil and cook for 10 minutes. Drain and stir in the split cardamom pods.

6 Remove the clay pot from the oven and stir in the chopped ready-to-eat apricots. Pile the cooked rice on top of the lamb and dot with the butter. Drizzle over 60ml/4 tbsp water, then sprinkle the cashew nuts or flaked almonds on top. Cover the pot, reduce the oven temperature to 150°C/300°F/Gas 2 and cook the meat and rice for 30 minutes. Remove the lid from the pot and fluff up the rice with a fork. Garnish with the fried onion and coriander, and serve.

Energy 427kcal/1784kJ; Fat 25.3g; Saturated fat 11.3g; Carbohydrate 14.4g; Fibre 2g.

Rogan Josh

This is one of the most popular lamb dishes to have originated in Kashmir. Traditionally, fatty meat on the bone is slow-cooked until most of the fat is separated from the meat. The fat that escapes from the meat is known as rogan, and josh refers to the red colour. This recipe, however, uses lean lamb.

Serves 4–6
45ml/3 tbsp lemon juice
250ml/8fl oz/1 cup natural
  (plain) yogurt
5ml/1 tsp salt
2 garlic cloves, crushed
2.5cm/1in piece fresh root ginger,
  finely grated
900g/2lb lean lamb fillet, cubed
60ml/4 tbsp vegetable oil
2.5ml/½ tsp cumin seeds
2 bay leaves
4 green cardamom pods
1 onion, finely chopped
10ml/2 tsp ground coriander
10ml/2 tsp ground cumin
5ml/1 tsp chilli powder
400g/14oz can chopped
  tomatoes
30ml/2 tbsp tomato purée
  (paste)
150ml/¼ pint/⅔ cup water
toasted cumin seeds and bay
  leaves, to garnish
plain boiled rice, to serve

1 In a large bowl, mix together the lemon juice, yogurt, salt, half the crushed garlic and the ginger. Add the lamb, cover and marinate in the refrigerator overnight.

2 Heat the oil in a karahi, wok or large pan and fry the cumin seeds for 2 minutes. Add the bay leaves and cardamom pods and fry for a further 2 minutes.

3 Add the onion and remaining garlic and fry for 5 minutes. Add the coriander, cumin and chilli powder. Fry for 2 minutes.

4 Add the marinated lamb to the pan and cook for a further 5 minutes, stirring occasionally to prevent the mixture from sticking to the base of the pan and starting to burn.

5 Stir in the tomatoes, tomato purée and water. Cover and simmer for 1–1½ hours. Garnish with toasted cumin seeds and bay leaves, and serve with the rice.

Energy 566kcal/2362kJ; Fat 37g; Saturated fat 13.3g; Carbohydrate 10.7g; Fibre 1.2g.

Curried Lamb & Lentils

This colourful curry is packed with protein and low in fat, so it makes a tasty yet healthy meal.

Serves 4
8 lean boned lamb leg steaks
  (about 500g/1¼lb
  total weight)
1 onion, chopped
2 carrots, diced
1 celery stick, chopped
15ml/1 tbsp hot curry paste
30ml/2 tbsp tomato
  purée (paste)
475ml/16fl oz/2 cups chicken or
  veal stock
175g/6oz/1 cup green lentils
salt and ground black pepper
fresh coriander (cilantro) leaves,
  to garnish
boiled rice, to serve

1 Cook the lamb steaks in a large, non-stick frying pan, without any added fat, for 2–3 minutes on each side, until browned.

2 Add the onion, carrots and celery and cook, stirring occasionally, for 2 minutes, then stir in the curry paste, tomato purée, stock and lentils.

3 Bring to the boil, lower the heat, cover with a tight-fitting lid and simmer gently for 30 minutes, until tender. Add some extra stock, if necessary.

4 Season to taste with salt and pepper. Spoon the curry on to warmed plates and serve immediately, garnished with coriander and accompanied by rice.

> **Cook's Tip**
> *Lentils are one of the few pulses (legumes) that do not require prolonged soaking in cold water before cooking. However, just like dried beans and peas, they should not be seasoned with salt until after cooking or their skins will become unpleasantly tough. Both green and brown lentils keep their shape well, as do the rather more expensive small Puy lentils. Red and yellow lentils are not suitable for this recipe as they tend to disintegrate during cooking.*

Energy 381kcal/1600kJ; Fat 14.7g; Saturated fat 6.6g; Carbohydrate 28.4g; Fibre 3.2g.

Minced Lamb with Curry Leaves & Chilli

The whole chillies pack quite a punch, but can be removed from the dish before serving.

Serves 4

10ml/2 tsp oil
2 medium onions, chopped
10 curry leaves
6 fresh green chillies
350g/12oz lean minced (ground) lamb
5ml/1 tsp crushed garlic
5ml/1 tsp grated fresh root ginger
5ml/1 tsp chilli powder
1.5ml/¼ tsp ground turmeric
5ml/1 tsp salt
2 tomatoes, peeled and quartered
15ml/1 tbsp chopped fresh coriander (cilantro)

1 Heat the oil in a karahi, wok or heavy pan and fry the onions with the curry leaves and 3 of the whole green chillies.

2 Put the lamb into a bowl. Mix with the crushed garlic, grated ginger and spices.

3 Add the minced lamb and salt to the onions and stir-fry for 7–10 minutes.

4 Add the tomatoes, coriander and remaining chillies and stir-fry for 2 minutes. Serve hot.

Cook's Tips
• *This aromatic curry also makes a terrific brunch if served with fried eggs.*
• *Curry leaves are available from Indian grocers and are best used fresh rather than dried as their flavour diminishes when dried. They will keep for several days in a plastic bag in the refrigerator. You can also freeze them.*

Energy 197kcal/821kJ; Fat 9.37g; Saturated fat 3.59g; Carbohydrate 8.57g; Fibre 1.63g.

Lamb with Peas & Mint

A simple dish for a family meal, this is easy to prepare and very versatile. It is equally delicious whether served with plain boiled rice or chapatis. Another excellent use for the lamb mixture is for filling samosas.

Serves 4

15ml/1 tbsp oil
1 medium onion, chopped
2.5ml/½ tsp crushed garlic
2.5ml/½ tsp grated fresh root ginger
2.5ml/½ tsp chilli powder
1.5ml/¼ tsp ground turmeric
5ml/1 tsp ground coriander
5ml/1 tsp salt
2 medium tomatoes, sliced
275g/10oz lean leg of lamb, minced (ground)
1 large carrot, sliced or cut into batons
75g/3oz/½ cup petits pois (baby peas)
15ml/1 tbsp chopped fresh mint
15ml/1 tbsp chopped fresh coriander (cilantro)
1 fresh green chilli, chopped
fresh coriander, to garnish

1 In a deep, heavy frying pan, heat the oil and fry the chopped onion over a medium heat for 5 minutes until golden.

2 Meanwhile, in a small mixing bowl, mix the garlic, ginger, chilli powder, turmeric, ground coriander and salt. Stir well.

3 Add the sliced tomatoes and the spice mixture to the onions in the frying pan and fry for 2–3 minutes, stirring continuously.

4 Add the minced lamb to the mixture and stir-fry for about 7–10 minutes to seal.

5 Break up any lumps of meat which may form in the pan, using a potato masher if necessary.

6 Finally add the carrot, petits pois, chopped fresh mint and coriander and the chopped green chilli and mix well.

7 Cook, stirring for 2–3 minutes until the carrot slices or batons and the petits pois are cooked, then serve immediately, garnished with fresh coriander sprigs.

Energy 178kcal/742kJ; Fat 9.4g; Saturated fat 3.32g; Carbohydrate 7.2g; Fibre 2.1g.

Rezala

This delectable lamb recipe is a legacy of the Muslim Mughal era. It comes from Bengal where there is a tradition of Muslim cuisine.

Serves 4

1 large onion, roughly chopped
10ml/2 tsp grated fresh root ginger
10ml/2 tsp crushed garlic
4 or 5 cloves
2.5ml/½ tsp black peppercorns
6 green cardamom pods
5cm/2in piece cinnamon stick, halved
8 lamb rib chops
60ml/4 tbsp vegetable oil
1 large onion, finely sliced
175ml/6fl oz/¾ cup natural (plain) yogurt
50g/2oz/¼ cup butter
2.5ml/1 tsp salt
2.5ml/½ tsp ground cumin
2.5ml/½ tsp hot chilli powder
whole nutmeg
2.5ml/½ tsp sugar
15ml/1 tbsp lime juice
pinch of saffron, steeped in 15ml/1 tbsp hot water for 10–15 minutes
15ml/1 tbsp rose water
rose petals, to garnish
naan bread or boiled basmatic rice, to serve (optional)

1 Process the onion in a blender or food processor. Add a little water if necessary to form a purée.

2 Put the purée in a glass bowl and add the grated ginger, crushed garlic, cloves, peppercorns, cardamom pods and cinnamon. Mix well.

3 Put the lamb chops in a large shallow glass dish and add the spice mixture. Mix thoroughly, cover the bowl and leave the lamb to marinate for 3–4 hours or overnight in the refrigerator. Bring back to room temperature before cooking.

4 In a karahi, wok or large pan, heat the oil over medium-high heat and fry the sliced onion for 6–7 minutes, until golden brown. Remove the onion slices with a slotted spoon, squeezing out as much oil as possible on the side of the pan. Drain the onions on kitchen paper.

5 In the remaining oil, fry the marinated lamb chops for 4–5 minutes, stirring frequently. Reduce the heat to low, cover and cook for 5–7 minutes.

6 Meanwhile, mix the yogurt and butter together in a small pan and place over a low heat. Cook for 5–6 minutes, stirring constantly, then stir into the lamb chops along with the salt. Add the cumin and chilli powder and cover the pan. Cook for 45–50 minutes until the chops are tender.

7 Using a nutmeg grater, or the finest cutting surface on a large, stainless steel grater, grate about 2.5ml/½ tsp nutmeg.

8 Add the nutmeg and sugar to the pan containing the lamb, cook for 1–2 minutes and add the lime juice, saffron and rose water. Stir and mix well, simmer for 2–3 minutes and remove from the heat. Spoon into a dish and garnish with the fried onion and rose petals. Serve with naan bread or boiled basmati rice, if you like.

Energy 637kcal/2630kJ; Fat 57.4g; Saturated fat 25.7g; Carbohydrate 12.8g; Fibre 1.7g.

Lamb with Apricots

Dried apricots are a useful store-cupboard ingredient and can really transform a curry or stew. Here they are combined with cinnamon, cardamom, cumin and coriander to make a delicious sauce with a hint of sweetness for lamb.

Serves 6

900g/2lb lean stewing lamb
15ml/1 tbsp oil
2.5cm/1in cinnamon stick
4 green cardamom pods
1 onion, chopped
15ml/1 tbsp curry paste
5ml/1 tsp ground cumin
5ml/1 tsp ground coriander
1.5ml/¼ tsp salt
175g/6oz/⅔ cup ready-to-eat dried apricots
350ml/12fl oz/1½ cups lamb stock
fresh coriander (cilantro), to garnish
saffron rice and mango chutney, to serve

1 Remove all the visible fat from the stewing lamb and cut into 2.5cm/1in cubes.

2 Heat the oil in a large, heavy pan and fry the cinnamon stick and cardamoms for 2 minutes. Add the onion and gently fry for about 6–8 minutes, stirring occasionally.

3 Add the curry paste and fry for 2 minutes. Stir in the ground cumin and coriander and the salt and stir-fry for a further 2–3 minutes.

4 Add the meat, apricots and the stock. Cover and cook for 1–1½ hours. Serve, garnished with fresh coriander, on yellow rice, with mango chutney in a separate bowl.

> **Cook's Tip**
> It is best to buy green cardamom pods from an Indian grocer or health food store, as the cardamoms sold in supermarkets are often bleached and do not have as full a flavour. Cardamom is a versatile spice in Indian cuisine, used in savoury and sweet dishes.

Energy 327kcal/1368kJ; Fat 16g; Saturated fat 6.59g; Carbohydrate 13.3g; Fibre 2.7g.

Mughlai-style Leg of Lamb

Legend has it that roasting a whole leg of lamb was first popularized by the Mongolian warrior Genghis Khan. Here the meat is permeated with spices.

Serves 4–6
4 large onions, chopped
4 garlic cloves
5cm/2in piece fresh root
   ginger, chopped
45ml/3 tbsp ground almonds
10ml/2 tsp ground cumin
10ml/2 tsp ground coriander

10ml/2 tsp ground turmeric
10ml/2 tsp garam masala
4–6 fresh green chillies
juice of 1 lemon
300ml/½ pint/1¼ cups natural
   (plain) yogurt, beaten
1.8kg/4lb leg of lamb
8–10 cloves
salt
15ml/1 tbsp flaked (sliced)
   almonds, to garnish
4 firm tomatoes, halved and
   grilled (broiled), to serve

1 Preheat the oven to 190°C/375°F/Gas 5. Place the onions, garlic, ginger, ground almonds, dry spices, chillies and lemon juice in a food processor or blender. Add salt to taste, and process to a smooth paste. Gradually add the yogurt and blend briefly to mix. Grease a large, deep roasting pan.

2 Remove most of the fat and skin from the lamb. Using a sharp knife, make deep pockets above the bone at each side of the thick end. Make deep diagonal gashes on both sides of the lamb.

3 Push the cloves firmly into the meat, spaced evenly on all sides.

4 Push some of the spice mixture into the pockets and gashes and spread the remainder evenly all over the meat. Place the meat on the roasting pan and loosely cover the whole pan with foil. Roast for 2–2½ hours, or until the meat is cooked, removing the foil for the last 10 minutes of cooking time.

5 Remove from the oven and leave to rest for about 10 minutes before carving. Garnish the roast with the almonds and serve with the tomatoes.

Energy 852kcal/3549kJ; Fat 51.2g; Saturated fat 17g; Carbohydrate 25.4g; Fibre 3.5g.

Kashmiri-style Lamb

This red-coloured, hot curry can be made milder by simply replacing the chilli powder with paprika and tomato purée.

Serves 4–6
60ml/4 tbsp vegetable oil
1.5ml/¼ tsp asafoetida
900g/2lb lean lamb, cubed
piece fresh root ginger,
   crushed
2 garlic cloves, crushed
60ml/4 tbsp rogan josh
   masala paste

5ml/1 tsp chilli powder, or
   10ml/2 tsp sweet paprika
   plus 10ml/2 tsp tomato
   purée (paste)
8–10 strands saffron (optional),
   plus extra to garnish
salt
about 150ml/¼ pint/⅔ cup
   natural (plain) yogurt, beaten

1 Heat the oil in a pan and fry the asafoetida and lamb, stirring well to seal the meat. Reduce the heat, cover and cook for about 10 minutes.

2 Add the ginger, garlic, rogan josh masala paste, chilli powder or paprika and tomato purée (if you want a milder curry), and saffron. Mix well and add salt. If the meat is too dry, add a very small amount of boiling water. Cover the pan and cook on a low heat for a further 10 minutes.

3 Remove the pan from the heat and leave to cool a little. Add the yogurt 15ml/1 tbsp at a time, stirring constantly to avoid curdling. Return to a low heat and cook uncovered until thick. Garnish with a spoonful of yogurt and a few saffron strands.

> **Cook's Tip**
> Asafoetida is made from the sap of the roots and stem of a large plant similar to fennel in appearance. The sap dries into a resin, which is ground for culinary use. As it has a strong aroma it is used in only small amounts.

Energy 547kcal/2280kJ; Fat 39.3g; Saturated fat 13.5g; Carbohydrate 2.8g; Fibre 0g.

Hot-&-sour Lamb & Lentil Curry

This dish has a hot, sweet-and-sour flavour, through which should rise the slightly bitter flavour of fenugreek leaves.

Serves 4–6

90ml/6 tbsp vegetable oil
2 fresh red chillies, chopped
2 fresh green chillies, chopped
2.5cm/1in piece fresh root
   ginger, crushed
3 garlic cloves, crushed
2 bay leaves
5cm/2in piece cinnamon
   stick
900g/2lb lean lamb, cubed
600ml/1 pint/2½ cups water
350g/12oz/1½ cups mixed
   lentils (see Cook's Tip)

2 potatoes, cubed
1 aubergine (eggplant), cubed
2 courgettes (zucchini), cubed
4 onions, thinly sliced, deep-fried
   and drained
115g/4oz frozen spinach,
   thawed and drained
25g/1oz fenugreek leaves,
   fresh or dried
115g/4oz pumpkin, cubed
115g/4oz/4 cups fresh coriander
   (cilantro), chopped
50g/2oz/2 cups fresh mint,
   chopped, or 15ml/1 tbsp
   mint sauce
45ml/3 tbsp garam masala
10ml/2 tsp brown sugar
lemon juice, to taste
1 garlic clove, sliced
salt

1 Heat 45ml/3 tbsp of the oil in a pan, wok or karahi and fry the chillies, ginger and garlic for 2 minutes. Add the bay leaves, cinnamon, lamb and water. Bring to the boil, then reduce the heat and simmer until the lamb is half cooked.

2 Drain the water into another pan and put the lamb aside. Add the lentils to the water and cook until they are tender. Mash the lentils with the back of a spoon.

3 Add the cubes of potatoes and aubergine and stir into the mashed lentils, then add the courgette cubes and deep-fried onions. Stir in the spinach, fenugreek and pumpkin. Add some hot water if the mixture is too thick. Cook until the vegetables are tender, then mash again with a spoon, keeping the vegetables a little coarse.

4 Heat 15ml/1 tbsp of the oil in a frying pan, and gently fry the fresh coriander and mint (saving a little to garnish) with the masala, sugar and salt. Add the reserved lamb and fry gently for about 5 minutes.

5 Return the lamb and spices to the lentil and vegetable mixture and stir well. If the mixture seems dry, add more water. Heat gently until the lamb is fully cooked.

6 Add the lemon juice and mix well. Heat the remaining oil and fry the sliced clove of garlic until golden brown. Pour over the curry. Garnish with the remaining deep-fried onion slices and the reserved coriander and mint. Serve hot.

> **Cook's Tip**
> *You might like to include bengal gram (a type of chickpea), moong dhal (small split yellow lentils) and masoor dhal (red split lentils). Cooking times will depend on the types chosen.*

Energy 1040kcal/4359kJ; Fat 53.5g; Saturated fat 14.9g; Carbohydrate 73.5g; Fibre 9.8g.

Hot Dry Meat Curry

This dish is nearly as hot as phaal (India's hottest curry) but the spices can still be distinguished above the fiery chilli.

Serves 4–6

30ml/2 tbsp vegetable oil
1 large onion, finely sliced
5cm/2in piece fresh root
   ginger, crushed
4 garlic cloves, crushed
6–8 curry leaves
45ml/3 tbsp extra-hot curry paste

15ml/1 tbsp chilli powder
5ml/1 tsp Indian five-spice
   powder
5ml/1 tsp ground turmeric
900g/2lb lean lamb, beef or pork,
   cubed
175ml/6fl oz/¾ cup thick
   coconut milk
salt
chopped tomato and coriander
   (cilantro) leaves, to garnish

1 Heat the oil in a large pan and fry the sliced onion, crushed ginger and garlic and the curry leaves until the onion is soft, stirring occasionally.

2 Stir in the curry paste, chilli, five-spice powder, turmeric and salt, and cook for a few moments, stirring frequently.

3 Add the meat and stir well over a medium heat to seal and evenly brown the meat pieces. Keep stirring until the oil separates. Cover and cook for about 20 minutes.

4 Add the coconut milk, mix well and simmer until the meat is cooked.

5 Towards the end of cooking, uncover the pan to reduce the excess liquid. Garnish and serve hot.

> **Cook's Tip**
> *Indian five-spice powder contains aniseed, cumin, fenugreek, mustard and nigella. If you are unable to find it you can substitute garam masala or curry powder instead.*

Energy 558kcal/2323kJ; Fat 39.2g; Saturated fat 13.4g; Carbohydrate 6.9g; Fibre 0.9g.

Spicy Spring Lamb Roast

Coating a leg of lamb with a spicy, fruity rub gives it a wonderful flavour.

Serves 6
1.6kg/3–3½lb lean leg of
    spring lamb
5ml/1 tsp chilli powder
5ml/1 tsp crushed garlic
5ml/1 tsp ground coriander
5ml/1 tsp ground cumin
5ml/1 tsp salt
15ml/1 tbsp dried breadcrumbs

45ml/3 tbsp natural (plain)
    low-fat yogurt
30ml/2 tbsp lemon juice
30ml/2 tbsp sultanas
    (golden raisins)
15ml/1 tbsp oil

For the garnish
mixed salad leaves
fresh coriander (cilantro)
2 tomatoes, quartered
1 large carrot, shredded
lemon wedges

1 Preheat the oven to 180°C/350°F/Gas 4. Trim any excess fat from the lamb. Rinse the joint, pat it dry and set aside on a sheet of foil large enough to enclose it completely.

2 In a medium bowl, mix together the chilli powder, garlic, ground coriander, ground cumin and salt.

3 Mix together in a food processor the breadcrumbs, yogurt, lemon juice and sultanas.

4 Add the contents of the food processor to the spice mixture together with the oil and mix together well. Pour this on to the leg of lamb and rub all over the meat.

5 Enclose the meat in the foil and place in an ovenproof dish. Cook in the oven for about 1½ hours.

6 Remove the lamb from the oven, open the foil and, using the back of a spoon, spread the mixture evenly over the meat. Return the lamb, uncovered, to the oven for another 45 minutes or until it is cooked right through and tender.

7 Slice the meat and serve with the mixed salad leaves, fresh coriander, tomatoes, carrot and lemon wedges.

Energy 265kcal/1109kJ; Fat 13.4g; Saturated fat 5.59g; Carbohydrate 8.9g; Fibre 0.7g.

Lamb Pilau

A pilau is a rice dish containing whole spices, which can either be plain or combined with meat, chicken or vegetables.

Serves 4–6
30ml/2 tbsp corn oil
15ml/1 tbsp unsalted (sweet)
    butter or ghee
2 medium onions, sliced
5ml/1 tsp crushed garlic
5ml/1 tsp chilli powder
1.5ml/¼ tsp crushed fresh
    root ginger
1.5ml/¼ tsp ground turmeric
5ml/1 tsp garam masala
5ml/1 tsp salt
30ml/2 tbsp natural (plain) yogurt
2 medium tomatoes, sliced
450g/1lb lean minced (ground)
    lamb

30ml/2 tbsp chopped fresh
    coriander (cilantro)
2 medium fresh chillies,
    chopped
tomato slices

For the rice
450g/1lb/2¼ cups basmati rice
1.2 litres/2 pints/5 cups water
4 cloves
4 green cardamom pods
2.5ml/½ tsp black cumin seeds
6 black peppercorns
7.5ml/1½ tsp salt
15ml/1 tbsp chopped fresh
    coriander (cilantro)
2 fresh green chillies, chopped
15ml/1 tbsp lime juice
2.5ml/½ tsp saffron strands
    soaked in 30ml/2 tbsp milk
    (optional)

1 Wash the rice twice, drain and set aside in a sieve (strainer).

2 Heat the oil and ghee in a deep, round-bottomed frying pan or a large karahi. Add the onions and fry until golden brown.

3 Lower the heat to medium and add the garlic, chilli powder, ginger, turmeric, garam masala, salt, yogurt and tomatoes and stir-fry gently for about 1 minute.

4 Add the minced lamb and turn up the heat to high. Use a slotted spoon to fry the lamb, scraping the bottom of the pan to prevent it from burning.

5 Add the fresh coriander and chillies, and continue to stir, breaking up any lumps in the meat as you work. Once the lamb is throughly cooked, set it to one side.

6 Put the rinsed and drained rice into a large pan with the water, cloves, cardamom pods, cumin seeds, peppercorns and salt, and bring to the boil. When the rice has boiled for 2 minutes, drain off the water along with half the rice, leaving the rest in the pan.

7 Spread the cooked lamb over the rice in the pan and cover with the rice left in the strainer.

8 Add the fresh coriander, green chillies, lime juice and saffron in milk, if using.

9 Cover the pan with a tight-fitting lid and cook over a very low heat for 15–20 minutes.

10 Check that the rice is cooked through and mix gently with a slotted spoon before serving. Garnish with slices of tomato if you like.

Energy 704kcal/2939kJ; Fat 22.1g; Saturated fat 8.7g; Carbohydrate 93.4g; Fibre 1.2g.

Pork with Vegetables

This is a basic recipe for stir-frying any meat with any vegetables, according to seasonal availability.

Serves 4
225g/8oz pork fillet (tenderloin)
15ml/1 tbsp light soy sauce
5ml/1 tsp soft light brown sugar
5ml/1 tsp Chinese rice wine or
   dry sherry
10ml/2 tsp cornflour (cornstarch)
   mixed to a paste with a
   little water
115g/4oz/1⅔ cups mangetouts
   (snow peas)
115g/4oz button (white)
   mushrooms
1 carrot
1 spring onion (scallion)
60ml/4 tbsp vegetable oil
5ml/1 tsp salt
stock (optional)
few drops sesame oil

1 Cut the pork into thin slices. Marinate with about 5ml/1 tsp of the soy sauce, the sugar, rice wine or sherry and cornflour paste.

2 Trim the mangetouts. Thinly slice the mushrooms. Cut the carrot into pieces roughly the same size as the pork and cut the spring onion into short sections.

3 Heat the oil in a preheated wok or large, heavy pan, and stir-fry the pork for about 1 minute or until its colour changes. Remove with a slotted spoon and keep warm while you cook the vegetables.

4 Add the vegetables to the wok and stir-fry for about 2 minutes. Add the salt and the partly cooked pork, and a little stock or water if necessary. Continue cooking and stirring for about 1 minute, then add the remaining soy sauce and blend well. Sprinkle with the sesame oil and serve.

Cook's Tip
When preparing vegetables for stir-frying, cut them to even sizes so that they will take the same amount of time to cook.

Energy 199kcal/826kJ; Fat 13.6g; Saturated fat 2.1g; Carbohydrate 5.7g; Fibre 1.6g.

Portuguese Pork

The Portuguese expanded their empire during the 15th century, establishing outposts in India and Malaysia. In these days, before refrigeration, spices were extremely valuable, and the Portuguese were keen to control the main trade routes both between Asia and Europe, and among different regions of Asia such as India, Indonesia, China and Japan. One major result of this Portuguese colonization was the influence of Portuguese cooking on Indian cuisine, as shown in this fiery pork curry recipe.

Serves 4–6
115g/4oz deep-fried onions,
   crushed
4 fresh red chillies
60ml/4 tbsp vindaloo
   curry paste
90ml/6 tbsp white wine vinegar
90ml/6 tbsp tomato purée
   (paste)
2.5ml/½ tsp fenugreek seeds
5ml/1 tsp ground turmeric
5ml/1 tsp crushed mustard
   seeds, or 2.5ml/½ tsp
   mustard powder
7.5ml/1½ tsp sugar
900g/2lb boneless pork spare
   ribs, cubed
250ml/8fl oz/1 cup water
salt
plain boiled rice, to serve

1 Place the crushed onions, chillies, curry paste, vinegar, tomato purée, fenugreek seeds, turmeric and mustard seeds or powder in a bowl, with sugar and salt to taste.

2 Add the pork cubes and mix well. Cover and marinate for 2 hours, then transfer to a large, heavy pan.

3 Stir in the water. Bring to the boil and simmer gently for 2 hours. Serve hot with the rice.

Cook's Tip
When preparing fresh chillies, it is a good idea to wear rubber gloves, especially if using the hotter varieties. Never touch your eyes, nose or mouth while handling them, and wash both the gloves and your hands with soap and warm water afterwards.

Energy 322kcal/1349kJ; Fat 12.2g; Saturated fat 3.6g; Carbohydrate 4.1g; Fibre 0.9g.

Chilli Pork with Curry Leaves

Curry leaves and chillies are two of the hallmark ingredients used in the southern states of India. This recipe is from the state of Andhra Pradesh, where the hottest chillies, known as *guntur* after the region where they are produced, are grown in abundance.

Serves 4–6
30ml/2 tbsp vegetable oil
1 large onion, finely sliced
5cm/2in piece fresh root ginger, grated
4 garlic cloves, crushed
12 curry leaves
45ml/3 tbsp extra-hot curry paste, or 60ml/4 tbsp hot curry powder
15ml/1 tbsp chilli powder
5ml/1 tsp five-spice powder
5ml/1 tsp ground turmeric
900g/2lb pork, cubed
175ml/6fl oz/¾ cup thick coconut milk
salt
red onion, finely sliced, to garnish
Indian bread and fruit raita, to serve

1 Heat the oil in a karahi, wok or large pan, and fry the onion, ginger, garlic and curry leaves until the onion is soft. Add the curry paste or powder, chilli and five-spice powder, turmeric and salt. Stir well.

2 Add the pork and stir well over a medium heat to seal and evenly brown the meat pieces. Keep stirring until the oil separates. Cover the pan and cook for about 20 minutes.

3 Stir in the coconut milk and simmer, covered, until the meat is cooked. Towards the end of cooking, uncover the pan to reduce the excess liquid. Garnish with onions and serve with any Indian bread, and with fruit raita, for a cooling effect.

Cook's Tip
For extra flavour, reserve half the curry leaves and add with the coconut milk in step 3.

Pork Balchao

This spicy stew is flavoured with vinegar and sugar, a combination that immediately identifies it as Goan.

Serves 4
60ml/4 tbsp vegetable oil
15ml/1 tbsp grated fresh root ginger
15ml/1 tbsp crushed garlic
2.5cm/1in piece cinnamon stick, broken up
2–4 dried red chillies, chopped or torn
4 cloves
10ml/2 tsp cumin seeds
10 black peppercorns
675g/1½lb cubed leg of pork, crackling and other visible fat removed
5ml/1 tsp ground turmeric
200ml/7fl oz/scant 1 cup warm water
25ml/1½ tbsp tomato purée (paste)
2.5ml/½ tsp chilli powder (optional)
1 large onion, finely sliced
5ml/1 tsp salt
5ml/1 tsp sugar
10ml/2 tbsp cider vinegar
fresh chillies, to garnish

1 Heat 30ml/2 tbsp of the oil in a karahi, wok or large pan, and add the ginger and garlic. Fry for 30 seconds.

2 Grind the cinnamon stick, dried chillies, cloves, cumin seeds and peppercorns to a fine powder, using a spice mill or coffee grinder reserved for spices. Add the spice mix to the pan and fry for a further 30 seconds, stirring.

3 Add the pork and turmeric and increase the heat slightly. Fry for 5–6 minutes or until the meat starts to release its juices, stirring regularly. Add the water, tomato purée and chilli powder, if using, and bring to the boil. Cover the pan and simmer gently for 35–40 minutes.

4 Heat the remaining oil and fry the sliced onion for 8–9 minutes until browned, stirring regularly. Add the fried onion to the pork along with the salt, sugar and cider vinegar. Stir, cover and simmer for 30–35 minutes or until the pork is tender. Remove from the heat and spoon into a serving dish. Garnish with fresh chillies and serve.

Energy 484kcal/2018kJ; Fat 31g; Saturated fat 12.5g; Carbohydrate 6.9g; Fibre 0.9g.

Energy 326kcal/1361kJ; Fat 17.9g; Saturated fat 3.7g; Carbohydrate 4.8g; Fibre 0.9g.

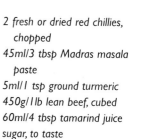

Pork & Pineapple Coconut Curry

The heat of this curry balances out the sweetness of the pineapple, and the coconut cream and spices make a smooth and fragrant dish. It takes very little time to cook, so is ideal for a quick supper before going out or for a midweek family meal on a busy evening.

Serves 4
400ml/14fl oz can coconut milk
10ml/2 tsp Thai red curry paste
400g/14oz pork loin steaks, trimmed and thinly sliced
15ml/1 tbsp Thai fish sauce
5ml/1 tsp palm sugar or light muscovado (brown) sugar
15ml/1 tbsp tamarind juice, made by mixing tamarind paste with warm water
2 kaffir lime leaves, torn
½ medium pineapple, peeled and chopped
1 fresh red chilli, seeded and finely chopped

1 Pour the coconut milk into a bowl and let it settle, so that the cream rises to the surface. Scoop the cream into a measuring jug (cup). You should have about 250ml/8fl oz/ 1 cup. If necessary, add a little of the coconut milk.

2 Pour the measured coconut cream into a large pan and bring it to the boil.

3 Cook the coconut cream for about 10 minutes, until it separates, stirring frequently to prevent it from sticking to the base of the pan and scorching. Add the red curry paste and stir until well mixed. Cook, stirring occasionally, for about 4 minutes, until the paste is fragrant.

4 Add the sliced pork and stir in the fish sauce, sugar and tamarind juice. Cook, stirring constantly, for 1–2 minutes, until the sugar has dissolved and the pork is no longer pink.

5 Add the reserved coconut milk and the lime leaves. Bring to the boil, then stir in the pineapple. Reduce the heat and simmer gently for 3 minutes, or until the pork is fully cooked. Sprinkle over the chilli and serve.

Energy 169kcal/712kJ; Fat 4.4g; Saturated fat 1.6g; Carbohydrate 11g; Fibre 0.6g.

Madras Beef Curry

Although Madras is renowned for the best vegetarian food in India, meat-based recipes such as this beef curry are also extremely popular there.

Serves 4–6
60ml/4 tbsp vegetable oil
1 large onion, finely sliced
3 or 4 cloves
4 green cardamom pods
2 whole star anise
4 fresh green chillies, chopped
2 fresh or dried red chillies, chopped
45ml/3 tbsp Madras masala paste
5ml/1 tsp ground turmeric
450g/1lb lean beef, cubed
60ml/4 tbsp tamarind juice
sugar, to taste
salt
a few fresh coriander (cilantro) leaves, chopped, to garnish

1 Heat the oil in a karahi, wok or large pan over a medium heat and fry the onion slices for about 8 minutes until they turn golden brown.

2 Lower the heat, add all the spice ingredients, and fry for a further 2–3 minutes.

3 Add the cubed beef and mix well with the spices. Cover and cook over a low heat until the beef is tender and fully cooked. Cook uncovered on a higher heat for the last few minutes to reduce any excess liquid.

4 Fold in the tamarind juice, sugar and salt. Reheat the dish and garnish with the chopped coriander leaves. Pilau rice and a tomato and onion salad would make excellent accompaniments for this dish.

Cook's Tip
To tenderize the meat, add 60ml/4 tbsp white wine vinegar in step 2, along with the meat, and omit the tamarind juice.

Energy 317kcal/1318kJ; Fat 21.6g; Saturated fat 5.6g; Carbohydrate 4.8g; Fibre 0.9g.

Pork Fillet with Eggs & Mushrooms

Traditionally, this dish is served as a filling wrapped in thin pancakes, but it can also be served on its own with plain rice. The beauty of this dish is that once the ingredients are prepared, it takes moments to cook.

Serves 4

15g/½oz dried Chinese
  mushrooms
175–225g/6–8oz pork fillet
  (tenderloin)
225g/8oz Chinese leaves
  (Chinese cabbage)
115g/4oz bamboo shoots,
  drained
2 spring onions (scallions)
3 eggs
5ml/1 tsp salt
60ml/4 tbsp vegetable oil
15ml/1 tbsp light soy sauce
15ml/1 tbsp Chinese rice wine
  or dry sherry
few drops sesame oil

1 Rinse the mushrooms thoroughly in cold water and then soak in warm water for 25–30 minutes.

2 Rinse thoroughly again and discard the hard stalks, if any. Dry the mushrooms and thinly shred them.

3 Cut the pork fillet into matchstick-size shreds. Thinly shred the Chinese leaves, bamboo shoots and spring onions.

4 Beat the eggs with a pinch of salt. Heat a little oil in a wok, add the eggs and lightly scramble, but do not allow to become too dry. Remove from the wok.

5 Heat the remaining oil in the wok and stir-fry the pork for about 1 minute, or until the colour changes.

6 Add the vegetables to the wok and stir-fry for 1 minute. Add the remaining salt, the soy sauce and rice wine or sherry. Stir for 1 further minute before adding the scrambled eggs. Break up the scrambled eggs and blend well. Sprinkle with sesame oil and serve.

Spicy Meat Loaf

This mixture is baked in the oven and provides a hearty meal on a cold winter day.

Serves 4–6

5 eggs
450g/1lb lean minced
  (ground) beef
30ml/2 tbsp grated fresh
  root ginger
30ml/2 tbsp crushed garlic
6 fresh green chillies, chopped
2 small onions, finely chopped
2.5ml/½ tsp ground turmeric
50g/2oz/2 cups fresh coriander
  (cilantro), chopped
175g/6oz potato, grated
salt
salad leaves, to serve
lemon twist, to garnish

1 Preheat the oven to 180°C/350°F/ Gas 4. Beat 2 eggs until fluffy and pour into a greased 900g/2lb loaf tin (pan).

2 Knead together the meat, ginger and garlic, 4 green chillies, 1 chopped onion, 1 beaten egg, the turmeric, fresh coriander, potato and salt.

3 Pack into the loaf tin and smooth the surface. Cook in the preheated oven for 45 minutes.

4 Meanwhile, beat the remaining eggs and fold in the remaining green chillies and onion. Remove the loaf tin from the oven and pour the mixture all over the meat.

5 Return to the oven and cook until the eggs have set. Serve the loaf hot on a bed of salad leaves, garnished with a twist of lemon.

Cook's Tip
It is always best to buy meat for mincing (grinding) by the piece if possible so that you can choose some with little fat and remove any remaining fat before you mince (grind) it.

Energy 232kcal/961kJ; Fat 17.5g; Saturated fat 3.2g; Carbohydrate 2.2g; Fibre 1.7g.

Energy 394kcal/1637kJ; Fat 25.4g; Saturated fat 9.8g; Carbohydrate 10.1g; Fibre 1g.

Stewing-beef Curry

Madras curries originate from southern India and are aromatic, robust and pungent in flavour. This recipe uses stewing beef, but you can replace it with lean lamb if you prefer.

Serves 4

900g/2lb lean stewing beef
15ml/1 tbsp oil
1 large onion, finely chopped
4 cloves
4 green cardamom pods
2 green chillies, finely chopped
2.5cm/1in piece fresh root ginger, finely chopped
2 garlic cloves, crushed
2 dried red chillies
15ml/1 tbsp curry paste
10ml/2 tsp ground coriander
5ml/1 tsp ground cumin
2.5ml/½ tsp salt
150ml/¼ pint/⅔ cup beef stock
fresh coriander (cilantro), to garnish
boiled rice, to serve

1 Remove any visible fat from the beef and cut the meat into 2.5cm/1in cubes.

2 Heat the oil in a large, heavy frying pan and stir-fry the onion, cloves and cardamom pods for about 5 minutes. Add the fresh green chillies, ginger, garlic and dried red chillies and fry for a further 2 minutes.

3 Add the curry paste and fry for about 2 minutes. Add the cubed beef and fry for 5–8 minutes until all the meat pieces are lightly browned.

4 Add the coriander, cumin, salt and stock. Cover and simmer gently for 1–1½ hours or until the meat is tender. Serve with Tomato Rice and garnish with fresh coriander.

> **Cook's Tip**
> When whole cardamom pods are used as a flavouring, they are not meant to be eaten. In India, they are left on the side of the plate, along with any bones.

Energy 355kcal/1487kJ; Fat 14.8g; Saturated fat 4.66g; Carbohydrate 7.7g; Fibre 1.8g.

Beef Koftas with Coriander & Mint

Serve these tasty treats piping hot with naan bread, raita and a salad. Leftover koftas can be chopped coarsely and packed into pitta bread.

Makes 20–25

450g/1lb lean minced (ground) beef
30ml/2 tbsp grated fresh root ginger
30ml/2 tbsp crushed garlic
4 fresh green chillies, finely chopped
1 small onion, finely chopped
1 egg
2.5ml/½ tsp ground turmeric
5ml/1 tsp garam masala
50g/2oz/2 cups fresh coriander (cilantro), chopped
4–6 fresh mint leaves, chopped
175g/6oz potato
vegetable oil, for deep-frying
salt

1 Mix the minced meat, ginger, garlic, chillies, onion, egg, spices and herbs in a large bowl.

2 Grate the potato into the bowl, and season with salt to taste. Knead together to blend well and form a soft dough.

3 Shape the mixture into portions the size of golf balls. Place on a plate, cover and leave the koftas to rest for about 25 minutes.

4 In a karahi, wok or frying pan, heat the oil to medium-hot and fry the koftas in small batches until they are golden brown in colour. Drain well and serve hot.

> **Variation**
> This dish works equally well with lamb, but make sure it is lean. As always it is best to buy lean meat and mince (grind) it yourself if you are able to.

Energy 63kcal/263kJ; Fat 4g; Saturated fat 1.7g; Carbohydrate 1.8g; Fibre 0.2g.

Beef Vindaloo

A fiery dish originally from Goa, a vindaloo is made using a unique blend of hot aromatic spices and vinegar to give it a distinctive flavour.

Serves 6

15ml/1 tbsp cumin seeds
4 dried red chillies
5ml/1 tsp black peppercorns
seeds from 5 green cardamom pods
5ml/1 tsp fenugreek seeds
5ml/1 tsp black mustard seeds
2.5ml/½ tsp salt
2.5ml/½ tsp demerara (raw) sugar
60ml/4 tbsp white wine vinegar
30ml/2 tbsp oil
1 large onion, finely chopped
900g/2lb lean stewing beef, cut into 2.5cm/1in cubes
2.5cm/1in piece fresh root ginger, finely chopped
1 garlic clove, crushed
10ml/2 tsp ground coriander
2.5ml/½ tsp ground turmeric
plain and yellow rice, to serve

1 Put the cumin seeds, chillies, peppercorns, cardamom seeds, fenugreek seeds and mustard seeds into a spice grinder (or a pestle and mortar) and grind to a fine powder.

2 Spoon into a bowl, add the salt, sugar and white wine vinegar and mix to a thin paste. Heat 15ml/1 tbsp of the oil in a large, heavy pan and fry the onion for 10 minutes.

3 Put the onions and the spice mixture into a food processor or blender and process to a coarse paste.

4 Heat the remaining oil in the frying pan and fry the meat cubes for about 10 minutes until lightly browned. Remove with a slotted spoon.

5 Add the ginger and garlic to the oil remaining in the pan and fry for 2 minutes. Stir in the ground coriander and turmeric and fry for a further 2 minutes.

6 Add the spice and onion paste and fry for about 5 minutes.

7 Return the beef cubes to the pan with 300ml/½ pint/ 1¼ cups water. Cover and simmer for about 1–1½ hours or until the meat is tender. Serve with plain and yellow rice.

Energy 269kcal/1127kJ; Fat 11.6g; Saturated fat 3.28g; Carbohydrate 7.3g; Fibre 0.6g.

Beef with Green Beans

Green beans cooked with beef is a variation on the traditional recipe which uses lamb. The sliced red pepper provides a contrast to the colour of the beans and chillies, and adds extra flavour.

Serves 4

275g/10oz fine green beans, cut into 2.5cm/1in pieces
15ml/1 tbsp oil
1 medium onion, sliced
5ml/1 tsp grated fresh root ginger
5ml/1 tsp crushed garlic
5ml/1 tsp chilli powder
6.5ml/1¼ tsp salt
1.5ml/¼ tsp ground turmeric
2 tomatoes, chopped
450g/1lb lean beef, cubed
475ml/16fl oz/2 cups water
1 red (bell) pepper, seeded and sliced
15ml/1 tbsp chopped fresh coriander (cilantro)
2 fresh green chillies, chopped
warm chapatis, to serve (optional)

1 Blanch the beans in boiling water for 3–4 minutes, then rinse under cold running water, drain and set aside.

2 Heat the oil in a large, heavy pan and gently fry the onion slices until golden brown.

3 In a bowl, mix the ginger, garlic, chilli powder, salt, turmeric and chopped tomatoes. Spoon the ginger and garlic mixture into the pan and stir-fry with the onion for 5–7 minutes.

4 Add the beef and stir-fry for a further 3 minutes. Pour in the water, bring to the boil and lower the heat. Half-cover the pan and cook for 1–1¼ hours until most of the water has evaporated and the meat is tender.

5 Add the green beans and mix everything together well.

6 Finally, add the red pepper, fresh coriander and green chillies. Cook the mixture, stirring, for a further 7–10 minutes, or until the beans are tender.

7 Spoon into a large bowl or individual plates. Serve the beef hot, with warm chapatis if you like.

Energy 242kcal/1012kJ; Fat 11.6g; Saturated fat 2.91g; Carbohydrate 9.3g; Fibre 3g.

Beef Biryani

Biryani is one of the easiest and most relaxing ways of cooking when entertaining.

Serves 4

2 large onions
2 garlic cloves, chopped
2.5cm/1in piece fresh root ginger, peeled and roughly chopped
½–1 fresh green chilli, seeded and chopped
small bunch of fresh coriander (cilantro)
60ml/4 tbsp flaked (sliced) almonds
30–45ml/2–3 tbsp water
15ml/1 tbsp ghee or butter, plus 25g/1oz/2 tbsp butter for the rice
45ml/3 tbsp vegetable oil
30ml/2 tbsp sultanas (golden raisins)
500g/1¼lb braising or stewing steak, cubed
5ml/1 tsp ground coriander
15ml/1 tbsp ground cumin
2.5ml/½ tsp ground turmeric
2.5ml/½ tsp ground fenugreek
good pinch of ground cinnamon
175ml/6fl oz/¾ cup natural (plain) yogurt, whisked
275g/10oz/1½ cups basmati rice
about 1.2 litres/2 pints/5 cups hot chicken stock or water
salt and ground black pepper
2 hard-boiled eggs, quartered, to garnish
chapatis, to serve

1 Roughly chop one onion and place it in a food processor or blender. Add the garlic, ginger, chilli, fresh coriander and half the flaked almonds. Pour in the water and process to a smooth paste. Transfer the paste to a small bowl and set aside.

2 Finely slice the remaining onion into rings. Heat half the ghee or butter with half the oil in a heavy flameproof casserole and fry the onion for 10–15 minutes until a deep golden brown. Transfer to a plate. Fry the remaining almonds briefly until golden. Set aside. Quickly fry the sultanas until they swell. Transfer to the plate.

3 Heat the remaining ghee or butter in the casserole with a further 15ml/1 tbsp of the oil. Fry the meat, in batches, until browned. Transfer to a plate. Wipe the casserole clean with kitchen paper, heat the remaining oil and pour in the spice paste. Cook over a medium heat for 2–3 minutes, stirring, until the mixture begins to brown lightly. Stir in all the spices, season and cook for 1 minute more.

4 Lower the heat, then stir in the yogurt, a little at a time. Return the meat to the casserole. Stir to coat, cover tightly and simmer for 40–45 minutes until the meat is tender. Meanwhile, soak the rice in a bowl of cold water for 20 minutes.

5 Preheat the oven to 160°C/325°F/Gas 3. Drain the rice, place in a pan and add the hot chicken stock or water, with a little salt. Bring back to the boil, cover and cook for 5 minutes.

6 Drain the rice, and pile it on top of the meat. Using the handle of a spoon, make a hole through the rice and meat mixture, to the bottom of the pan. Place the fried onions, almonds and sultanas over the top and dot with butter.

7 Cover the casserole tightly with a double layer of foil and a lid. Cook in the oven for 30–40 minutes. Garnish and serve with chapatis.

Energy 741kcal/3090kJ; Fat 29.3g; Saturated fat 10.9g; Carbohydrate 79.1g; Fibre 3.1g.

Beef & Kidney with Spinach

Here, spinach is coarsely chopped and added towards the end of cooking, which retains the nutritional value of the spinach and gives the dish a lovely appearance.

Serves 4–6

5cm/2in piece fresh root ginger
30ml/2 tbsp vegetable oil
1 large onion, finely chopped
4 garlic cloves, crushed
60ml/4 tbsp mild curry paste, or 60ml/4 tbsp mild curry powder
1.5ml/¼ tsp ground turmeric
salt
900g/2lb steak and kidney, cubed
450g/1lb fresh spinach, trimmed, washed and chopped, or 450g/1lb frozen spinach, thawed and drained
60ml/4 tbsp tomato purée (paste)
2 large tomatoes, finely chopped

1 Using a sharp knife or vegetable peeler, remove the skin from the ginger. Grate it on the fine side of a metal grater.

2 Heat the oil in a frying pan, wok or karahi and fry the onion, ginger and garlic until the onion is soft and the ginger and garlic turn golden brown.

3 Lower the heat and add the curry paste or powder, turmeric and salt. Add the steak and kidney to the pan and mix well. Cover and cook, stirring frequently to prevent the mixture from sticking to the pan, for 20–30 minutes over a medium heat, until the meat is just tender.

4 Add the spinach and tomato purée and mix well. Cook uncovered until the spinach is softened and most of the liquid has evaporated.

5 Fold in the chopped tomatoes. Increase the heat, as the tomatoes will have a cooling effect on the other ingredients, and cook the mixture for a further 5 minutes, until they are soft.

6 Spoon into shallow bowls and serve piping hot with a simple accompaniment to offset the rich, gamey flavour of the dish, like plain boiled basmati rice. Go easy on any side portions though, as this is a very rich and filling dish.

Energy 362kcal/1515kJ; Fat 13.5g; Saturated fat 3.5g; Carbohydrate 11.7g; Fibre 4.4g.

Citrus Beef Curry

This superbly aromatic curry is not exceptionally hot but it is full of flavour.

Serves 4
450g/1lb rump (round) steak
30ml/2 tbsp vegetable oil
30ml/2 tbsp medium curry paste
2 bay leaves
400ml/14fl oz/1²⁄₃ cups coconut milk
300ml/¹⁄₂ pint/1¹⁄₄ cups beef stock
30ml/2 tbsp lemon juice
grated rind and juice of ¹⁄₂ orange
15ml/1 tbsp sugar

115g/4oz baby (pearl) onions, peeled but left whole
225g/8oz new potatoes, halved
115g/4oz/1 cup unsalted roasted peanuts, roughly chopped
115g/4oz fine green beans, halved
1 red (bell) pepper, seeded and thinly sliced
unsalted roasted peanuts, to garnish (optional)

1 Trim any visible fat from the beef and cut the meat into 5cm/2in strips.

2 Heat the vegetable oil in a large, heavy pan, add the medium curry paste and cook over medium heat for 30 seconds, stirring constantly.

3 Add the beef and cook, stirring, for 2 minutes until it is beginning to brown and is thoroughly coated with the spices.

4 Stir in the bay leaves, coconut milk, stock, lemon juice, orange rind and juice, and sugar. Bring to the boil, stirring frequently.

5 Add the onions and potatoes, then bring back to the boil, reduce the heat and simmer, uncovered, for 5 minutes.

6 Stir in the peanuts, beans and pepper and simmer for a further 10 minutes, or until the beef and potatoes are tender. Serve in shallow bowls, with a spoon and fork, to enjoy all the rich and creamy juices. Sprinkle with extra unsalted roasted peanuts, if you like.

Energy 444kcal/1858kJ; Fat 24.2g; Saturated fat 5.4g; Carbohydrate 23.5g; Fibre 4.2g.

Chilli Beef with Basil

This is a dish for chilli lovers! It is very easy to prepare – all you need is a karahi or a wok.

Serves 2
about 90ml/6 tbsp vegetable oil
16–20 large fresh basil leaves
275g/10oz rump steak
30ml/2 tbsp Worcestershire sauce
5ml/1 tsp soft dark brown sugar
1 or 2 fresh red chillies, sliced into rings
3 garlic cloves, chopped

5ml/1 tsp chopped fresh root ginger
1 shallot, thinly sliced
30ml/2 tbsp finely chopped fresh basil leaves, plus extra to garnish
squeeze of lemon juice
salt and ground black pepper
rice, to serve

1 Heat the oil in a karahi or wok. Add the whole basil leaves and fry for about 1 minute until crisp and golden. Drain on kitchen paper. Remove the pan from the heat and pour off all but 30ml/2 tbsp of the oil.

2 Cut the steak across the grain into thin strips. Mix the Worcestershire sauce and sugar in a bowl. Add the beef, mix well, then cover and leave to marinate for about 30 minutes.

3 Reheat the oil until hot, add the chilli, garlic, ginger and shallot and stir-fry for 30 seconds. Add the beef and chopped basil, then stir-fry for about 3 minutes. Flavour with lemon juice, and add salt and pepper to taste.

4 Transfer the chilli beef to a warmed serving plate, sprinkle over the basil leaves to garnish and serve immediately with rice.

Cook's Tip
Although Worcestershire sauce is often thought of as archetypally English, it is actually based on an Indian recipe. Ingredients include molasses, anchovies and tamarind extract.

Energy 469kcal/1943kJ; Fat 38.6g; Saturated fat 9g; Carbohydrate 0g; Fibre 0g.

Beef Rendang

This spicy dish is usually served with the meat quite dry; if you prefer more sauce, add more water.

Serves 6–8

2 onions or 5 or 6 shallots, chopped
4 garlic cloves, chopped
2.5cm/1in piece fresh galangal, peeled and sliced, or 15ml/ 1 tbsp galangal paste
2.5cm/1in piece fresh root ginger, peeled and sliced
4–6 fresh red chillies, seeded and roughly chopped
lower part only of 1 lemon grass stalk, sliced
2.5cm/1in piece fresh turmeric, peeled and sliced, or 5ml/1 tsp ground turmeric

1kg/2¼lb prime beef in one piece
5ml/1 tsp coriander seeds, dry-fried
5ml/1 tsp cumin seeds, dry-fried
2 kaffir lime leaves, torn into pieces
2 × 400ml/14fl oz cans coconut milk
300ml/½ pint/1¼ cups water
30ml/2 tbsp dark soy sauce
5ml/1 tsp tamarind pulp, soaked in 60ml/4 tbsp warm water
8–10 small new potatoes, scrubbed
salt and ground black pepper
deep-fried onions, sliced fresh red chillies and spring onions (scallions), to garnish

1 Put the onions or shallots in a food processor. Add the garlic, galangal, ginger, chillies, sliced lemon grass and turmeric. Process to a fine paste or grind in a mortar, using a pestle.

2 Cut the meat into cubes using a large sharp knife, then place the cubes in a bowl. Grind the dry-fried coriander and cumin seeds, then add to the meat with the onion, chilli paste and kaffir lime leaves; stir well. Cover and leave in a cool place to marinate.

3 Pour the coconut milk and water into a wok, then stir in the spiced meat and the soy sauce. Strain the tamarind water and add to the wok. Stir over medium heat until the liquid boils, then simmer gently, half-covered, for 1½ hours. Add the potatoes and simmer for 20–25 minutes, or until meat and potatoes are tender. Add water if liked. Season and serve, garnished with deep-fried onions, chillies and spring onions.

Venison with Lentils & Tomatoes

Venison curries well and tastes good in this simple dish. Serve it with pilau rice, naan bread or bhaturas.

Serves 4

60ml/4 tbsp corn oil
1 bay leaf
2 cloves
4 black peppercorns
1 medium onion, sliced
450g/1lb diced venison
2.5ml/½ tsp ground turmeric
7.5ml/1½ tsp chilli powder

5ml/1 tsp garam masala
5ml/1 tsp crushed coriander seeds
2.5cm/1in cinnamon stick
5ml/1 tsp crushed garlic
5ml/1 tsp grated fresh root ginger
7.5ml/1½ tsp salt
1.5 litres/2½ pints/6 cups water
50g/2oz/⅓ cup split red lentils
2 medium tomatoes, quartered
2 fresh green chillies, chopped
15ml/1 tbsp chopped fresh coriander (cilantro)

1 Heat the oil in a karahi, wok or deep pan. Lower the heat slightly and add the bay leaf, cloves, peppercorns and onion slices. Fry for about 5 minutes, or until the onions are golden brown, stirring occasionally. Add the diced venison, turmeric, chilli powder, garam masala, coriander seeds, cinnamon stick, garlic, ginger and most of the salt, and stir-fry for about 5 minutes over a medium heat.

2 Pour in 900ml/1½ pints/3½ cups of the water and cover the pan with a lid. Simmer over a low heat for about 35–40 minutes, or until the water has evaporated and the meat is tender.

3 Put the lentils into a pan with the remaining 600ml/1 pint/ 2½ cups water and boil for about 12–15 minutes, or until the water has almost evaporated and the lentils are soft enough to mash. If the lentils are too thick, add up to 150ml/¼ pint/⅔ cup more water to loosen the mixture.

4 When the meat is tender, stir-fry the mixture using a wooden spoon, until some free oil begins to appear on the sides of the pan. Add the cooked lentils to the venison and mix together well. Add the tomatoes, chillies and fresh coriander and serve.

Energy 388kcal/1629kJ; Fat 16.3g; Saturated fat 6.7g; Carbohydrate 21.5g; Fibre 1.6g.

Energy 277kcal/1160kJ; Fat 13.9g; Saturated fat 2.6g; Carbohydrate 11.6g; Fibre 1.6g.

Balti Potatoes with Aubergines

Using baby potatoes adds to the attractiveness of this dish. Choose the smaller variety of aubergines, too, as they are tastier than the large ones, which contain a lot of water and little flavour. You can buy small aubergines from specialist grocers.

Serves 4

10–12 baby potatoes
6 small aubergines (eggplants)
1 medium red (bell) pepper
15ml/1 tbsp oil
2 medium onions, sliced
4–6 curry leaves
2.5ml/½ tsp onion seeds
5ml/1 tsp crushed coriander seeds
2.5ml/½ tsp cumin seeds
5ml/1 tsp grated fresh root ginger
5ml/1 tsp crushed garlic
5ml/1 tsp crushed dried red chillies
15ml/1 tbsp chopped fresh fenugreek leaves
5ml/1 tsp chopped fresh coriander (cilantro)
15ml/1 tbsp natural (plain) low-fat yogurt
fresh coriander leaves, to garnish

1 Cook the unpeeled potatoes in a pan of boiling water until they are just soft, but still whole.

2 Cut the aubergines into quarters if very small, or eighths if using larger aubergines.

3 Cut the pepper in half, remove the seeds and ribs, then slice the flesh into thin even strips.

4 Heat the oil in a karahi, wok or heavy pan and fry the sliced onions, curry leaves, onion seeds, crushed coriander seeds and cumin seeds until the onion slices are a soft golden brown, stirring constantly.

5 Add the ginger, garlic, crushed chillies and fenugreek, followed by the aubergines and potatoes. Stir everything together and cover the pan with a lid. Lower the heat and cook the vegetables for 5–7 minutes.

6 Remove the lid, add the fresh coriander followed by the yogurt and stir well. Serve garnished with coriander leaves.

Energy 183kcal/773kJ; Fat 4.42g; Saturated fat 0.70g; Carbohydrate 33.02g; Fibre 5.43g.

Balti Stir-fried Vegetables with Cashew Nuts

This quick and versatile stir-fry will accommodate most other combinations of vegetables – you do not have to use the selection suggested here.

Serves 4

2 medium carrots
1 medium red (bell) pepper, seeded
1 medium green (bell) pepper, seeded
2 courgettes (zucchini)
115g/4oz green beans
1 medium bunch spring onions (scallions)
15ml/1 tbsp oil
4–6 curry leaves
2.5ml/½ tsp cumin seeds
4 dried red chillies
10–12 cashew nuts
5ml/1 tsp salt
30ml/2 tbsp lemon juice
fresh mint leaves, to garnish

1 Prepare the vegetables: cut the carrots, peppers and courgettes into matchsticks, halve the beans and chop the spring onions. Set aside.

2 Heat the oil in a karahi, wok or heavy pan and fry the curry leaves, cumin seeds and dried red chillies for about 1 minute.

3 Add the vegetables and nuts, and stir them around gently. Add the salt and lemon juice. Continue to stir and cook for about 3–5 minutes.

4 Transfer the vegetables to a serving dish, garnish with fresh mint leaves and serve immediately.

> **Variation**
> Small florets of broccoli or cauliflower are delicious cooked in a stir-fry so that they retain their crunch. You could use them in place of the courgettes (zucchini). Or you could use mushrooms, mangetouts (snow peas) and beansprouts.

Energy 98kcal/406kJ; Fat 5.28g; Saturated fat 0.88g; Carbohydrate 10.36g; Fibre 3.94g.

Karahi Potatoes with Whole Spices

The potato is transformed into something quite exotic when it is cooked like this.

Serves 4
15ml/1 tbsp oil
5ml/1 tsp cumin seeds
3 curry leaves
5ml/1 tsp crushed dried
  red chillies
2.5ml/½ tsp mixed onion,
  mustard and fenugreek seeds
2.5ml/½ tsp fennel seeds
3 garlic cloves, sliced
2.5cm/1in piece fresh root ginger,
  grated
2 onions, sliced
6 new potatoes, thinly sliced
15ml/1 tbsp chopped fresh
  coriander (cilantro)
1 fresh red chilli, seeded
  and sliced
1 fresh green chilli, seeded
  and sliced

1 Heat the oil in a karahi, wok or heavy pan. Lower the heat slightly and add the cumin seeds, curry leaves, dried red chillies, mixed onion, mustard and fenugreek seeds, fennel seeds, garlic slices and ginger. Fry for 1 minute.

2 Add the onions and fry for a further 5 minutes, or until the onions are golden brown.

3 Add the potatoes, fresh coriander and sliced fresh red and green chillies and mix well. Cover the pan tightly with a lid or foil; if using foil, make sure that it does not touch the food. Cook over a very low heat for about 7 minutes or until the potatoes are tender.

4 Remove the pan from the heat, and take off the lid or foil cover. Serve hot straight from the pan.

Cook's Tip
Choose a waxy variety of new potato for this fairly hot vegetable dish; if you use a very soft potato, it will not be possible to cut it into thin slices without it breaking up. Suitable varieties are often labelled "salad potatoes" when sold at supermarkets. Leave the skin on for a tastier result.

Energy 110kcal/462kJ; Fat 3.6g; Saturated fat 0.39g; Carbohydrate 17.1g; Fibre 1.6g.

Balti Mushrooms in a Creamy Garlic Sauce

This is a simple and delicious Balti recipe which could be accompanied by bread or one of the rice side dishes from this book.

Serves 4
350g/12oz/4½ cups button
  (white) mushrooms
15ml/1 tbsp oil
1 bay leaf
3 garlic cloves, roughly chopped
2 green chillies, seeded and
  chopped
225g/8oz/1 cup low-fat fromage
  frais or ricotta cheese
15ml/1 tbsp chopped fresh
  mint
15ml/1 tbsp chopped fresh
  coriander (cilantro)
5ml/1 tsp salt
fresh mint and coriander leaves,
  to garnish

1 Cut the button mushrooms in half, or in quarters if large, and set aside.

2 Heat the oil in a karahi, wok or heavy pan, then add the bay leaf, chopped garlic and chillies, and quickly stir-fry for about 1 minute.

3 Add the mushrooms. Stir-fry for another 2 minutes.

4 Remove from the heat and stir in the fromage frais or ricotta cheese, followed by the mint, coriander and salt. Return to the heat and stir-fry for 2–3 minutes, then transfer to a warmed serving dish and garnish with mint and coriander leaves.

Cook's Tip
Balti curries have their origins in Baltistan, the area that is now North Pakistan. They are traditionally aromatic but not heavily flavoured with chilli, and bread is usually used to scoop up the food. However, rice also goes well with all the dishes.

Energy 76kcal/321kJ; Fat 3.4g; Saturated fat 0.55g; Carbohydrate 5.2g; Fibre 1.1g.

Balti Dhal with Spring Onions & Tomatoes

This rich-tasting dish is made using toor dhal, a shiny, yellow split lentil which resembles chana dhal. Fresh fenugreek leaves are perfect with pulses and impart a stunning aroma.

Serves 4

115g/4oz/½ cup toor dhal
   or yellow split peas
30ml/2 tbsp oil
1.5ml/¼ tsp onion seeds
1 medium bunch spring onions
   (scallions), roughly chopped
5ml/1 tsp crushed garlic
1.5ml/¼ tsp ground turmeric
7.5ml/1½ tsp grated fresh
   root ginger
5ml/1 tsp chilli powder
30ml/2 tbsp fresh fenugreek
   leaves
5ml/1 tsp salt
150ml/¼ pint/⅔ cup
   water
6–8 cherry tomatoes
30ml/2 tbsp fresh coriander
   (cilantro) leaves
½ green (bell) pepper, seeded
   and sliced
15ml/1 tbsp lemon juice
shredded spring onion tops
   and fresh coriander leaves,
   to garnish

1 Cook the dhal in a pan of boiling water for 40–45 minutes until soft and mushy. Drain and set aside.

2 Heat the oil with the onion seeds in a karahi, wok or heavy pan for a few seconds until hot.

3 Add the drained dhal to the wok or frying pan and stir-fry with the onion seeds for about 3 minutes.

4 Add the spring onions followed by the garlic, turmeric, ginger, chilli powder, fenugreek leaves and salt, and continue to stir-fry for 5–7 minutes.

5 Pour in just enough of the water to loosen the mixture.

6 Add the whole cherry tomatoes, coriander leaves, green pepper and lemon juice. Stir well and serve garnished with shredded spring onion tops and coriander leaves.

Balti Corn with Cauliflower & Mint

This quick and tasty vegetable side dish can be made with frozen corn, so it is an excellent store-cupboard standby. If you do not have any cauliflower, substitute broccoli or another vegetable such as slices of courgette.

Serves 4

3 small onions
1 fresh red chilli
15ml/1 tbsp oil
4 curry leaves
1.5ml/¼ tsp onion seeds
175g/6oz/1 cup frozen
   corn
½ small cauliflower, separated
   into florets
3–7 mint leaves

1 Using a sharp knife dice the onions finely. Slit the chilli, scrape out the seeds and then slice the flesh thinly.

2 Heat the oil in a karahi, wok or heavy pan and stir-fry the curry leaves and onion seeds for about 30 seconds.

3 Add the diced onions to the pan and fry them for 5–8 minutes until golden brown.

4 Add the chilli, frozen corn and cauliflower florets and stir-fry for 5–8 minutes more.

5 Toss with the mint leaves and serve immediately.

> **Cook's Tips**
> • It is best to eat this dish immediately after it has been cooked, as the flavour tends to spoil if it is kept warm.
> • Whole mint leaves can be frozen in the summer when they are plentiful for use during the winter. They are then added while frozen to dishes such as this where they are mixed in with other ingredients. Frozen herbs are not suitable for garnishes, however.

Balti Dhal with Green & Red Chillies

The white urad dhal which is used in this recipe should ideally be soaked overnight as this makes it easier to cook. Serve with freshly made chapatis.

Serves 4
115g/4oz/½ cup urad dhal
10ml/2 tsp low-fat spread
10ml/2 tsp oil
1 bay leaf
2 onions, sliced
1 piece cinnamon stick
2.5cm/1in piece fresh root ginger, grated
2 garlic cloves
2 green chillies, seeded and sliced lengthways
2 red chillies, seeded and sliced lengthways
15ml/1 tbsp chopped fresh mint

1 Soak the dhal overnight in enough cold water to cover. Boil in water until the individual grains are soft enough to break into two. Set aside.

2 Heat the spread with the oil in a wok or heavy frying pan over a medium heat. Fry the bay leaf with the onions and the cinnamon.

3 Add the grated ginger, whole garlic cloves and half the green and red chillies.

4 Drain almost all the water from the lentils. Add the lentils to the wok or frying pan, then add the remaining green and red chillies and finally the chopped fresh mint. Heat through briefly and serve while piping hot.

Cook's Tip
If you like your curries milder, replace some of the chillies with some finely chopped green or red (bell) peppers.

Energy 159kcal/663kJ; Fat 3.19g; Saturated fat 0.51g; Carbohydrate 24.39g; Fibre 1.15g.

Chunky Fish Balti with Peppers

Try to find peppers in different colours to make this dish as colourful as possible.

Serves 2–4
450g/1lb cod, or any other firm white fish, such as haddock
7.5ml/1½ tsp ground cumin
10ml/2 tsp mango powder (amchur)
5ml/1 tsp ground coriander
2.5ml/½ tsp chilli powder
5ml/1 tsp salt
5ml/1 tsp grated fresh root ginger
45ml/3 tbsp cornflour (cornstarch)
150ml/¼ pint/⅔ cup corn oil
1 each green, orange and red (bell) peppers, seeded and chopped
8–10 cherry tomatoes

1 Skin the fish and cut it into small cubes. Put the cubes in a large mixing bowl and add the ground cumin, mango powder, ground coriander, chilli powder, salt, grated ginger and cornflour. Mix together thoroughly until the fish is well coated with the spice mix.

2 Heat the oil in a karahi, wok or large, deep pan. Lower the heat slightly and add the fish pieces, 3 or 4 at a time. Fry for about 3 minutes, turning constantly.

3 Drain the cooked fish pieces on kitchen paper and transfer to a serving dish. Keep hot while you fry the remaining fish pieces.

4 Fry the chopped peppers in the oil remaining in the pan for about 2 minutes. They should still be slightly crisp. Drain on kitchen paper.

5 Add the cooked peppers to the fish and garnish with the cherry tomatoes. Serve immediately.

Cook's Tip
Amchur is made from unripe mangoes and is used to add sourness.

Energy 495kcal/2058kJ; Fat 30g; Saturated fat 3.8g; Carbohydrate 13.3g; Fibre 3.4g.

Balti Fish Fillets in Spicy Coconut Sauce

Although coconut milk is a familiar ingredient in Indian fish dishes, it is quite unusual to find desiccated coconut in a starring role. It makes for a delicious and most unusual dish.

Serves 4

30ml/2 tbsp corn oil
5ml/1 tsp onion seeds
4 dried red chillies
3 garlic cloves, sliced
1 medium onion, sliced

2 medium tomatoes, sliced
30ml/2 tbsp desiccated
 (dry unsweetened shredded)
 coconut
5ml/1 tsp salt
5ml/1 tsp ground coriander
4 flat fish fillets, such as plaice,
 sole or flounder, about 75g/
 3oz each
150ml/1/4 pint/2/3 cup
 water
15ml/1 tbsp lime juice
15ml/1 tbsp chopped fresh
 coriander (cilantro)

1 Heat the oil in a karahi, wok or deep pan. Lower the heat slightly and add the onion seeds, dried red chillies, garlic slices and onion. Cook for 3–4 minutes, stirring once or twice.

2 Add the sliced tomatoes, coconut, salt and ground coriander and stir thoroughly.

3 Cut each fish fillet into 3 pieces. Drop the fish pieces into the mixture and turn them over gently until they are well coated.

4 Cook for 5–7 minutes, lowering the heat if necessary. Add the water, lime juice and fresh coriander and cook for a further 3–5 minutes until most of the water has evaporated. Serve immediately, with rice, if you like.

Cook's Tip
Use fresh fish fillets to make this dish if you can, as the flavour and texture will probably be superior. If you must use frozen fillets, ensure that they are completely thawed before cooking.

Energy 175kcal/731kJ; Fat 11.4g; Saturated fat 5g; Carbohydrate 4.9g; Fibre 2g.

Sizzling Balti Prawns in Hot Sauce

This sizzling prawn dish is cooked in a fiery hot and spicy sauce. This sauce not only contains chilli powder, but is further enhanced by the addition of ground fresh green chillies mixed with other spices. If the heat seems extreme, offer a cooling raita to moderate the piquant flavour.

Serves 4

2 medium onions, roughly
 chopped
30ml/2 tbsp tomato purée
 (paste)

5ml/1 tsp ground coriander
1.5ml/1/4 tsp ground turmeric
5ml/1 tsp chilli powder
2 fresh green chillies
45ml/3 tbsp chopped fresh
 coriander (cilantro)
30ml/2 tbsp lemon juice
5ml/1 tsp salt
45ml/3 tbsp corn oil
16 cooked king prawns
 (jumbo shrimp)
sliced green chillies, to garnish
 (optional)

1 Put the onions, tomato purée, ground coriander, turmeric, chilli powder, 2 whole green chillies, 30ml/2 tbsp of the fresh coriander, the lemon juice and salt into the bowl of a food processor. Process for about 1 minute. If the mixture seems too thick, add a little water to loosen it.

2 Heat the oil in a karahi, wok or deep pan. Lower the heat slightly and add the spice mixture. Fry the mixture for 3–5 minutes or until the sauce has thickened slightly.

3 Add the prawns and stir-fry briefly over a medium heat.

4 As soon as the prawns are heated through, transfer them to a serving dish. Garnish with the rest of the fresh coriander and the chopped green chilli, if using. Serve immediately.

Cook's Tip
Don't overcook the prawns or they will become tough.

Energy 139kcal/578kJ; Fat 8.7g; Saturated fat 1.3g; Carbohydrate 5.9g; Fibre 1.1g.

Prawn & Vegetable Balti

This makes a delicious light lunch or supper, and is quick and simple to make.

Serves 4

175g/6oz frozen cooked
   peeled prawns (shrimp)
30ml/2 tbsp oil
1.5ml/¼ tsp onion seeds
4–6 curry leaves
115g/4oz/1 cup frozen peas
115g/4oz/ ⅔ cup frozen
   corn
1 large courgette (zucchini),
   sliced

1 medium red (bell) pepper,
   seeded and roughly diced
5ml/1 tsp crushed coriander
   seeds
5ml/1 tsp crushed dried
   red chillies
1.5ml/ ½ tsp salt
15ml/1 tbsp lemon juice
15ml/1 tbsp fresh coriander
   (cilantro) leaves, to garnish

1 Thaw the prawns and drain them of any excess liquid.

2 Heat the oil with the onion seeds and curry leaves in a karahi, wok or heavy frying pan.

3 Add the prawns to the spicy mixture in the wok and stir-fry until the liquid has evaporated.

4 Next, add the peas, corn, courgette and red pepper. Continue to stir for 3–5 minutes.

5 Finally, add the crushed coriander seeds and chillies, salt to taste and the lemon juice.

6 Serve immediately, garnished with fresh coriander leaves.

> **Cook's Tip**
> *Freshly crushed spices have a strong and vibrant flavour. The best way to crush whole seeds is to use an electric spice grinder or a small marble pestle and mortar.*

Karahi Prawns & Fenugreek

The black-eyed beans, prawns and paneer in this recipe ensure that it is rich in protein. The combination of both ground and fresh fenugreek makes this a very fragrant and delicious dish. When preparing fresh fenugreek, use the leaves whole, but discard the stalks which would add a bitter flavour to the dish.

Serves 4–6

60ml/4 tbsp corn oil
2 medium onions, sliced
2 medium tomatoes, sliced
7.5ml/1½ tsp crushed garlic

5ml/1 tsp chilli powder
5ml/1 tsp grated fresh
   root ginger
5ml/1 tsp ground cumin
5ml/1 tsp ground coriander
5ml/1 tsp salt
150g/5oz paneer, cubed
5ml/1 tsp ground fenugreek
1 bunch fresh fenugreek leaves
115g/4oz cooked prawns
   (shrimp)
2 fresh red chillies, sliced
30ml/2 tbsp chopped fresh
   coriander (cilantro)
50g/2oz/ ⅓ cup canned
   black-eyed beans (peas),
   drained
15ml/1 tbsp lemon juice

1 Heat the oil in a karahi, wok or deep pan. Lower the heat slightly and add the onions and tomatoes. Fry for about 3 minutes.

2 Add the garlic, chilli powder, ginger, ground cumin, ground coriander, salt, paneer and the ground and fresh fenugreek. Lower the heat and stir-fry for about 2 minutes.

3 Add the prawns, red chillies, fresh coriander and black-eyed beans, and mix well. Toss over the heat for a further 3–5 minutes, or until the prawns are heated through. Sprinkle with the lemon juice and serve.

> **Cook's Tip**
> *Paneer is a type of cheese made with the curds from boiling milk which has been acidified with lemon juice. If you cannot locate paneer, tofu makes a good substitute.*

Energy 171kcal/714kJ; Fat 7.7g; Saturated fat 1.05g; Carbohydrate 11.8g; Fibre 2.8g.

Energy 206kcal/858kJ; Fat 13g; Saturated fat 2.6g; Carbohydrate 10.7g; Fibre 2.3g.

Paneer Balti with Prawns

Paneer is a protein food and makes an excellent substitute for red meat. Here it is combined with king prawns to make a dish with unforgettable flavour.

Serves 4

12 cooked king prawns (jumbo shrimp)
175g/6oz paneer
30ml/2 tbsp tomato purée (paste)
60ml/4 tbsp Greek (US strained plain) yogurt
7.5ml/1½ tsp garam masala
5ml/1 tsp chilli powder
5ml/1 tsp crushed garlic
5ml/1 tsp salt
10ml/2 tsp mango powder (amchur)
5ml/1 tsp ground coriander
115g/4oz/½ cup butter
15ml/1 tbsp vegetable oil
3 fresh green chillies, chopped
45ml/3 tbsp chopped fresh coriander (cilantro)
150ml/¼ pint/⅔ cup single (light) cream

1 Peel and remove the black intestinal vein from the king prawns. Cut the paneer into small cubes.

2 Put the tomato purée, yogurt, garam masala, chilli powder, garlic, salt, mango powder and ground coriander in a mixing bowl. Mix to a paste and set aside.

3 Melt the butter with the oil in a karahi, wok or deep pan. Lower the heat slightly and quickly fry the paneer and prawns for about 2 minutes. Remove with a slotted spoon and drain on kitchen paper.

4 Pour the spice paste into the fat left in the pan and cook for about 1 minute, stirring constantly.

5 Add the paneer and prawns, and cook for 7–10 minutes, stirring occasionally, until the prawns are heated through.

6 Add the fresh chillies and most of the coriander, and pour in the cream. Heat through for about 2 minutes, garnish with the remaining coriander and serve.

Energy 416kcal/1720kJ; Fat 36g; Saturated fat 21.2g; Carbohydrate 5.4g; Fibre 0g.

Seafood Balti with Vegetables

In this dish, the spicy seafood is cooked separately and combined with the melange of vegetables at the last minute to give a truly delicious combination of flavours.

Serves 4

225g/8oz cod, or any other firm white fish
225g/8oz cooked prawns (shrimp)
6 seafood sticks, halved lengthways, or 115g/4oz white crab meat
15ml/1 tbsp lemon juice
5ml/1 tsp ground coriander
5ml/1 tsp chilli powder
5ml/1 tsp salt
5ml/1 tsp ground cumin
60ml/4 tbsp cornflour (cornstarch)
150ml/¼ pint/⅔ cup corn oil
lime slices, to garnish

For the vegetables

150ml/¼ pint/⅔ cup corn oil
2 medium onions, chopped
5ml/1 tsp onion seeds
½ medium cauliflower, cut into florets
115g/4oz green beans, cut into 2.5cm/1in lengths
175g/6oz/1 cup corn
5ml/1 tsp shredded fresh root ginger
5ml/1 tsp chilli powder
5ml/1 tsp salt
4 fresh green chillies, sliced
30ml/2 tbsp chopped fresh coriander (cilantro)

1 Skin the fish and cut into small cubes. Put into a medium mixing bowl with the prawns and seafood sticks or crab meat.

2 In a separate bowl, mix together the lemon juice, ground coriander, chilli powder, salt and ground cumin. Pour this over the seafood and mix together thoroughly, using your hands.

3 Sprinkle on the cornflour and mix again until the seafood is well coated. Place in the refrigerator for about 1 hour to allow the flavours to develop.

4 To make the vegetable mixture, heat the oil in a karahi, wok or deep pan. Add the onions and the onion seeds, and stir-fry until lightly browned.

5 Add the cauliflower, green beans, corn, ginger, chilli powder, salt, green chillies and fresh coriander. Stir-fry for about 7–10 minutes over a medium heat, making sure that the pieces of cauliflower retain their shape.

6 Spoon the fried vegetables around the edge of a shallow serving dish, leaving a space in the middle for the seafood, and keep hot.

7 Wash and dry the pan, then heat the oil to fry the seafood pieces. Fry the seafood pieces in 2 or 3 batches, until they turn a golden brown. Remove with a slotted spoon and drain on kitchen paper.

8 Arrange the seafood in the middle of the dish of vegetables and keep hot while you fry the remaining seafood. Garnish with lime slices and serve. Plain boiled rice and raita make ideal accompaniments for this dish.

Energy 279kcal/1165kJ; Fat 11g; Saturated fat 1.6g; Carbohydrate 18.5g; Fibre 4g.

Classic Balti Chicken

This recipe has a beautifully delicate flavour, and is probably the most popular of all Balti dishes. Choose a young chicken as it will be more flavoursome.

Serves 4–6

1–1.3kg/2¼–3lb chicken
45ml/3 tbsp corn oil
3 medium onions, sliced
3 medium tomatoes, halved and sliced
2.5cm/1in cinnamon stick
2 large black cardamom pods
4 black peppercorns
2.5ml/½ tsp black cumin seeds
5ml/1 tsp grated fresh root ginger
5ml/1 tsp crushed garlic
5ml/1 tsp garam masala
5ml/1 tsp chilli powder
5ml/1 tsp salt
30ml/2 tbsp natural (plain) yogurt
60ml/4 tbsp lemon juice
30ml/2 tbsp chopped fresh coriander (cilantro)
2 fresh green chillies, chopped

1 Skin the chicken, then use a sharp knife to cut it into eight pieces. Wash and trim the chicken pieces, and set to one side.

2 Heat the oil in a large karahi, wok or deep pan. Add the onions and fry until they are golden brown. Add the tomatoes and stir well.

3 Add the piece of cinnamon stick, cardamoms, peppercorns, black cumin seeds, ginger, garlic, garam masala, chilli powder and salt. Lower the heat and stir-fry for 3–5 minutes.

4 Add the chicken pieces, two at a time, and stir-fry for at least 7 minutes or until the spice mixture has completely penetrated the chicken pieces and they are beginning to brown. Add the yogurt to the chicken and mix well.

5 Lower the heat and cover the pan with a piece of foil, making sure that the foil does not touch the food. Cook very gently for about 15 minutes, checking once to make sure the food is not catching on the bottom of the pan.

6 Finally, add the lemon juice, fresh coriander and green chillies. Serve immediately, straight from the pan.

Energy 569kcal/2362kJ; Fat 38.2g; Saturated fat 9.5g; Carbohydrate 13.2g; Fibre 2.3g.

Sweet-&-sour Balti Chicken

This dish combines a sweet-and-sour flavour with a creamy texture. It is delicious served with pilau rice or naan bread.

Serves 4

45ml/3 tbsp tomato purée (paste)
30ml/2 tbsp Greek (US strained plain) yogurt
7.5ml/1½ tsp garam masala
5ml/1 tsp chilli powder
5ml/1 tsp crushed garlic
30ml/2 tbsp mango chutney
5ml/1 tsp salt
2.5ml/½ tsp sugar
60ml/4 tbsp corn oil
675g/1½lb skinned boneless chicken, cubed
150ml/¼ pint/⅔ cup water
2 fresh green chillies, chopped
30ml/2 tbsp chopped fresh coriander (cilantro)
30ml/2 tbsp single (light) cream

1 Mix the tomato purée, Greek yogurt, garam masala, chilli powder, crushed garlic, mango chutney, salt and sugar in a medium mixing bowl. Stir well.

2 Heat the oil in a karahi, wok or deep pan. Lower the heat slightly and pour in the spice mixture. Bring to the boil and cook for about 2 minutes, stirring occasionally.

3 Add the chicken pieces and stir until they are well coated.

4 Stir in the water to thin the sauce slightly. Continue cooking for 5–7 minutes, or until the chicken is fully cooked and tender.

5 Finally, add the fresh chillies, coriander and cream, cook for a further 2 minutes over a low heat, then serve.

Variation
If you like, you could lightly fry 1 sliced green (bell) pepper and 115g/4oz/1½ cups whole small button (white) mushrooms in 15ml/1 tbsp oil and add to the spice mixture with the chicken pieces in step 3.

Energy 227kcal/957kJ; Fat 4.2g; Saturated fat 1.7g; Carbohydrate 6.7g; Fibre 0.3g.

Khara Masala Balti Chicken

Whole spices (*khara*) are used in this recipe, giving it a wonderful, rich flavour. This is a dry dish so it is best served with plenty of creamy raita.

Serves 4

3 curry leaves
1.5ml/ ¼ tsp mustard seeds
1.5ml/ ¼ tsp fennel seeds
1.5ml/ ¼ tsp onion seeds
2.5ml/ ½ tsp crushed dried
   red chillies
2.5ml/ ½ tsp white cumin seeds
1.5ml/ ¼ tsp fenugreek seeds

2.5ml/ ½ tsp crushed
   pomegranate seeds
5ml/1 tsp salt
5ml/1 tsp shredded fresh
   root ginger
3 garlic cloves, sliced
60ml/4 tbsp corn oil
4 fresh green chillies, slit
1 large onion, sliced
1 medium tomato, sliced
675g/1 ½lb skinless, boneless
   chicken, cubed
15ml/1 tbsp chopped fresh
   coriander (cilantro)

1 Mix together the curry leaves, mustard seeds, fennel seeds, onion seeds, crushed red chillies, cumin seeds, fenugreek seeds, crushed pomegranate seeds and salt in a large bowl.

2 Add the shredded ginger and garlic cloves to the spice mixture in the bowl and stir well.

3 Heat the oil in a medium karahi, wok or deep pan. Add the spice mixture, then tip in the green chillies.

4 Spoon the sliced onion into the pan and fry over a medium heat for 5–7 minutes, stirring constantly to flavour the onion with the spices.

5 Finally add the tomato and chicken pieces, and cook over a medium heat for about 7 minutes. The chicken should be cooked through and the sauce reduced.

6 Stir everything together over the heat for a further 3–5 minutes. Serve from the pan, garnished with chopped fresh coriander.

Balti Chicken Pasanda

Yogurt and cream give this tasty dish its characteristic richness. Serve it with garlic and coriander naan to complement the almonds.

Serves 4

60ml/4 tbsp Greek (US strained
   plain) yogurt
2.5ml/ ½ tsp black cumin seeds
4 cardamom pods
6 whole black peppercorns
10ml/2 tsp garam masala
2.5cm/1in cinnamon stick
15ml/1 tbsp ground almonds
5ml/1 tsp crushed garlic

5ml/1 tsp grated fresh root ginger
5ml/1 tsp chilli powder
5ml/1 tsp salt
675g/1 ½lb skinless, boneless
   chicken, cubed
75ml/5 tbsp corn oil
2 medium onions, diced
3 fresh green chillies, chopped
30ml/2 tbsp chopped fresh
   coriander (cilantro), plus extra
   to garnish
120ml/4fl oz/ ½ cup single (light)
   cream

1 Mix the Greek yogurt, black cumin seeds, cardamom pods, whole black peppercorns, garam masala and cinnamon stick together in a medium mixing bowl. Add the ground almonds, garlic, ginger, chilli powder and salt and mix together well.

2 Add the cubed chicken pieces, stir to coat, and leave in the spice mixture to marinate for about 2 hours.

3 Heat the oil in a large karahi, wok or deep pan. Add the onions and fry for 2–3 minutes.

4 Tip in the chicken mixture and stir until it is well blended with the onions.

5 Cook for 12–15 minutes over a medium heat until the sauce thickens and the chicken is cooked through.

6 Add the chopped green chillies and fresh coriander to the chicken in the wok, and pour in the single cream. Bring to the boil, stirring constantly, and serve the dish garnished with more coriander, if you like.

Energy 313kcal/1310kJ; Fat 13.7g; Saturated fat 2.3g; Carbohydrate 8.1g; Fibre 2.3g.

Energy 453kcal/1888kJ; Fat 26.8g; Saturated fat 8.7g; Carbohydrate 10.9g; Fibre 1.1g.

Balti Chicken Pieces with Cumin & Coriander

The potatoes are tossed in spices and cooked separately in the oven before being added to the chicken.

Serves 4

150ml/¼ pint/⅔ cup natural (plain) low-fat yogurt
25g/1oz/¼ cup ground almonds
7.5ml/1½ tsp ground coriander
2.5ml/½ tsp chilli powder
5ml/1 tsp garam masala
15ml/1 tbsp coconut milk
5ml/1 tsp crushed garlic
5ml/1 tsp grated fresh root ginger
30ml/2 tbsp chopped fresh coriander (cilantro)

1 fresh red chilli, seeded and chopped
225g/8oz skinned chicken breast fillets, cubed
15ml/1 tbsp oil
2 medium onions, sliced
3 green cardamom pods
2.5cm/1in cinnamon stick
2 cloves

For the potatoes

15ml/1 tbsp oil
8 baby potatoes, thickly sliced
1.5ml/¼ tsp cumin seeds
15ml/1 tbsp finely chopped fresh coriander (cilantro)

1 In a large bowl, mix together the first eight ingredients with half the fresh coriander and half the red chilli. Place the chicken pieces in the mixture, mix well, then cover and leave to marinate for about 2 hours.

2 Meanwhile, start to prepare the spicy potatoes. Heat the oil in a karahi, wok or heavy pan. Add the sliced potatoes, cumin seeds and fresh coriander and quickly stir-fry for 2–3 minutes.

3 Preheat the oven to 180°C/350°F/Gas 4. Spoon the potatoes into a baking dish, cover and bake for about 30 minutes or until they are cooked through.

4 Halfway through the potatoes' cooking time, heat the oil and fry the onions, cardamoms, cinnamon and cloves for 1½ minutes. Add the chicken mixture to the fried onions and stir-fry for 5–7 minutes. Lower the heat, cover and cook for 5–7 minutes. Top with the potatoes and garnish with coriander and red chilli.

Chicken & Tomato Balti

If you like tomatoes, you will love this chicken recipe. It makes a delicious semi-dry Balti and is good served with a lentil dish and plain boiled rice.

Serves 4

60ml/4 tbsp corn oil
6 curry leaves
2.5ml/½ tsp mixed onion and mustard seeds
8 medium tomatoes, sliced

5ml/1 tsp ground coriander
5ml/1 tsp chilli powder
5ml/1 tsp salt
5ml/1 tsp ground cumin
5ml/1 tsp crushed garlic
675g/1½lb skinless, boneless chicken, cubed
150ml/¼ pint/⅔ cup water
15ml/1 tbsp sesame seeds, roasted
15ml/1 tbsp chopped fresh coriander (cilantro)

1 Heat the oil in a karahi, wok or deep round-bottomed frying pan. Add the curry leaves and mixed onion and mustard seeds.

2 Toss the seeds over the heat for 1–2 minutes so that they become fragrant. Do not let the seeds burn.

3 Lower the heat slightly and add the tomatoes.

4 While the tomatoes are gently cooking, mix together the ground coriander, chilli powder, salt, ground cumin and crushed garlic in a bowl.

5 Tip the spices on to the tomatoes in the wok or pan and stir well to mix thoroughly.

6 Add the chicken pieces and stir well. Stir-fry for about 5 minutes more.

7 Stir in the water and continue cooking, stirring occasionally, until the sauce thickens and the chicken is fully cooked and tender.

8 Sprinkle the roasted sesame seeds and chopped fresh coriander over the chicken and tomato Balti. Serve immediately, from the pan.

Energy 2783kcal/1166kJ; Fat 10.76g; Saturated fat 1.58g; Carbohydrate 27.43g; Fibre 2.78g.

Energy 360kcal/1508kJ; Fat 18.3g; Saturated fat 3g; Carbohydrate 8.6g; Fibre 2.3g.

Balti Chicken in a Lentil Sauce

Traditionally, this dish is made with lamb, but it is equally delicious made with chicken breast.

Serves 4

30ml/2 tbsp chana dhal or yellow
   split peas
50g/2oz/¼ cup masoor dhal
   or red split peas
15ml/1 tbsp oil
2 medium onions, chopped
5ml/1 tsp crushed garlic
5ml/1 tsp grated fresh root ginger
2.5ml/½ tsp ground turmeric
7.5ml/1½ tsp chilli powder
5ml/1 tsp garam masala
2.5ml/½ tsp ground coriander

7.5ml/1½ tsp salt
175g/6oz skinned chicken breast
   fillets, cubed
45ml/3 tbsp fresh coriander
   (cilantro) leaves
1 or 2 fresh green chillies, seeded
   and chopped
30–45ml/2–3 tbsp lemon
   juice
300ml/½ pint/1¼ cups water
2 tomatoes, peeled and halved

For the tarka
5ml/1 tsp oil
2.5ml/½ tsp cumin seeds
2 garlic cloves
2 dried red chillies
4 curry leaves

1 Put the pulses in a pan with water and bring to the boil. Cook for 30–45 minutes until soft and mushy. Drain and set aside. Heat the oil in a karahi, wok or heavy frying pan and fry the onions until soft and golden brown. Stir in the garlic, ginger, turmeric, chilli powder, garam masala, ground coriander and salt.

2 Next, add the chicken pieces and fry for 5–7 minutes, stirring constantly over a medium heat to seal in the juices and lightly brown the meat.

3 Add half the fresh coriander, the green chillies, lemon juice and water and cook for 3–5 minutes. Stir in the cooked pulses, then add the tomatoes. Sprinkle over the remaining coriander leaves. Take the pan off the heat and set aside.

4 To make the tarka, heat the oil and add the cumin seeds, whole garlic cloves, dried red chillies and curry leaves. Heat for about 30 seconds then pour over the top of the chicken and lentils. Serve the dish immediately.

Energy 207kcal/868kJ; Fat 7.07g; Saturated fat 1.03g; Carbohydrate 20.37g; Fibre 2.84g.

Balti Chicken with Paneer & Peas

This is rather an unusual combination, but it really works well. Serve with plain boiled rice.

Serves 4

1 small chicken, about
   675g/1½lb
30ml/2 tbsp tomato purée
   (paste)
45ml/3 tbsp natural (plain)
   low-fat yogurt
7.5ml/1½ tsp garam masala
5ml/1 tsp crushed garlic
5ml/1 tsp grated fresh root
   ginger
pinch of ground cardamom

15ml/1 tbsp chilli powder
1.5ml/¼ tsp ground turmeric
5ml/1 tsp salt
5ml/1 tsp sugar
10ml/2 tsp oil
2.5cm/1in cinnamon stick
2 black peppercorns
300ml/½ pint/1¼ cups water
115g/4oz paneer, cubed
30ml/2 tbsp fresh coriander
   (cilantro) leaves
2 fresh green chillies, seeded
   and chopped
50g/2oz/¼ cup low-fat fromage
   frais or ricotta cheese
75g/3oz/¾ cup frozen peas,
   thawed

1 Skin the chicken and cut it into six to eight equal pieces.

2 Mix the tomato purée, yogurt, garam masala, garlic, ginger, cardamom, chilli powder, turmeric, salt and sugar in a bowl.

3 Heat the oil with the whole spices in a karahi, wok or heavy pan, then pour the yogurt mixture into the oil. Lower the heat and cook gently for about 3 minutes, then pour in the water and bring to a simmer.

4 Add the chicken pieces to the pan. Stir-fry for 2 minutes, then cover the pan and cook over medium heat for about 10 minutes.

5 Add the paneer cubes to the pan, followed by half the coriander and half the green chillies. Mix well and cook for a further 5–7 minutes.

6 Stir in the fromage frais or ricotta and peas, heat through and serve with the reserved coriander and chillies.

Energy 233kcal/977kJ; Fat 10.28g; Saturated fat 4.64g; Carbohydrate 8.14g; Fibre 1.49g.

Balti Chicken with Green & Red Chillies

Minced or ground chicken is seldom cooked in Indian homes. However, it works very well in this recipe.

Serves 4

275g/10oz skinned chicken breast fillet, cubed
2 plump fresh red chillies
3 plump fresh green chillies
30ml/2 tbsp oil
6 curry leaves
3 medium onions, sliced
7.5ml/1½ tsp crushed garlic
7.5ml/1½ tsp ground coriander
7.5ml/1½ tsp grated fresh root ginger
5ml/1 tsp chilli powder
5ml/1 tsp salt
15ml/1 tbsp lemon juice
30ml/2 tbsp chopped fresh coriander (cilantro)
chapatis and lemon wedges, to serve

1 Cook the chicken breast fillet in a pan of water for about 10 minutes until soft and cooked through. Remove with a slotted spoon and place in the bowl of a food processor fitted with a metal blade.

2 Roughly mince or grind the cooked chicken breast fillet.

3 Cut the chillies in half lengthways and remove the seeds, if you like. Cut the flesh into strips and set aside.

4 Heat the oil in a karahi, wok or heavy pan and fry the curry leaves and onions until the onions are a soft golden brown. Lower the heat and stir in the garlic, ground coriander, ginger, chilli powder and salt.

5 Add the minced (ground) chicken to the onion and spices, and stir-fry for 3–5 minutes.

6 Add the lemon juice, the prepared chilli strips and most of the fresh coriander. Stir-fry for a further 3–5 minutes.

7 Serve, garnished with the remaining fresh coriander and accompanied by warm chapatis and lemon wedges.

Energy 184kcal/767kJ; Fat 8.4g; Saturated fat 1.57g; Carbohydrate 10.1g; Fibre 1.3g.

Balti Chicken with Dhal & Leeks

This dish has rather an unusual combination of flavours. Slightly sour mango powder gives it a deliciously tangy flavour.

Serves 4–6

2 medium leeks
75g/3oz/⅓ cup chana dhal or yellow split peas
60ml/4 tbsp corn oil
6 large dried red chillies
4 curry leaves
5ml/1 tsp mustard seeds
10ml/2 tsp mango powder (amchur)
2 medium tomatoes, chopped
2.5ml/½ tsp chilli powder
5ml/1 tsp ground coriander
5ml/1 tsp salt
450g/1lb skinless, boneless chicken, cubed
15ml/1 tbsp chopped fresh coriander (cilantro), to garnish

1 Using a sharp knife, slice the leeks thinly into rounds. Separate the slices, rinse them in a colander under cold water to wash away any grit, then drain well.

2 Wash the chana dhal or split peas carefully and remove any stones or sticks.

3 Put the pulses into a pan with enough water to cover, and boil for about 10 minutes until they are soft but not mushy. Drain and set to one side in a bowl.

4 Heat the oil in a karahi, wok or deep pan. Lower the heat slightly and add the leeks, dried red chillies, curry leaves and mustard seeds. Stir-fry gently for a few minutes.

5 Add the mango powder, tomatoes, chilli powder, ground coriander, salt and chicken, and stir-fry for 7–10 minutes.

6 Mix in the cooked chana dhal or split peas and fry for a further 2 minutes, or until you are sure that the chicken is cooked right through.

7 Garnish with fresh coriander and serve immediately, from the pan.

Energy 309kcal/1295kJ; Fat 13.4g; Saturated fat 2.2g; Carbohydrate 16.1g; Fibre 2.8g.

Balti Chicken in Hara Masala Sauce

This chicken dish can be served as an accompaniment to any of the rice dishes in this book.

Serves 4

1 crisp green eating apple, peeled, cored and cut into small cubes
60ml/4 tbsp fresh coriander (cilantro) leaves
30ml/2 tbsp fresh mint leaves
120ml/4fl oz/½ cup natural (plain) low-fat yogurt
45ml/3 tbsp low-fat fromage frais or ricotta cheese
2 fresh green chillies, seeded and chopped
1 bunch spring onions (scallions), chopped
5ml/1 tsp salt
5ml/1 tsp sugar
5ml/1 tsp crushed garlic
5ml/1 tsp grated fresh root ginger
15ml/1 tbsp oil
225g/8oz skinned chicken breast fillets, cubed
25g/1oz/2 tbsp sultanas (golden raisins)

1 Place the apple, 45ml/3 tbsp of the fresh coriander, the mint, yogurt, fromage frais or ricotta, chillies, spring onions, salt, sugar, garlic and ginger in a food processor and pulse for about 1 minute.

2 Heat the oil in a karahi, wok or heavy pan, pour in the yogurt mixture and cook over a low heat for about 2 minutes.

3 Next, add the chicken pieces and blend everything together. Cook over a medium to low heat for 12–15 minutes or until the chicken is fully cooked.

4 Stir in the sultanas and the remaining 15ml/1 tbsp fresh coriander leaves and serve.

> **Cook's Tip**
> This dish makes an attractive centrepiece for a dinner party.

Balti Butter Chicken

Butter Chicken is one of the most popular Balti chicken dishes, especially in the West. Cooked in butter, with aromatic spices, cream and almonds, this mild dish will be enjoyed by everyone. Serve with pilau rice.

Serves 4

150ml/¼ pint/⅔ cup natural (plain) yogurt
50g/2oz/½ cup ground almonds
7.5ml/1½ tsp chilli powder
1.5ml/¼ tsp crushed bay leaves
1.5ml/¼ tsp ground cloves
1.5ml/¼ tsp ground cinnamon
5ml/1 tsp garam masala
4 green cardamom pods
5ml/1 tsp grated fresh root ginger
5ml/1 tsp crushed garlic
400g/14oz/2 cups canned tomatoes
7.5ml/1¼ tsp salt
1kg/2¼lb skinless, boneless chicken, cubed
75g/3oz/6 tbsp butter
15ml/1 tbsp corn oil
2 medium onions, sliced
30ml/2 tbsp chopped fresh coriander (cilantro)
60ml/4 tbsp single (light) cream
coriander sprigs, to garnish

1 Put the yogurt in a bowl and add the ground almonds, chilli powder, crushed bay leaves, ground cloves, cinnamon, garam masala, cardamoms, ginger and garlic.

2 Chop the tomatoes and add them to the bowl with the salt. Mix thoroughly.

3 Put the chicken into a large mixing bowl and pour over the yogurt mixture. Set aside.

4 Melt together the butter and oil in a karahi, wok or deep pan. Add the onions and fry for about 3 minutes.

5 Add the chicken mixture and stir-fry for 7–10 minutes.

6 Sprinkle over about half of the coriander and mix well.

7 Pour over the single cream and stir in well. Heat through and serve, garnished with the remaining chopped fresh coriander and coriander sprigs.

Energy 158kcal/666kJ; Fat 4.37g; Saturated fat 1.69g; Carbohydrate 14.54g; Fibre 1.08g.

Energy 592kcal/2474kJ; Fat 32.2g; Saturated fat 13.7g; Carbohydrate 12.1g; Fibre 1.6g.

Balti Chicken in Thick Creamy Coconut Sauce

If you like the flavour of coconut, you will really love this aromatic curry.

Serves 4

15ml/1 tbsp ground almonds
15ml/1 tbsp desiccated (dry unsweetened shredded) coconut
75ml/2½fl oz/⅓ cup coconut milk
175g/6oz/⅔ cup low-fat fromage frais or ricotta cheese
7.5ml/1½ tsp ground coriander
5ml/1 tsp chilli powder
5ml/1 tsp crushed garlic
7.5ml/1½ tsp grated fresh root ginger
5ml/1 tsp salt
15ml/1 tbsp oil
225g/8oz skinned chicken fillet, cubed
3 green cardamom pods
1 bay leaf
1 dried red chilli, crushed
30ml/2 tbsp chopped fresh coriander (cilantro)

1 Using a heavy pan, dry-roast the ground almonds and desiccated coconut, stirring frequently, until they turn just a shade darker. Transfer the nut mixture to a mixing bowl.

2 Add the coconut milk, fromage frais or ricotta cheese, ground coriander, chilli powder, crushed garlic, ginger and salt to the mixing bowl.

3 Heat the oil in a karahi, wok or heavy pan and add the chicken cubes, cardamoms and bay leaf. Stir-fry for about 2 minutes to seal the chicken but not cook it.

4 Pour in the coconut milk mixture and blend everything together. Lower the heat, add the chilli and fresh coriander, cover and cook for 10–12 minutes, stirring occasionally. Uncover, then stir and cook for a further 2 minutes before serving, making sure the chicken is cooked.

Energy 166kcal/696kJ; Fat 8.30g; Saturated fat 2.84g; Carbohydrate 6.38g; Fibre 0.95g.

Balti Chicken in Saffron Sauce

This is a beautifully aromatic chicken dish that is partly cooked in the oven.

Serves 4

50g/2oz/¼ cup butter
30ml/2 tbsp corn oil
1.2–1.3kg/2½–3lb chicken, skinned and cut into 8 pieces
1 medium onion, chopped
5ml/1 tsp crushed garlic
2.5ml/½ tsp crushed black peppercorns
2.5ml/½ tsp crushed cardamom pods
2.5ml/¼ tsp ground cinnamon
7.5ml/1½ tsp chilli powder
150ml/¼ pint/⅔ cup natural (plain) yogurt
50g/2oz/½ cup ground almonds
15ml/1 tbsp lemon juice
5ml/1 tsp salt
5ml/1 tsp saffron strands
150ml/¼ pint/⅔ cup water
150ml/¼ pint/⅔ cup single (light) cream
30ml/2 tbsp chopped fresh coriander (cilantro)

1 Preheat the oven to 180°C/350°F/Gas 4. Melt the butter with the oil in a karahi, wok or deep pan. Add the chicken pieces and fry until lightly browned, about 5 minutes. Remove the chicken using a slotted spoon, leaving behind the fat.

2 Add the onion to the same pan, and fry over a medium heat. Meanwhile, mix together the next 10 ingredients in a bowl. When the onions are lightly browned, pour the spice mixture into the pan and stir-fry for about 1 minute.

3 Add the chicken pieces, and continue to fry for a further 2 minutes stirring constantly. Pour in the water and bring to a simmer. Transfer the contents of the pan to a casserole and cover with a lid, or, if using a karahi with heatproof handles, cover with foil. Transfer to the oven and cook for 30–35 minutes.

4 Once you are sure that the chicken is cooked right through, remove it from the oven. Transfer the mixture to a frying pan or place the karahi on the stove and stir in the cream.

5 Reheat gently for about 2 minutes. Garnish with fresh coriander and serve with a fruity pilau or plain boiled rice.

Energy 525kcal/2190kJ; Fat 33g; Saturated fat 13.3g; Carbohydrate 11g; Fibre 1.5g.

Balti Chicken with Vegetables

This is an excellent recipe for making a small amount of chicken go a long way. The carrots and courgettes add colour and boost the dish's nutritional value.

Serves 4–6
60ml/4 tbsp corn oil
2 medium onions, sliced
4 garlic cloves, thickly sliced
450g/1lb skinned chicken breast
   fillets, cut into strips
5ml/1 tsp salt

30ml/2 tbsp lime juice
3 fresh green chillies, chopped
2 medium carrots, cut into batons
2 medium potatoes, peeled and
   cut into 1cm/½in strips
1 medium courgette (zucchini),
   cut into batons
4 lime slices
15ml/1 tbsp chopped fresh
   coriander (cilantro)
2 fresh green chillies, cut into
   strips (optional)

1 Heat the oil in a large karahi, wok or deep pan. Lower the heat slightly and add the sliced onions. Fry until the onions are lightly browned and softened.

2 Add half the garlic slices and fry for a few seconds before adding the chicken strips and salt. Cook everything together, stirring, until all the moisture has evaporated and the chicken is lightly browned.

3 Add the lime juice, green chillies and all the vegetables to the pan. Increase the heat and add the rest of the garlic. Stir-fry for 7–10 minutes, or until the chicken is cooked through and the vegetables are just tender.

4 Transfer to a serving dish and garnish with the lime slices, fresh chopped coriander and green chilli strips, if you like. Serve the Balti immediately.

Cook's Tip
Try other fresh vegetables in this dish, such as green beans, mangetouts (snow peas) and (bell) peppers.

Energy 308kcal/1289kJ; Fat 13.1g; Saturated fat 2.1g; Carbohydrate 20.1g; Fibre 2.8g.

Balti Chilli Chicken

Hot and spicy would be the best way of describing this mouthwatering Balti dish. The smell of the fresh chillies while they are cooking is simply irresistible.

Serves 4–6
75ml/5 tbsp corn oil
8 large fresh green chillies, slit
2.5ml/½ tsp mixed onion seeds
   and cumin seeds
4 curry leaves
5ml/1 tsp grated fresh root ginger
5ml/1 tsp chilli powder
5ml/1 tsp ground coriander

5ml/1 tsp crushed garlic
5ml/1 tsp salt
2 medium onions, chopped
675g/1½lb skinned chicken
   fillets, cubed
15ml/1 tbsp lemon juice
15ml/1 tbsp roughly chopped
   fresh mint
15ml/1 tbsp roughly chopped
   fresh coriander (cilantro)
8–10 cherry tomatoes

1 Heat the oil in a karahi, wok or deep pan. Lower the heat slightly and add the slit green chillies. Fry until the skin starts to change colour.

2 Add the onion seeds and cumin seeds, curry leaves, ginger, chilli powder, ground coriander, garlic, salt and onions, and fry for a few seconds, stirring continuously.

3 Add the chicken pieces to the pan. Stir-fry over a medium heat for 7–10 minutes, or until the chicken is cooked right through. Do not overcook the chicken or it will become tough in texture.

4 Sprinkle on the lemon juice and add the roughly chopped fresh mint and coriander. Dot with the cherry tomatoes and serve from the pan.

Cook's Tip
Frying the whole spices releases their lovely aromas.

Energy 346kcal/1448kJ; Fat 16.5g; Saturated fat 2.7g; Carbohydrate 9.9g; Fibre 1.3g.

Balti Chicken in Tamarind Sauce

The tamarind in this recipe gives the dish a sweet-and-sour flavour; this is also quite a hot Balti.

Serves 4–6

60ml/4 tbsp tomato ketchup
15ml/1 tbsp tamarind paste
60ml/4 tbsp water
7.5ml/1½ tsp chilli powder
7.5ml/1½ tsp salt
15ml/1 tbsp sugar
7.5ml/1½ tsp grated fresh root ginger
7.5ml/1½ tsp crushed garlic
30ml/2 tbsp desiccated (dry unsweetened shredded) coconut
30ml/2 tbsp sesame seeds
5ml/1 tsp poppy seeds
5ml/1 tsp ground cumin
7.5ml/1½ tsp ground coriander
2 × 450g/1lb baby chickens, skinned and cut into 6–8 pieces each
75ml/5 tbsp corn oil
120ml/8 tbsp curry leaves
2.5ml/½ tsp onion seeds
3 large dried red chillies
2.5ml/½ tsp fenugreek seeds
10–12 cherry tomatoes
45ml/3 tbsp chopped fresh coriander (cilantro)
2 fresh green chillies, chopped

1 Put the tomato ketchup, tamarind paste and water into a large mixing bowl and use a fork to blend everything together. Add the chilli powder, salt, sugar, ginger, garlic, coconut, sesame and poppy seeds, cumin and coriander to the mixture. Stir to mix. Add the chicken pieces and stir until they are well coated with the spice mixture. Set aside.

2 Heat the oil in a karahi, wok or deep pan. Add the curry leaves, onion seeds, dried red chillies and fenugreek seeds and fry for about 1 minute.

3 Lower the heat to medium and add 2 or 3 chicken pieces at a time, with their sauce, mixing as you go. When all the pieces have been added to the pan, stir well, using a slotted spoon.

4 Simmer gently for about 12–15 minutes, or until the chicken is thoroughly cooked. Finally, add the tomatoes, fresh coriander and green chillies, and serve from the pan.

Energy 348kcal/1454kJ; Fat 19.9g; Saturated fat 6.4g; Carbohydrate 11.9g; Fibre 1.5g.

Balti Chicken Madras

This is a fairly hot chicken curry which is good served with either plain boiled rice, pilau rice or naan bread.

Serves 4

275g/10oz skinned chicken breast fillets
45ml/3 tbsp tomato purée (paste)
large pinch of ground fenugreek
1.5ml/¼ tsp ground fennel seeds
5ml/1 tsp grated fresh root ginger
7.5ml/1½ tsp ground coriander
5ml/1 tsp crushed garlic
5ml/1 tsp chilli powder
1.5ml/¼ tsp ground turmeric
30ml/2 tbsp lemon juice
5ml/1 tsp salt
300ml/½ pint/1¼ cups water
15ml/1 tbsp oil
2 medium onions, diced
2–4 curry leaves
2 fresh green chillies, seeded and chopped
15ml/1 tbsp fresh coriander (cilantro) leaves

1 Remove any visible fat from the chicken breasts and cut the meat into bitesize cubes.

2 Mix the tomato purée in a bowl with the fenugreek, fennel seeds, ginger, coriander, garlic, chilli powder, turmeric, lemon juice, salt and water.

3 Heat the oil in a karahi, wok or heavy pan and fry the diced onions together with the curry leaves until the onions are golden brown and softened.

4 Add the chicken pieces to the onions and stir over the heat for about 1 minute to seal the meat.

5 Next, pour in the prepared spice mixture and continue to stir the chicken for about 2 minutes.

6 Lower the heat and cook the spicy chicken for 8–10 minutes, stirring frequently to prevent the mixture from catching on the bottom of the pan.

7 Add the chopped chillies and fresh coriander leaves and serve the Balti immediately.

Energy 141kcal/591kJ; Fat 4.11g; Saturated fat 0.6g; Carbohydrate 8.6g; Fibre 1.53g.

Balti Chicken Vindaloo

This version of a popular dish from Goa is not as fiery as some, but will still suit those who like their curry to have a definite spicy impact.

Serves 4

1 large potato	5ml/1 tsp crushed garlic
150ml/¼ pint/²⁄₃ cup malt vinegar	5ml/1 tsp grated fresh root ginger
7.5ml/1½ tsp crushed coriander seeds	5ml/1 tsp salt
	7.5ml/1½ tsp paprika
5ml/1 tsp crushed cumin seeds	15ml/1 tbsp tomato purée (paste)
7.5ml/1½ tsp chilli powder	large pinch of ground fenugreek
1.5ml/¼ tsp ground turmeric	300ml/½ pint/1¼ cups water
	225g/8oz skinned chicken breast fillets, cubed
	15ml/1 tbsp oil
	2 medium onions, sliced
	4 curry leaves
	2 fresh green chillies, chopped

1 Peel the potato, cut it into large, irregular shapes, place these in a bowl of water and set aside.

2 In a bowl, mix the vinegar, crushed coriander seeds, cumin, chilli powder, turmeric, garlic, ginger, salt, paprika, tomato purée, fenugreek and water.

3 Pour this spice mixture over the chicken, stir and set aside.

4 Heat the oil in a karahi, wok or heavy pan and quickly fry the onions with the curry leaves for 3–4 minutes without burning.

5 Lower the heat and add the chicken mixture to the pan with the spices. Continue to stir-fry for a further 2 minutes.

6 Drain the potato pieces and add to the pan. Cover with a lid and cook over a medium to low heat for 5–7 minutes or until the sauce has thickened slightly and the chicken and potatoes are cooked through.

7 Stir in the chopped green chillies and serve.

Energy 168kcal/704kJ; Fat 4.2g; Saturated fat 0.6g; Carbohydrate 17.65g; Fibre 2.04g.

Balti Lamb Tikka

This is a traditional tikka recipe, in which the lamb is marinated in yogurt and spices. The lamb is usually cut into cubes, but the cooking time can be halved by cutting it into strips.

Serves 4

450g/1lb lean boneless lamb, cut into strips	5ml/1 tsp ground coriander
	5ml/1 tsp chilli powder
175ml/6fl oz/¾ cup natural (plain) yogurt	5ml/1 tsp crushed garlic
	5ml/1 tsp salt
5ml/1 tsp ground cumin	5ml/1 tsp garam masala
	30ml/2 tbsp chopped fresh coriander (cilantro)
	30ml/2 tbsp lemon juice
	30ml/2 tbsp corn oil
	15ml/1 tbsp tomato purée (paste)
	1 large green (bell) pepper, seeded and sliced
	3 large fresh red chillies

1 Put the lamb strips, yogurt, ground cumin, ground coriander, chilli powder, garlic, salt, garam masala, fresh coriander and lemon juice into a large mixing bowl and stir thoroughly. Cover and marinate at cool room temperature for 1 hour.

2 Heat the oil in a karahi, wok or deep pan. Lower the heat slightly and stir in the tomato purée.

3 Add the lamb strips to the pan, a few at a time, leaving any excess marinade behind in the bowl.

4 Cook the lamb, stirring frequently, for 7–10 minutes or until it is well browned.

5 Finally, add the green pepper slices and the whole red chillies. Heat through, checking that the lamb is fully cooked, spoon into a serving dish and serve hot.

Cook's Tip
Coriander leaves can easily go soggy after washing, so dry them quickly on kitchen paper.

Energy 289kcal/1207kJ; Fat 18.7g; Saturated fat 6.9g; Carbohydrate 6.1g; Fibre 0.7g.

Balti Lamb Koftas with Vegetables

These mouthwatering koftas look very attractive served on their bed of vegetables, especially if you make them quite small.

Serves 4
450g/1lb lean minced (ground) lamb
5ml/1 tsp garam masala
5ml/1 tsp ground cumin
5ml/1 tsp ground coriander
5ml/1 tsp crushed garlic
5ml/1 tsp chilli powder
5ml/1 tsp salt
15ml/1 tbsp chopped fresh coriander (cilantro)
1 small onion, finely diced
150ml/¼ pint/⅔ cup corn oil

For the vegetables
45ml/3 tbsp corn oil
1 bunch spring onions (scallions), roughly chopped

½ large red (bell) pepper, seeded and chopped
½ large green (bell) pepper, seeded and chopped
175g/6oz/1 cup corn
225g/8oz/1½ cups canned butter (lima) beans
½ small cauliflower, cut into florets
4 fresh green chillies, chopped

To garnish
5ml/1 tsp chopped fresh mint
15ml/1 tbsp chopped fresh coriander (cilantro)
15ml/1 tbsp shredded fresh root ginger
lime slices
15ml/1 tbsp lemon juice

1 Put the minced lamb into a food processor or blender and process for about 1 minute.

2 Transfer the lamb to a medium bowl. Add the dry spices, garlic, chilli powder, salt, fresh coriander and onion, and use your fingers to blend the kofta mixture thoroughly. Cover and set aside in the refrigerator.

3 Heat the oil for the vegetables in a karahi, wok or deep pan. Add the spring onions and stir-fry for 2 minutes.

4 Add the peppers, corn, butter beans, cauliflower and green chillies, and stir-fry over a high heat for about 2 minutes. Set to one side.

5 Using your hands, roll small pieces of the kofta mixture into round golf-ball size portions. You should have between 12 and 16 koftas.

6 Heat the oil for the koftas in a frying pan. Lower the heat slightly and add the koftas, a few at a time. Shallow-fry each batch, turning the koftas occasionally, until they are evenly browned. Remove from the oil with a slotted spoon, and drain on kitchen paper.

7 Put the vegetable mixture back over a medium heat, and add the cooked koftas. Stir the mixture gently for about 5 minutes, or until everything is heated through.

8 Garnish with the chopped mint and coriander, shredded ginger and lime slices. Just before serving, sprinkle over the lemon juice.

Energy 515kcal/2146kJ; Fat 35g; Saturated fat 9.9g; Carbohydrate 22g; Fibre 5.7g.

Balti Lamb with Potatoes & Fenugreek

The combination of lamb with fresh fenugreek works very well in this dish, which is delicious accompanied by plain boiled rice and Mango Chutney. Use only the fenugreek leaves, as the stalks can be rather bitter. This dish is traditionally served with rice.

Serves 4
450g/1lb lean minced (ground) lamb
5ml/1 tsp grated fresh root ginger
5ml/1 tsp crushed garlic
7.5ml/1½ tsp chilli powder
5ml/1 tsp salt

1.5ml/¼ tsp turmeric
45ml/3 tbsp corn oil
2 medium onions, sliced
2 medium potatoes, peeled, par-boiled and roughly diced
1 bunch fresh fenugreek, chopped
2 tomatoes, chopped
50g/2oz/½ cup frozen peas
30ml/2 tbsp chopped fresh coriander (cilantro)
3 fresh red chillies, seeded and sliced

1 Put the minced lamb, grated ginger, garlic, chilli powder, salt and turmeric into a large bowl, and mix together thoroughly. Set to one side.

2 Heat the oil in a karahi, wok or deep pan. Add the onion slices and fry for about 5 minutes until golden brown.

3 Add the minced lamb and fry over a medium heat for 5–7 minutes, stirring.

4 Stir in the potatoes, chopped fenugreek, tomatoes and peas and cook for a further 5–7 minutes, stirring continuously.

5 Just before serving, stir in the fresh coriander. Spoon into a large dish or on to individual plates and serve hot. Garnish with fresh red chillies.

Energy 386kcal/1610kJ; Fat 23.7g; Saturated fat 8.2g; Carbohydrate 20.3g; Fibre 2.5g.

Balti Mini Lamb Kebabs

In this unusual Balti dish the meat patties are cooked on skewers before being added to the karahi.

Serves 6
450g/1lb lean minced (ground) lamb
1 medium onion, finely chopped
5ml/1 tsp garam masala
5ml/1 tsp crushed garlic
2 medium fresh green chillies, finely chopped
30ml/2 tbsp chopped fresh coriander (cilantro), plus extra to garnish
5ml/1 tsp salt
15ml/1 tbsp plain (all-purpose) flour
60ml/4 tbsp corn oil
12 baby (pearl) onions
4 fresh green chillies, sliced
12 cherry tomatoes

1 Mix the lamb, onion, garam masala, garlic, green chillies, fresh coriander, salt and flour in a medium bowl, using your hands. Transfer the mixture to a food processor and process for about 1 minute, to make the mixture even finer in texture.

2 Put the mixture back into the bowl. Break off small pieces and wrap them around skewers to form small sausage shapes. Put about 2 of these shapes on each skewer.

3 Continue making up the sausage shapes until you have used up all the mixture. Preheat the grill (broiler) to its maximum setting. Baste the meat with 15ml/1 tbsp of the oil and grill (broil) the kebabs for 12–15 minutes, turning and basting occasionally, until the meat is evenly browned.

4 Heat the remaining 45ml/3 tbsp of the oil in a karahi, wok or deep pan. Lower the heat slightly and add the whole baby onions. As soon as they start to darken, add the fresh chillies and tomatoes.

5 Slide the lamb patties from their skewers and add them to the onion and tomato mixture. Stir gently for about 3 minutes to heat them through. Transfer to a serving dish and garnish with fresh coriander.

Energy 252kcal/1047kJ; Fat 17.6g; Saturated fat 5.7g; Carbohydrate 8.5g; Fibre 1.2g.

Balti Lamb with Cauliflower

This tasty curry is given a final tarka, a dressing of oil, cumin seeds and curry leaves, to enhance the flavour.

Serves 4
10ml/2 tsp oil
2 medium onions, sliced
7.5ml/1½ tsp grated fresh root ginger
5ml/1 tsp chilli powder
5ml/1 tsp crushed garlic
1.5ml/¼ tsp ground turmeric
2.5ml/½ tsp ground coriander
30ml/2 tbsp fresh fenugreek leaves
275g/10oz boneless lean spring lamb, cut into strips
1 small cauliflower, cut into small florets
300ml/½ pint/1¼ cups water
30ml/2 tbsp fresh coriander (cilantro) leaves
½ red (bell) pepper, seeded and sliced
15ml/1 tbsp lemon juice

For the tarka
10ml/2 tsp oil
2.5ml/½ tsp cumin seeds
4–6 curry leaves

1 Heat the oil in a karahi, wok or heavy pan and gently fry the onions until they are golden brown. Lower the heat and then add the ginger, chilli powder, garlic, turmeric and ground coriander. Stir well, then add the fenugreek leaves and mix well.

2 Add the lamb strips to the wok and stir-fry until the lamb is completely coated with the spices. Add half the cauliflower florets and stir the mixture well. Pour in the water, cover the wok, lower the heat and cook for 5–7 minutes until the cauliflower and lamb are almost cooked through.

3 Add the remaining cauliflower, half the fresh coriander, the red pepper and lemon juice and stir-fry for about 5 minutes, ensuring the sauce does not catch on the bottom of the pan. Check that the lamb is completely cooked, then remove the pan from the heat and set it aside.

4 To make the tarka, heat the oil and fry the seeds and curry leaves for about 30 seconds. While it is still hot, pour the seasoned oil over the cauliflower and lamb and serve garnished with the remaining fresh coriander leaves.

Energy 202kcal/839kJ; Fat 9.88g; Saturated fat 3.24g; Carbohydrate 10.86g; Fibre 2.88g.

Balti Bhoona Lamb

Bhooning is a very traditional way of stir-frying which simply involves semi-circular movements, scraping the bottom of the pan each time in the centre. Serve this dish of spring lamb with freshly made chapatis.

Serves 4
225–275g/8–10oz boneless lean spring lamb
3 medium onions
15ml/1 tbsp oil
15ml/1 tbsp tomato purée (paste)
5ml/1 tsp crushed garlic
7.5ml/1½ tsp finely grated fresh root ginger, plus 15ml/1 tbsp shredded
5ml/1 tsp salt
1.5ml/¼ tsp ground turmeric
600ml/1 pint/2½ cups water
15ml/1 tbsp lemon juice
15ml/1 tbsp chopped fresh coriander (cilantro)
15ml/1 tbsp chopped fresh mint
1 fresh red chilli, chopped

1 Using a sharp knife, remove any excess fat from the lamb and cut the meat into small cubes.

2 Dice the onions finely. Heat the oil in a karahi, wok or heavy pan and fry the onions until soft.

3 Meanwhile, mix together the tomato purée, garlic and ginger, salt and turmeric. Pour the spice mixture on to the onions in the pan and stir-fry for a few seconds.

4 Add the lamb and continue to stir-fry for about 2–3 minutes. Stir in the water, lower the heat, cover the pan and cook for 15–20 minutes, stirring occasionally.

5 When the water has almost evaporated, start bhooning over a medium heat, making sure that the sauce does not catch on the bottom of the pan. Continue for 5–7 minutes.

6 Pour in the lemon juice, followed by the shredded ginger, chopped fresh coriander, mint and red chilli. Stir to mix, then serve straight from the pan.

Energy 198kcal/825kJ; Fat 10.37g; Saturated fat 3.24g; Carbohydrate 11.05g; Fibre 1.84g.

Balti Lamb with Peas & Potatoes

Fresh mint leaves are used in this dish, but if they are unobtainable, use ready-minted frozen peas to bring an added freshness. Serve with plain rice.

Serves 4
225g/8oz boneless lean spring lamb
120ml/4fl oz/½ cup natural (plain) low-fat yogurt
1 cinnamon stick
2 green cardamom pods
3 black peppercorns
5ml/1 tsp crushed garlic
5ml/1 tsp grated fresh root ginger
5ml/1 tsp chilli powder
5ml/1 tsp garam masala
5ml/1 tsp salt
30ml/2 tbsp roughly chopped fresh mint
15ml/1 tbsp oil
2 medium onions, sliced
300ml/½ pint/1¼ cups water
1 large potato, diced
115g/4oz/1 cup frozen peas
1 firm tomato, peeled, seeded and diced

1 Using a sharp knife, trim any excess fat from the lamb and cut the meat into strips. Place it in a bowl.

2 Add the yogurt, cinnamon, cardamoms, peppercorns, garlic, ginger, chilli powder, garam masala, salt and half the mint. Stir well, cover the bowl and leave in a cool place to marinate for about 2 hours.

3 Heat the oil in a karahi, wok or heavy pan and fry the onions until golden brown. Stir in the lamb and the marinade and stir-fry for about 3 minutes.

4 Pour in the water, lower the heat and cook for about 15 minutes until the meat is cooked right through. Meanwhile, cook the potato in boiling water until just soft, but not mushy.

5 Add the peas and potato to the lamb and stir gently to mix.

6 Finally, add the remaining mint and the tomato and cook for a further 5 minutes before serving.

Energy 231kcal/968kJ; Fat 8.47g; Saturated fat 2.79g; Carbohydrate 22.72g; Fibre 3.73g.

Balti Lamb in Yogurt

The lamb is first marinated in spices then cooked slowly in a hot yogurt sauce. The dish is served with dried apricots which have been lightly sautéed in ghee with cinnamon and cardamom.

Serves 4

15ml/1 tbsp tomato purée (paste)
175ml/6fl oz/³⁄₄ cup natural (plain) low-fat yogurt
5ml/1 tsp garam masala
1.5ml/¹⁄₄ tsp cumin seeds
5ml/1 tsp salt
5ml/1 tsp crushed garlic
5ml/1 tsp grated fresh root ginger
5ml/1 tsp chilli powder
225g/8oz boneless lean spring lamb, cut into strips
15ml/1 tbsp oil
2 medium onions, finely sliced
25g/1oz/2 tbsp ghee or unsalted (sweet) butter
2.5cm/1in cinnamon stick
2 green cardamom pods
5 dried apricots, quartered
15ml/1 tbsp fresh coriander (cilantro) leaves, to garnish

1 In a bowl blend together the tomato purée, yogurt, garam masala, cumin seeds, salt, garlic, ginger and chilli powder. Add the lamb to the sauce and mix well. Cover and leave to marinate in a cool place for about 1 hour.

2 Heat 10ml/2 tsp of the oil in a wok or heavy frying pan and fry the onions over a medium heat until they are crisp and golden brown. Remove the onions using a slotted spoon, allow to cool and then grind down by processing briefly in a food processor or with a pestle and mortar. Reheat the oil remaining in the pan and return the onions to the wok.

3 Add the lamb and stir-fry for about 2 minutes. Cover with a lid, lower the heat and cook, stirring occasionally, for about 15 minutes or until the meat is cooked through. If required, add about 150ml/¹⁄₄ pint/²⁄₃ cup water during the cooking. Remove from the heat and set aside.

4 Heat the ghee or butter with the remaining 5ml/1 tsp of oil and drop in the cinnamon stick and cardamoms. Add the dried apricots and stir over a low heat for about 2 minutes. Pour this over the lamb. Serve garnished with the fresh coriander leaves.

Energy 221kcal/922kJ; Fat 11.2g; Saturated fat 3.64g; Carbohydrate 14.6g; Fibre 1.8g.

Balti Lamb with Stuffed Vegetables

Aubergines and bright, mixed peppers are stuffed with an aromatic lamb filling and served on a bed of sautéed onions. The presentation is very attractive.

Serves 4–6

3 small aubergines (eggplants)
1 each red, green and yellow (bell) peppers

For the stuffing

45ml/3 tbsp corn oil
3 medium onions, sliced
5ml/1 tsp chilli powder
1.5ml/¹⁄₄ tsp ground turmeric
5ml/1 tsp ground coriander
5ml/1 tsp ground cumin
5ml/1 tsp grated fresh root ginger
5ml/1 tsp crushed garlic
5ml/1 tsp salt
450g/1lb lean minced (ground) lamb
3 fresh green chillies, chopped
30ml/2 tbsp chopped fresh coriander (cilantro)

For the sautéed onions

45ml/3 tbsp corn oil
5ml/1 tsp mixed onion, mustard, fenugreek and white cumin seeds
4 dried red chillies
3 medium onions, roughly chopped
5ml/1 tsp salt
5ml/1 tsp chilli powder
2 medium tomatoes, sliced
2 fresh green chillies, chopped
30ml/2 tbsp chopped fresh coriander

1 Prepare the vegetables. Slit the aubergines lengthways up to the stalks; keep the stalks intact. Cut the tops off the peppers and remove the seeds.

2 Make the stuffing. Heat the oil in a medium pan. Add the onions and fry for about 3 minutes. Lower the heat and add the chilli powder, turmeric, ground coriander, ground cumin, ginger, garlic and salt, and stir-fry for about 1 minute. Add the lamb to the pan and increase the heat.

3 Stir-fry for 7–10 minutes or until the lamb is cooked, using a wooden spoon to scrape the bottom of the pan. Add the green chillies and fresh coriander towards the end. Remove from the heat, cover and set to one side.

4 Make the sautéed onions. Heat the oil in a karahi, wok or deep pan and add the mixed onion, mustard, fenugreek and white cumin seeds. Stir in the dried red chillies, and fry for about 1 minute. Add the onions and fry for about 2 minutes or until soft.

5 Add the salt, chilli powder, tomatoes, green chillies and fresh coriander. Cook for a further minute. Remove from the heat and set to one side.

6 The minced lamb should by now be cool enough to stuff the prepared aubergines and peppers. Fill the vegetables quite loosely with the meat mixture. As you stuff the vegetables, place them on top of the sautéed onions in the karahi. Cover with foil, making sure the foil doesn't touch the food, and cook over a low heat for about 15 minutes.

7 The dish is ready as soon as the aubergines and peppers are tender. Serve with a dish of plain boiled rice or a colourful pilau rice to complement the colours of the peppers.

Energy 606kcal/2521kJ; Fat 40.8g; Saturated fat 10.6g; Carbohydrate 35g; Fibre 7.4g.

Balti Lamb Chops with Potatoes

These chops are marinated before being cooked in a deliciously spicy sauce.

Serves 6–8

8 lamb chops, about
   50–75g/2–3oz each
30ml/2 tbsp olive oil
150ml/¼ pint/⅔ cup lemon juice
5ml/1 tsp salt
15ml/1 tbsp chopped fresh mint
   and coriander (cilantro)
150ml/¼ pint/⅔ cup corn oil
fresh mint sprigs and lime slices,
   to garnish

For the sauce

45ml/3 tbsp corn oil
8 medium tomatoes, roughly
   chopped
1 bay leaf
5ml/1 tsp garam masala
30ml/2 tbsp natural (plain)
   yogurt
5ml/1 tsp crushed garlic
5ml/1 tsp chilli powder
5ml/1 tsp salt
2.5ml/½ tsp black cumin seeds
3 black peppercorns
2 medium potatoes, peeled,
   roughly chopped and boiled

1 Put the chops into a large bowl. Mix together the olive oil, lemon juice, salt and fresh mint and coriander. Pour the oil mixture over the chops and rub it in well. Cover and leave to marinate for at least 3 hours in the refrigerator.

2 To make the sauce, heat the corn oil in a karahi, wok or deep pan. Lower the heat and add the chopped tomatoes. Stir-fry for about 2 minutes. Add the bay leaf, garam masala, yogurt, garlic, chilli powder, salt, black cumin seeds and black peppercorns, and stir-fry for a further 2–3 minutes. Lower the heat again and add the cooked potatoes, mixing everything together well. Remove from the heat and set to one side.

3 Heat 150ml/¼ pint/⅔ cup corn oil in a separate frying pan. Lower the heat slightly and fry the marinated chops until they are cooked through. This will take about 10–12 minutes. Remove and drain the cooked chops on kitchen paper.

4 Heat the sauce in the karahi, bringing it to the boil. Add the chops and lower the heat. Simmer for 5–7 minutes. Transfer to a warmed serving dish and garnish with the mint sprigs and lime slices.

Energy 327kcal/1367kJ; Fat 18.7g; Saturated fat 6.3g; Carbohydrate 14.8g; Fibre 2g.

Balti Beef

There's no marinating involved with this simple recipe, which can be prepared and cooked in under an hour.

Serves 4

1 red (bell) pepper
1 green (bell) pepper
15ml/1 tbsp oil
5ml/1 tsp cumin seeds
2.5ml/½ tsp fennel seeds
1 onion, cut into thick
   wedges
1 garlic clove, crushed
2.5cm/1in piece fresh root ginger,
   finely chopped
1 fresh red chilli, finely chopped
15ml/1 tbsp curry paste
2.5ml/½ tsp salt
675g/1½lb lean rump (round)
   or fillet steak (beef tenderloin),
   cut into thick strips
naan bread, to serve

1 Cut the red and green peppers into 2.5cm/1in chunks.

2 Heat the oil in a karahi, wok or frying pan and fry the cumin and fennel seeds for 2 minutes or until they begin to splutter. Add the onion, garlic, ginger and chilli and fry for a further 5 minutes.

3 Stir in the curry paste and salt and fry for a further 3–4 minutes.

4 Add the peppers and toss over the heat for about 5 minutes. Stir in the beef strips and continue to fry for 10–12 minutes or until the meat is tender. Serve from the pan, with warm naan bread.

Variations
• *This recipe would also work well with chicken breast fillet.*
• *You could add mangetouts (snow peas), trimmed and left whole, to the dish for added crunch. As they need only the minimum amount of cooking, add them for the last 5 minutes of cooking only.*

Energy 278kcal/1166kJ; Fat 11.6g; Saturated fat 3.52g; Carbohydrate 7.7g; Fibre 2.5g.

Mushroom & Okra Curry

The sliced okra not only flavours this unusual curry, but thickens it, too.

Serves 4

4 garlic cloves, roughly chopped
2.5cm/1in piece fresh root ginger, roughly chopped
1 or 2 fresh red chillies, seeded and chopped
175ml/6fl oz/¾ cup cold water
15ml/1 tbsp sunflower oil
5ml/1 tsp coriander seeds
5ml/1 tsp cumin seeds
5ml/1 tsp ground cumin
seeds from 2 green cardamom pods, ground
pinch of ground turmeric
400g/14oz can chopped tomatoes
450g/1lb/6 cups mushrooms, quartered if large
225g/8oz okra, trimmed and sliced
30ml/2 tbsp chopped fresh coriander (cilantro)
basmati rice, to serve

For the mango relish
1 large ripe mango, about 500g/1¼lb
1 small garlic clove, crushed
1 small onion, finely chopped
10ml/2 tsp grated fresh root ginger
1 fresh red chilli, seeded and finely chopped
a pinch each of salt and sugar

1 To make the mango relish, peel the mango, cut the flesh off the stone and chop it finely. Put it in a bowl. Mash with a fork and mix in the garlic, onion, ginger, chilli, salt and sugar. Set aside.

2 Put the garlic, ginger, chillies and 45ml/3 tbsp of the water in a blender or food processor and blend to a smooth paste.

3 Heat the oil in a large pan. Add the coriander and cumin seeds, and the ground cumin, ground cardamom and turmeric, and cook for 1 minute, until aromatic. Scrape in the garlic paste, then add the tomatoes, mushrooms and okra. Pour in the remaining water. Stir to mix well, and bring to the boil. Reduce the heat, cover and simmer the curry for 5 minutes.

4 Remove the lid, increase the heat slightly and cook for 5–10 minutes more, until the okra is tender. Stir in the fresh coriander and serve with the rice and the mango relish.

Mushrooms, Peas & Paneer

Paneer is a traditional cheese made from rich milk and is most popular with northern Indians. Rajasthani farmers eat this dish for lunch with thick parathas as they work in the fields.

Serves 4–6
75ml/6 tbsp ghee or vegetable oil
225g/8oz paneer, cubed
1 onion, finely chopped
a few fresh mint leaves, chopped
50g/2oz/2 cups fresh coriander (cilantro), chopped
3 fresh green chillies, chopped
3 garlic cloves, roughly chopped
2.5cm/1in piece fresh root ginger, sliced
5ml/1 tsp ground turmeric
5ml/1 tsp chilli powder (optional)
5ml/1 tsp garam masala
salt
225g/8oz/3 cups tiny button (white) mushrooms
225g/8oz/2 cups frozen peas, thawed and drained
175ml/6fl oz/¾ cup natural (plain) yogurt, mixed with 5ml/1 tsp cornflour (cornstarch)
fresh mint sprig, to garnish

1 Heat the ghee or vegetable oil in a frying pan and fry the paneer cubes until they are golden brown on all sides. Remove and drain on kitchen paper.

2 Grind the onion, mint, coriander, chillies, garlic and ginger in a pestle and mortar or food processor to a fairly smooth paste. Remove and mix in the turmeric, chilli powder if using, garam masala and salt.

3 Remove the excess ghee or oil from the pan, leaving about 15ml/1 tbsp. Heat and fry the paste until the raw onion smell disappears and the oil separates.

4 Add the mushrooms, peas and paneer. Mix together well. Cool the mixture and gradually fold in the yogurt. Simmer for about 10 minutes. Garnish with a sprig of mint and serve hot.

Energy 152kcal/645kJ; Fat 4.4g; Saturated fat 0.7g; Carbohydrate 24.2g; Fibre 8g.

Energy 294kcal/1217kJ; Fat 20.3g; Saturated fat 3.7g; Carbohydrate 14g; Fibre 3.5g.

Okra with Green Mango & Lentils

If you like okra, you'll love this spicy tangy dish. Serve with rice for a main course.

Serves 4

115g/4oz/½ cup toor dhal or
   yellow split peas
450g/1lb okra
15ml/1 tbsp oil
2.5ml/½ tsp onion seeds
2 onions, sliced
2.5ml/½ tsp ground fenugreek
1.5ml/¼ tsp ground turmeric
5ml/1 tsp ground coriander
7.5ml/1½ tsp chilli powder
5ml/1 tsp grated fresh
   root ginger
5ml/1 tsp crushed garlic
1 green mango, peeled and sliced
7.5ml/1½ tsp salt
2 red chillies, seeded and sliced
30ml/2 tbsp chopped fresh
   coriander (cilantro)
1 tomato, sliced

1 Wash the toor dhal thoroughly to remove any grit and place in a large pan with enough cold water to cover. Bring to the boil and cook for 30–45 minutes until soft but not mushy.

2 Trim the okra and cut the pods into 1cm/½in pieces.

3 Heat the oil in a karahi, wok or heavy pan and fry the onion seeds until they begin to pop. Add the onions and fry until golden brown. Lower the heat and stir in the ground fenugreek, turmeric and coriander, and the chilli powder, ginger and garlic.

4 Add the mango slices and the okra pieces. Stir well and then add the salt, red chillies and fresh coriander. Stir-fry together for 3–4 minutes or until the okra is well cooked and tender.

5 Finally, add the cooked dhal and sliced tomato, and cook for a further 3 minutes. Serve hot.

> **Cook's Tip**
> *When buying okra, always choose small, bright-green ones with no brown patches. If cooking whole, trim off the conical cap, taking care not to pierce through to the seed pod where there are tiny edible seeds and a sticky juice.*

Energy 229kcal/963kJ; Fat 5g; Saturated fat 0.55g; Carbohydrate 36g; Fibre 8.1g.

Corn & Pea Curry

Tender corn cooked in a spicy tomato sauce makes a flavoursome curry. It is perfect served with chapatis.

Serves 4

6 frozen corn cobs, thawed
15ml/1 tbsp oil
2.5ml/½ tsp cumin seeds
1 onion, finely chopped
2 garlic cloves, crushed
1 fresh green chilli, finely chopped
15ml/1 tbsp curry paste
5ml/1 tsp ground coriander
5ml/1 tsp ground cumin
1.5ml/¼ tsp ground turmeric
2.5ml/½ tsp salt
2.5ml/½ tsp sugar
400g/14oz can chopped
   tomatoes
15ml/1 tbsp tomato purée
   (paste)
150ml/¼ pint/⅔ cup
   water
115g/4oz/1 cup frozen peas,
   thawed
30ml/2 tbsp chopped fresh
   coriander (cilantro)
chapatis, to serve (optional)

1 Using a sharp knife, cut each piece of corn in half crossways to make 12 equal pieces in total.

2 Bring a large pan of water to the boil and cook the corn cob pieces for 10–12 minutes. Drain well.

3 Heat the oil in a large, heavy pan and fry the cumin seeds for 2 minutes or until they begin to splutter. Add the onion, garlic and chilli and fry for about 5–6 minutes until the onion is golden.

4 Add the curry paste and fry for 2 minutes. Stir in the remaining spices, the salt and sugar, and fry for a further 2–3 minutes, adding some water if the mixture is too dry.

5 Add the chopped tomatoes and tomato purée together with the water and simmer for 5 minutes or until the sauce thickens. Add the peas and cook for a further 5 minutes.

6 Stir in the pieces of corn and the fresh coriander and cook for 6–8 minutes more, until the corn and peas are tender. Serve with chapatis for mopping up the rich sauce, if you like.

Energy 159kcal/669kJ; Fat 5.2g; Saturated fat 0.48g; Carbohydrate 23g; Fibre 4.6g.

Spinach & Potato Curry

Spinach, potatoes and traditional Indian spices are the main ingredients in this simple but authentic curry.

Serves 4

450g/1lb spinach
15ml/1 tbsp oil
5ml/1 tsp black mustard seeds
1 onion, thinly sliced
2 garlic cloves, crushed
2.5cm/1in piece fresh root ginger, finely chopped
675g/1½lb potatoes, cut into 2.5cm/1in chunks
5ml/1 tsp chilli powder
5ml/1 tsp salt
120ml/4fl oz/½ cup water

1 Wash and trim the spinach, then blanch it in a pan of boiling water for about 3–4 minutes.

2 Drain the spinach thoroughly and set aside. When it is cool enough to handle, use your hands to squeeze out any remaining liquid (see Cook's Tip) and set aside.

3 Heat the oil in a large, heavy pan and fry the mustard seeds for 2 minutes or until they splutter.

4 Add the sliced onion, garlic cloves and chopped ginger to the mustard seeds and fry for 5 minutes, stirring.

5 Add the potato chunks, chilli powder, salt and water, and cook for a further 8 minutes.

6 Add the drained spinach. Cover the pan with a lid and simmer for 10–15 minutes or until the potatoes are tender. Serve hot.

Cook's Tips
• To make certain that the spinach is completely dry, put it in a clean dish towel, roll up tightly and squeeze gently to remove any excess liquid.
• Use a waxy variety of potato for this dish so that the pieces do not break up during cooking.

Spicy Potato & Tomato Curry

Diced potatoes are cooked gently in a fresh tomato sauce, which is flavoured with curry leaves, green chillies and ginger.

Serves 4

2 medium potatoes
15ml/1 tbsp oil
2 medium onions, finely chopped
4 curry leaves
1.5ml/¼ tsp onion seeds
1 fresh green chilli, seeded and chopped
4 tomatoes, sliced
5ml/1 tsp grated fresh root ginger
5ml/1 tsp crushed garlic
5ml/1 tsp chilli powder
5ml/1 tsp ground coriander
1.5ml/¼ tsp salt
5ml/1 tsp lemon juice
15ml/1 tbsp chopped fresh coriander (cilantro)
3 hard-boiled eggs, to garnish

1 Peel the potatoes and cut them into small cubes.

2 Heat the oil in a karahi, wok or heavy pan and stir-fry the onions, curry leaves, onion seeds and green chilli for about 40 seconds.

3 Add the tomatoes and cook for about 2 minutes over a low heat.

4 Add the ginger and garlic, chilli powder, ground coriander and salt to taste. Continue to stir-fry for 1–2 minutes, then add the potatoes and cook over a low heat for 5–7 minutes until the potatoes are tender.

5 Add the lemon juice and fresh coriander and stir to mix together.

6 Shell the hard-boiled eggs, cut into quarters, and add as a garnish to the finished dish.

Cook's Tip
Use vine-ripened tomatoes, if possible, for the best flavour. Locally grown tomatoes in season are also more likely to have a full flavour than those bought out of season.

Energy 203kcal/851kJ; Fat 4.6g; Saturated fat 0.65g; Carbohydrate 34.4g; Fibre 5.1g.

Energy 188kcal/790kJ; Fat 7.62g; Saturated fat 1.66g; Carbohydrate 23.41g; Fibre 3.1g.

Courgette Curry with Tomatoes

Thickly sliced courgettes are combined with authentic Indian spices for a tasty vegetable curry.

Serves 4

675g/1½lb courgettes (zucchini)
30ml/2 tbsp oil
2.5ml/½ tsp cumin seeds
2.5ml/½ tsp mustard seeds
1 onion, thinly sliced
2 garlic cloves, crushed
1.5ml/¼ tsp ground turmeric
1.5ml/¼ tsp chilli powder
5ml/1 tsp ground coriander
5ml/1 tsp ground cumin
2.5ml/½ tsp salt
15ml/1 tbsp tomato purée (paste)
400g/14oz can chopped tomatoes
150ml/¼ pint/⅔ cup water
15ml/1 tbsp chopped fresh coriander (cilantro)
5ml/1 tsp garam masala
rice or naan bread, to serve

1 Trim the ends from the courgettes and then cut them evenly into 1cm/½in thick slices.

2 Heat the oil in a large, heavy pan and fry the cumin and the mustard seeds for 2 minutes until they begin to splutter.

3 Add the sliced onion and crushed garlic to the seeds in the pan, and fry for about 5–6 minutes.

4 Add the turmeric, chilli powder, ground coriander, cumin and salt, and fry for 2–3 minutes.

5 Add the sliced courgettes all at once, and cook for 5 minutes, stirring so that they do not burn.

6 Mix together the tomato purée and chopped tomatoes and add to the pan with the water. Cover and simmer for 10 minutes until the sauce thickens.

7 Stir in the fresh coriander and garam masala, then cook for 5 minutes or until the courgettes are tender. Serve the curry with rice or naan bread.

Potatoes Stuffed with Cottage Cheese

This makes an excellent low-fat snack at any time of the day.

Serves 4

4 medium baking potatoes
225g/8oz/1 cup low-fat cottage cheese
10ml/2 tsp tomato purée (paste)
2.5ml/½ tsp ground cumin
2.5ml/½ tsp ground coriander
2.5ml/½ tsp chilli powder
2.5ml/½ tsp salt
15ml/1 tbsp oil
2.5ml/½ tsp mixed onion and mustard seeds
3 curry leaves
30ml/2 tbsp water

For the garnish
mixed salad leaves
fresh coriander (cilantro) sprigs
lemon wedges
2 tomatoes, quartered

1 Preheat the oven to 180°C/350°F/Gas 4. Wash each potato and pat dry. Make a slit in the middle of each potato. Prick the potatoes a few times with a fork or skewer, then wrap them individually in foil. Bake in the oven directly on the shelf for about 1 hour, or until soft. Put the cottage cheese into a heatproof dish and set aside.

2 In a separate bowl, mix the tomato purée, ground cumin, ground coriander, chilli powder and salt.

3 Heat the oil in a small pan for about 1 minute. Add the mixed onion and mustard seeds and the curry leaves. When the curry leaves turn a shade darker, pour the tomato purée mixture into the pan and turn the heat immediately to low. Add the water and mix well. Cook for a further minute, then pour the spicy tomato mixture on to the cottage cheese and stir together well.

4 Check that the baked potatoes are cooked right through, by inserting a knife or skewer into the middle of the flesh. If it is soft, unwrap the potatoes from the foil and divide the cottage cheese equally between them.

5 Garnish the filled potatoes with mixed salad leaves, coriander sprigs, lemon wedges and tomato quarters and serve hot.

Energy 133kcal/550kJ; Fat 7.2g; Saturated fat 0.91g; Carbohydrate 11.6g; Fibre 2.8g.

Energy 175kcal/740kJ; Fat 4.3g; Saturated fat 0.43g; Carbohydrate 24.4g; Fibre 1.9g.

Spicy Root Vegetable Gratin

Subtly spiced, this rich gratin is substantial enough to serve on its own for lunch or supper.

Serves 4

2 large potatoes, total weight about 450g/1lb
2 sweet potatoes, total weight about 275g/10oz
175g/6oz celeriac
15ml/1 tbsp unsalted (sweet) butter
5ml/1 tsp curry powder
5ml/1 tsp ground turmeric
2.5ml/½ tsp ground coriander
5ml/1 tsp mild chilli powder
3 shallots, chopped
150ml/¼ pint/⅔ cup single (light) cream
150ml/¼ pint/⅔ cup milk
salt and ground black pepper
chopped fresh flat leaf parsley, to garnish

1 Peel the potatoes, sweet potatoes and celeriac and cut into thin, even slices using a sharp knife or the slicing attachment on a food processor. Immediately place the vegetables in a bowl of cold water to prevent them from discolouring.

2 Preheat the oven to 180°C/350°F/Gas 4. Heat half the butter in a heavy pan, add the curry powder, ground turmeric and coriander and half the chilli powder. Cook for 2 minutes, then leave to cool slightly. Drain the vegetables, then pat them dry with kitchen paper. Place in a bowl, add the spice mixture and the shallots, and mix well.

3 Arrange the vegetables in a shallow baking dish, seasoning well with salt and pepper between the layers. Mix the cream and milk together, pour the mixture over the vegetables, then sprinkle the remaining chilli powder on top.

4 Cover the dish with baking parchment and bake for 45 minutes. Remove the baking parchment, dot the vegetables with the remaining butter and bake for a further 50 minutes, or until the top is golden brown. Serve the gratin garnished with chopped parsley.

Energy 205kcal/863kJ; Fat 5.1g; Saturated fat 2.9g; Carbohydrate 36.9g; Fibre 4.7g.

Stuffed Baby Vegetables

The combination of potatoes and aubergines is popular in Indian cooking.

Serves 4

12 small potatoes
8 baby aubergines (eggplants)

For the stuffing

15ml/1 tbsp sesame seeds
30ml/2 tbsp ground coriander
30ml/2 tbsp ground cumin
2.5ml/½ tsp salt
1.5ml/¼ tsp chilli powder
2.5ml/½ tsp ground turmeric
10ml/2 tsp sugar
1.5ml/¼ tsp garam masala
15ml/1 tbsp gram flour
2 garlic cloves, crushed
15ml/1 tbsp lemon juice
30ml/2 tbsp chopped fresh coriander (cilantro)

For the sauce

15ml/1 tbsp oil
2.5ml/½ tsp black mustard seeds
400g/14oz can chopped tomatoes
30ml/2 tbsp chopped fresh coriander
150ml/¼ pint/⅔ cup water

1 Preheat the oven to 200°C/400°F/Gas 6. Make deep slits in the potatoes and aubergines to hold the stuffing, ensuring that you do not cut right through.

2 Mix all the ingredients for the stuffing together on a plate.

3 Carefully spoon the spicy stuffing mixture into each of the slits in the potatoes and aubergines.

4 Arrange the stuffed potatoes and aubergines in a greased ovenproof dish, filling side up.

5 For the sauce, heat the oil in a heavy pan and fry the mustard seeds for 2 minutes until they begin to splutter, then add the canned tomatoes, chopped coriander and any leftover stuffing. Stir in the water. Bring to the boil and simmer for 5 minutes until the sauce thickens.

6 Pour the sauce over the potatoes and aubergines. Cover and bake in the oven for 25–30 minutes until the potatoes and aubergines are soft.

Energy 259kcal/1088kJ; Fat 7.6g; Saturated fat 0.73g; Carbohydrate 41.3g; Fibre 4g.

Mixed Vegetable Curry

You can use any combination of vegetables that are in season for this basic recipe.

Serves 4
15ml/1 tbsp oil
2.5ml/½ tsp black mustard seeds
2.5ml/½ tsp cumin seeds
1 onion, thinly sliced
2 curry leaves
1 fresh green chilli, finely chopped
2.5cm/1in piece fresh root ginger, finely chopped
30ml/2 tbsp curry paste

1 small cauliflower, broken into florets
1 large carrot, thickly sliced
115g/4oz green beans, cut into 2.5cm/1in lengths
1.5ml/¼ tsp ground turmeric
1.5ml/¼ tsp chilli powder
2.5ml/½ tsp salt
2 tomatoes, finely chopped
50g/2oz/½ cup frozen peas, thawed
150ml/¼ pint/⅔ cup vegetable stock
fresh curry leaves, to garnish

1 Heat the oil in a large, heavy pan and fry the mustard seeds and cumin seeds for 2 minutes until they begin to splutter. If they are very lively, put a lid on the pan.

2 Add the onion and the curry leaves and fry for 5 minutes.

3 Add the chopped chilli and fresh ginger and fry for 2 minutes. Stir in the curry paste, mix well and fry for 3–4 minutes.

4 Add the cauliflower florets, sliced carrot and beans, and cook for 4–5 minutes. Add the turmeric, chilli powder, salt and tomatoes and cook for 2–3 minutes.

5 Finally add the thawed peas and cook for a further 2–3 minutes. Pour in the stock. Cover and simmer over a low heat for 10–15 minutes until all the vegetables are tender. Serve garnished with curry leaves.

> **Variation**
> *To turn this dish into a non-vegetarian main course, add some prawns (shrimp) or cubes of cooked chicken with the stock.*

Energy 130kcal/540kJ; Fat 6.2g; Saturated fat 0.61g; Carbohydrate 12.3g; Fibre 6.2g.

Vegetable Korma

Here the aim is to produce a subtle, aromatic curry rather than an assault on the senses.

Serves 4
50g/2oz/¼ cup butter
2 onions, sliced
2 garlic cloves, crushed
2.5cm/1in piece fresh root ginger, grated
5ml/1 tsp ground cumin
15ml/1 tbsp ground coriander
6 cardamom pods
5cm/2in piece of cinnamon stick
5ml/1 tsp ground turmeric
1 fresh red chilli, seeded and finely chopped

1 potato, peeled and cut into 2.5cm/1in cubes
1 small aubergine (eggplant), chopped
115g/4oz/1½ cups mushrooms, thickly sliced
175ml/6fl oz/¾ cup water
115g/4oz green beans, cut into 2.5cm/1in lengths
60ml/4 tbsp natural (plain) yogurt
150ml/¼ pint/⅔ cup double (heavy) cream
5ml/1 tsp garam masala
salt and ground black pepper
fresh coriander (cilantro) sprigs, to garnish
boiled rice and poppadums, to serve

1 Melt the butter in a heavy pan. Add the onions and cook for 5 minutes until soft. Add the garlic and ginger and cook for 2 minutes, then stir in the cumin, coriander, cardamom pods, cinnamon stick, turmeric and finely chopped chilli. Cook, stirring constantly, for 30 seconds.

2 Add the potato cubes, aubergine and mushrooms and the water. Cover the pan, bring to the boil, then lower the heat and simmer for 15 minutes.

3 Add the beans and cook, uncovered, for 5 minutes. With a slotted spoon, remove the vegetables to a warmed serving dish and keep hot.

4 Allow the cooking liquid to bubble up until it has reduced a little. Season with salt and pepper to taste, then stir in the yogurt, double cream and garam masala. Pour the sauce over the vegetables and garnish with fresh coriander. Serve with boiled rice and poppadums.

Energy 361kcal/1494kJ; Fat 31.3g; Saturated fat 19.3g; Carbohydrate 16.7g; Fibre 3.2g.

Spiced Vegetable Curry with Yogurt

This is a very delicately spiced vegetable dish that is particularly appetizing when served with plain yogurt. It is also a good accompaniment to a main course of heavily spiced curries.

Serves 4–6

350g/12oz mixed vegetables, such as beans, peas, potatoes, cauliflower, carrots, cabbage, mangetouts (snow peas) and mushrooms
30ml/2 tbsp vegetable oil
5ml/1 tsp cumin seeds, freshly roasted
2.5ml/½ tsp mustard seeds
2.5ml/½ tsp onion seeds
5ml/1 tsp ground turmeric
2 garlic cloves, crushed
6–8 curry leaves
1 dried red chilli
salt
5ml/1 tsp sugar
150ml/¼ pint/⅔ cup natural (plain) yogurt mixed with 5ml/1 tsp cornflour (cornstarch)

1 Prepare all the vegetables you have chosen: string the beans; thaw the peas, if frozen; peel and cube the potatoes; cut the cauliflower into florets; dice the carrots; shred the cabbage; trim the mangetouts; wipe the mushrooms and leave whole.

2 Heat a large pan with enough water to cook all the vegetables and bring to the boil. First add the potatoes and carrots and cook until nearly tender then add all the other vegetables and cook until crisp-tender. All the vegetables should be crunchy except the potatoes. Drain.

3 Heat the oil in a frying pan and fry the cumin, mustard and onion seeds, the turmeric, garlic, curry leaves and dried chilli gently until the garlic is golden brown and the chilli nearly burnt. Reduce the heat.

4 Fold in the drained vegetables, add the sugar and salt and gradually add the yogurt and cornflour mixture. Heat until piping hot, and serve immediately.

Energy 99kcal/411kJ; Fat 6.1g; Saturated fat 0.9g; Carbohydrate 6.5g; Fibre 2g.

Vegetable Kashmiri

This is a wonderful vegetable curry, in which fresh mixed vegetables are cooked in a spicy aromatic yogurt sauce. The spicing is quite gentle, so it will appeal to most palates.

Serves 4

10ml/2 tsp cumin seeds
8 black peppercorns
seeds from 2 green cardamom pods
5cm/2in piece cinnamon stick
2.5ml/½ tsp grated nutmeg
30ml/2 tbsp oil
1 fresh green chilli, chopped
2.5cm/1in piece fresh root ginger, grated
5ml/1 tsp chilli powder
2.5ml/½ tsp salt
2 large potatoes, cut into 2.5cm/1in chunks
225g/8oz cauliflower, broken into florets
225g/8oz okra, trimmed and thickly sliced
150ml/¼ pint/⅔ cup natural (plain) low-fat yogurt
150ml/¼ pint/⅔ cup vegetable stock
toasted flaked (sliced) almonds and fresh coriander (cilantro) sprigs, to garnish

1 Grind the cumin seeds and peppercorns, cardamom seeds, cinnamon stick and nutmeg to a fine powder using a spice blender or a pestle and mortar.

2 Heat the oil in a large, heavy pan and fry the chilli and ginger for 2 minutes, stirring all the time.

3 Add the chilli powder, salt and ground spice mixture, and fry for about 2–3 minutes, stirring all the time to prevent the spices from sticking to the bottom of the pan.

4 Stir in the potatoes, cover and cook for 10 minutes over a low heat, stirring from time to time.

5 Add the cauliflower and okra and cook for 5 minutes.

6 Add the yogurt and stock. Bring to the boil, then reduce the heat. Cover and simmer for 20 minutes, or until all the vegetables are tender. Garnish with the toasted almonds and the coriander sprigs.

Energy 220kcal/920kJ; Fat 8.2g; Saturated fat 1.02g; Carbohydrate 29.1g; Fibre 4.7g.

Vegetable Biryani

This is a good-tempered dish made from everyday ingredients, and thus indispensable for the cook catering for an unexpected vegetarian guest.

Serves 4–6

175g/6oz/scant 1 cup long-grain rice, rinsed
2 whole cloves
seeds from 2 cardamom pods
450ml/³/₄ pint/scant 2 cups vegetable stock
2 garlic cloves
1 small onion, roughly chopped
5ml/1 tsp cumin seeds
5ml/1 tsp ground coriander
2.5ml/¹/₂ tsp ground turmeric
2.5ml/¹/₂ tsp chilli powder
1 large potato, cut into 2.5cm/ 1in cubes
2 carrots, sliced
¹/₂ cauliflower, broken into florets
50g/2oz green beans, cut into 2.5cm/1in lengths
30ml/2 tbsp chopped fresh coriander (cilantro), plus extra to garnish
30ml/2 tbsp lime juice
salt and ground black pepper

1 Put the rice, cloves and cardamom seeds into a large, heavy pan. Pour over the stock and bring to the boil. Reduce the heat, cover the pan and simmer for 20 minutes or until all the stock has been absorbed.

2 Meanwhile, put the garlic cloves, onion, cumin seeds, ground coriander, turmeric, chilli powder and seasoning into a blender or food processor together with 30ml/2 tbsp water. Blend to a smooth paste. Scrape the paste into a large flameproof casserole.

3 Preheat the oven to 180°C/350°F/Gas 4. Cook the spicy paste in the casserole over a low heat for 2 minutes, stirring occasionally. Add the potato cubes, carrots, cauliflower, beans and 90ml/6 tbsp water. Cover and cook over a low heat for 12 minutes, stirring occasionally. Add the chopped fresh coriander.

4 Remove the cloves from the rice. Spoon the rice over the vegetables. Sprinkle with the lime juice. Cover and cook in the oven for 25 minutes or until the vegetables are tender. Fluff up the rice with a fork before serving, garnished with coriander.

Energy 260kcal/1100kJ Fat 1.9g Saturated fat 0.07g Carbohydrate 55.8g Fibre 3.2g.

Broad Bean & Cauliflower Curry

This is a hot and spicy vegetable curry, tasty when served with cooked rice (especially a brown basmati variety), a few poppadums and cucumber raita.

Serves 4

2 garlic cloves, chopped
2.5cm/1in piece fresh root ginger
1 fresh green chilli, seeded and chopped
30ml/2 tbsp oil
1 onion, sliced
1 large potato, chopped
15ml/1 tbsp curry powder, mild or hot
1 cauliflower, cut into small florets
600ml/1 pint/2¹/₂ cups vegetable stock
275g/10oz can broad (fava) beans
juice of ¹/₂ lemon (optional)
salt and ground black pepper
fresh coriander (cilantro) sprig, to garnish
plain rice, to serve

1 Blend the chopped garlic, ginger, chopped chilli and 15ml/ 1 tbsp of the oil in a food processor or blender until the mixture forms a smooth paste.

2 In a large, heavy pan, fry the sliced onion and chopped potato in the remaining oil for 5 minutes, then stir in the spice paste and curry powder. Cook for another minute.

3 Add the cauliflower florets to the onion and potato and stir well until they are thoroughly combined with the spicy mixture, then pour in the stock and bring to the boil over medium to high heat.

4 Season well, cover and simmer for 10 minutes. Add the beans with the liquid from the can and cook, uncovered, for a further 10 minutes.

5 Check the seasoning and adjust if necessary. Add a good squeeze of lemon juice, if you like, and serve hot, garnished with coriander and accompanied by plain boiled rice.

Energy 216kcal/906kJ; Fat 7.7g; Saturated fat 0.75g; Carbohydrate 25.8g; Fibre 7.9g.

Plain Boiled Rice

Always use basmati rice for the best flavour and texture. It is easy to cook and produces an excellent finished result. It is slimmer than other long grain rice and has a delicate flavour. Although slightly more expensive, it is well worth buying as it is the perfect rice for accompanying curries.

Serves 4–6
150ml/1 tbsp ghee, unsalted (sweet) butter or olive oil
350g/12oz/1¾ cups basmati rice, washed and drained
450ml/¾ pint/scant 2 cups water
salt

1 Rinse the basmati rice well in cold water until most of the starch is removed and the water runs clear.

2 Heat the ghee, butter or oil in a pan and sauté the drained rice thoroughly for about 2–3 minutes.

3 Add the water and salt and bring to the boil. Reduce the heat to low, cover and cook gently for 10–15 minutes. To serve, fluff the grains gently with a fork.

> **Cook's Tips**
> • *Always test the rice after it has cooked for about 10 minutes; it should be just cooked.*
> • *As a guide, 75g/3oz/scant ½ cup raw rice will give you an ample helping for one person.*

> **Variation**
> *To make a fragrantly spiced version, sauté 4–6 green cardamom pods, 4 cloves, 5cm/2in piece cinnamon stick, 2.5ml/½ tsp black cumin seeds and 2 bay leaves. Add 350g/12oz/1¾ cups drained basmati rice and proceed as for plain boiled rice. For an even more luxurious rice, add 6–8 strands of saffron and sauté with the spices.*

Energy 342kcal/1429kJ; Fat 3.5g; Saturated fat 2g; Carbohydrate 69.9g; Fibre 0g.

Indian Pilau Rice

This traditional spiced rice is the perfect accompaniment for meat, fish or vegetarian dishes.

Serves 4
225g/8oz/1¼ cups basmati rice
15ml/1 tbsp oil
1 small onion, finely chopped
1 garlic clove, crushed
5ml/1 tsp fennel seeds
15ml/1 tbsp sesame seeds
2.5ml/½ tsp ground turmeric
5ml/1 tsp ground cumin
1.5ml/¼ tsp salt
2 whole cloves
4 cardamom pods, lightly crushed
5 black peppercorns
450ml/¾ pint/scant 2 cups chicken stock
fresh coriander (cilantro), to garnish

1 Wash the rice well and leave to soak in water for 30 minutes. Heat the oil in a heavy pan, add the onion and garlic and fry gently for 5–6 minutes until softened.

2 Stir in the fennel and sesame seeds, the turmeric, cumin, salt, cloves, cardamom pods and peppercorns and fry for about a minute. Drain the rice well, add to the pan and stir-fry for a further 3 minutes.

3 Pour on the chicken stock. Bring to the boil, then cover. Reduce the heat to very low and simmer gently for 20 minutes, without removing the lid, until all the liquid has been absorbed.

4 Remove from the heat and leave to stand for 2–3 minutes. Fluff up the rice with a fork, garnish with coriander and transfer to a warmed dish to serve.

> **Cook's Tip**
> *In South India, where large quantities of rice are eaten, people prefer a rice which will absorb the spicy flavours of seasonings. In this recipe, basmati rice is cooked in the traditional way to seal in all the flavour.*

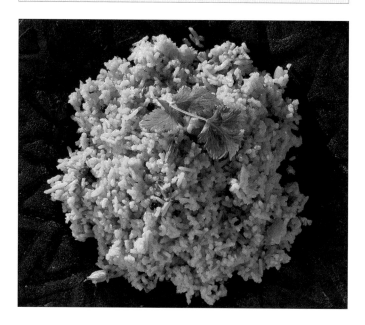

Energy 265kcal/1108kJ Fat 6g Saturated fat 0.68g Carbohydrate 49.5g Fibre 0.6g.

Colourful Pilau Rice

This lightly spiced rice makes an extremely attractive accompaniment to many Balti dishes, and is easily made.

Serves 4–6

450g/1lb/2 1/3 cups basmati rice
75g/3oz/6 tbsp unsalted (sweet) butter
4 cloves
4 green cardamom pods
1 bay leaf
5ml/1 tsp salt
1 litre/1 3/4 pints/4 cups water
a few drops each of yellow, green and red food colouring

1 Wash the basmati rice twice, drain well and set aside in a sieve (strainer).

2 Melt the butter in a medium pan, and add the cloves, cardamoms, bay leaf and salt. Lower the heat and add the rice. Fry for about 1 minute, stirring constantly.

3 Add the water to the rice and spices and bring to the boil. As soon as it has boiled, cover the pan and reduce the heat. Cook for 10–15 minutes. Taste a grain of rice after 10 minutes; it should be slightly *al dente* (soft but with a bite in the centre).

4 Just before you are ready to serve the rice, pour a few drops of each colouring at different sides of the pan. Leave to stand for 5 minutes so that the colours can "bleed" into the rice. Mix gently with a fork and serve.

> **Variation**
> *For Nut Pilau, fry 1.5ml/1/4 tsp cumin seeds with the cloves and cardamoms at step 2. When the rice has almost cooked, drain it and gently stir in a pinch of saffron threads and 15ml/ 1 tbsp ground almonds. Leave the rice to stand for a few minutes before serving. Omit the food colouring.*

Fruity Pilau

Sultanas and almonds make this a flavoursome rice to serve alongside rich curries.

Serves 4–6

450g/1lb/2 1/3 cups basmati rice
75g/3oz/6 tbsp unsalted (sweet) butter
15ml/1 tbsp corn oil
1 bay leaf
6 black peppercorns
4 green cardamom pods
5ml/1 tsp salt
75g/3oz/1/2 cup sultanas (golden raisins)
50g/2oz/1/2 cup flaked (sliced) almonds
1 litre/1 3/4 pints/4 cups water

1 Wash the basmati rice twice, drain well and set aside in a sieve (strainer).

2 Heat the butter and oil in a medium pan. Lower the heat and throw in the bay leaf, peppercorns and cardamoms, and fry for about 30 seconds.

3 Add the rice, salt, sultanas and flaked almonds. Stir-fry for about 1 minute, then pour in the water. Bring to the boil, then cover with a tightly fitting lid and lower the heat. Cook for 15–20 minutes. Taste a grain of rice after 10 minutes; it should be slightly *al dente* (soft but with a bite in the centre).

4 Turn off the heat and leave the rice to stand, still covered, for about 5 minutes. The rice will continue cooking gently during this time. Serve.

> **Variation**
> *For Mushroom Pilau, boil the rice without any of the flavourings for 15 minutes and then drain. Stir-fry 10ml/2 tsp cumin seeds, 1.5ml/1/2 tsp fennel seeds and 1 star anise for 30 seconds. Add half a chopped onion and 75g/3oz/1 cup sliced mushrooms, and cook over medium-high heat for 5 minutes. Add to the rice and transfer to a casserole. Heat in the oven at 190°C/ 375°F/Gas 5 for 30 minutes.*

Energy 544kcal/2263kJ; Fat 16g; Saturated fat 9.8g; Carbohydrate 89.9g; Fibre 0g.

Energy 696kcal/2901kJ; Fat 25.8g; Saturated fat 10.7g; Carbohydrate 103.8g; Fibre 1.3g.

Nut Pilau

Versions of this rice dish are cooked throughout Asia, always with the best-quality long grain rice. In India, basmati rice is the natural choice. In this particular interpretation of the recipe, walnuts and cashew nuts are added. Serve the pilau with a raita or yogurt.

Serves 4

15–30ml/1–2 tbsp vegetable oil
1 onion, chopped
1 garlic clove, crushed
1 large carrot, coarsely grated
225g/8oz/generous 1 cup
  basmati rice, soaked for
  20–30 minutes
5ml/1 tsp cumin seeds
10ml/2 tsp ground coriander
10ml/2 tsp black mustard seeds
4 green cardamom pods
450ml/ ¾ pint/scant 2 cups
  vegetable stock
1 bay leaf
75g/3oz/ ¾ cup unsalted walnuts
  and cashew nuts
salt and ground black pepper
fresh coriander (cilantro) sprigs,
  to garnish

1 Heat the oil in a karahi, wok or large pan. Fry the onion, garlic and carrot for 3–4 minutes. Drain the rice and add to the pan with the spices. Cook for 2 minutes, stirring to coat the grains in oil.

2 Pour in the stock, stirring. Add the bay leaf and season well.

3 Bring to the boil, lower the heat, cover and simmer very gently for 10–12 minutes without stirring.

4 Remove the pan from the heat without lifting the lid. Leave to stand for 5 minutes, then check the rice. If it is cooked, there will be small steam holes on the surface of the rice. Discard the bay leaf and the cardamom pods.

5 Stir in the walnuts and cashew nuts and check the seasoning. Spoon on to a warmed platter, garnish with the fresh coriander and serve.

Energy 376kcal/1562kJ; Fat 16g; Saturated fat 1.4g; Carbohydrate 50g; Fibre 1.6g.

Sultana & Cashew Pilau

The secret of a perfect pilau is to wash the rice thoroughly, then soak it briefly. This softens and moistens the grains, enabling the rice to absorb moisture during cooking, which results in fluffier rice.

Serves 4

600ml/1 pint/2½ cups hot
  chicken or vegetable stock
generous pinch of saffron threads
50g/2oz/¼ cup butter
1 onion, chopped
1 garlic clove, crushed
2.5cm/1in piece cinnamon stick
6 green cardamom pods
1 bay leaf
250g/9oz/1⅓ cups basmati
  rice, soaked in water for
  20–30 minutes
50g/2oz/⅓ cup sultanas
  (golden raisins)
15ml/1 tbsp vegetable oil
50g/2oz/½ cup cashew nuts
naan bread and tomato and
  onion salad, to serve

1 Pour the hot chicken stock into a jug (pitcher). Stir in the saffron threads and set aside.

2 Heat the butter in a pan and fry the onion and garlic for 5 minutes. Stir in the cinnamon stick, cardamoms and bay leaf and cook for 2 minutes.

3 Drain the rice and add to the pan, then cook, stirring, for 2 minutes more. Pour in the saffron stock and add the sultanas. Bring to the boil, stir, then lower the heat, cover and cook gently for 10 minutes or until the rice is tender and all the liquid has been absorbed.

4 Meanwhile, heat the oil in a wok, karahi or large pan and fry the cashew nuts until browned. Drain on kitchen paper, then sprinkle the cashew nuts over the rice. Serve with naan bread and tomato and onion salad.

> **Cook's Tip**
> Saffron powder can be used instead of saffron threads, if you prefer. Dissolve it in the hot stock.

Energy 462kcal/1922kJ Fat 19.5g Saturated fat 8g Carbohydrate 63.9g Fibre 1.2g.

Herby Rice Pilau

A quick and easy recipe to make, this simple pilau is delicious to eat. Serve with a main course meat, poultry or vegetarian curry accompanied by a selection of fresh seasonal vegetables such as broccoli florets, baby corn, asparagus and carrots.

Serves 4

1 onion
1 garlic clove
225g/8oz/generous 1 cup mixed
  brown basmati and wild rice
15ml/1 tbsp olive oil
5ml/1 tsp ground cumin

5ml/1 tsp ground turmeric
50g/2oz/¹/₃ cup sultanas
  (golden raisins)
750ml/1¹/₄ pints/3 cups vegetable
  stock
30–45ml/2–3 tbsp chopped
  fresh mixed herbs
salt and ground black pepper
sprigs of fresh herbs and 25g/
  1oz/¹/₄ cup pistachio nuts,
  chopped, to garnish

1 Chop the onion and crush the garlic cloves.

2 Wash the rice under cold running water until the water runs clear, then drain well.

3 Heat the oil, add the onion and garlic, and cook gently for 5 minutes, stirring occasionally.

4 Add the ground cumin and turmeric and drained rice and cook gently for 1 minute, stirring. Stir in the sultanas and vegetable stock, bring to the boil, cover and simmer gently for 20–25 minutes, stirring occasionally.

5 Stir in the chopped mixed herbs and season with salt and pepper to taste.

6 Spoon the pilau into a warmed serving dish and garnish with fresh herb sprigs and a sprinkling of chopped pistachio nuts. Serve immediately.

Energy 271kcal/1133kJ; Fat 3.3g; Saturated fat 0.4g; Carbohydrate 55.1g; Fibre 1.1g.

Tomato & Spinach Pilau

A tasty and nourishing dish for vegetarians and meat-eaters alike.

Serves 4

225g/8oz/generous 1 cup brown
  basmati rice
30ml/2 tbsp vegetable oil
15ml/1 tbsp ghee or unsalted
  (sweet) butter
1 onion, chopped
2 garlic cloves, crushed
3 tomatoes, peeled and chopped

10ml/2 tsp dhana jeera powder,
  or 5ml/1 tsp ground coriander
  and 5ml/1 tsp ground cumin
2 carrots, coarsely grated
900ml/1¹/₂ pints/3³/₄ cups
  vegetable stock
275g/10oz young spinach leaves
50g/2oz/¹/₂ cup unsalted
  cashew nuts
salt and ground black pepper
naan bread, to serve

1 Wash the basmati rice. Place it in a bowl, cover with cold water and leave to soak for 20 minutes. Drain the rice and place it in a large pan of boiling salted water, bring back to the boil and cook for 10 minutes.

2 Heat the oil and ghee or butter in a karahi, wok or large pan, and fry the onion and garlic for 4–5 minutes until soft. Add the tomatoes and cook for 3–4 minutes, stirring, until the mixture thickens. Drain the rice, add it to the pan and cook for a further 1–2 minutes, stirring, until the grains of rice are coated.

3 Stir in the dhana jeera powder or coriander and cumin, then add the carrots. Season with salt and pepper. Pour in the stock and stir well to mix.

4 Bring to the boil, then cover tightly and simmer over a very gentle heat for 20–25 minutes, until the rice is tender.

5 Lay the spinach on the surface of the rice, cover again, and cook for a further 2–3 minutes, until the spinach has wilted. Fold the spinach into the rest of the rice.

6 Dry-fry the cashew nuts until lightly browned and sprinkle over the rice mixture. Serve with naan bread.

Energy 402kcal/1687kJ Fat 17.1g Saturated fat 4.4g Carbohydrate 56.4g Fibre 4.8g.

Fragrant Meat Pilau

This rice dish acquires its delicious taste not only from the spices but the richly flavoured meat stock.

Serves 4–6

450g/1lb/2⅓ cups basmati
  rice
900g/2lb boned chicken pieces,
  or lean lamb, cubed
600ml/1 pint/2½ cups water
4 green cardamom pods
2 black cardamom pods
10 black peppercorns
4 cloves
1 medium onion, sliced
8–10 saffron strands

2 garlic cloves, crushed
5cm/2in piece fresh root ginger
5cm/2in piece cinnamon stick
salt
175g/6oz/1 cup sultanas
  (golden raisins) and sautéed
  blanched almonds, to garnish

1 Wash the rice under cold running water until the water runs clear. Drain the rice well and set aside.

2 In a large pan, cook the cubed chicken or lamb in the measured water with the cardamom pods, peppercorns, cloves, onion and salt, until the meat is cooked.

3 Remove the meat with a slotted spoon and keep warm. Strain the stock if you wish, and return to the pan.

4 Add the rice, saffron, garlic, ginger and cinnamon to the stock and bring the contents to the boil.

5 Quickly add the meat and stir well. Bring back to the boil, reduce the heat and cover. Cook covered for about 15–20 minutes.

6 Remove the pan from the heat and leave to stand for 5 minutes. Garnish with sultanas and sautéed blanched almonds and serve.

Tricolour Pilau

Most Indian restaurants in the West serve this popular vegetable pilau, which has three different vegetables. The effect is easily achieved with canned or frozen vegetables, but for entertaining or a special occasion dinner, you may prefer to use fresh produce.

Serves 4–6

225g/8oz/generous 1 cup
  basmati rice
30ml/2 tbsp vegetable
  oil
2.5ml/½ tsp cumin seeds
2 dried bay leaves

4 green cardamom pods
4 cloves
1 onion, finely chopped
1 carrot, finely diced
50g/2oz/½ cup frozen peas,
  thawed
50g/2oz/⅓ cup frozen corn,
  thawed
25g/1oz/¼ cup cashew nuts,
  lightly fried
475ml/16fl oz/2 cups water
1.5ml/¼ tsp ground cumin
salt

1 Wash the rice, then soak it in cold water for 20 minutes.

2 Heat the oil in a karahi, wok, or large pan over a medium heat, and fry the cumin seeds for 2 minutes. Add the bay leaves, cardamoms and cloves, and fry gently for 2 minutes more, stirring the spices from time to time.

3 Add the onion and fry until lightly browned. Stir in the diced carrot and cook, stirring, for 3–4 minutes.

4 Drain the soaked basmati rice and add to the contents in the pan. Stir well to mix. Add the peas, corn and fried cashew nuts.

5 Add the measured water and the ground cumin, and stir in salt to taste. Bring to the boil, cover and simmer for 15 minutes over a low heat until all the water is absorbed.

6 Leave to stand, covered, for 10 minutes. Fluff up the rice with a fork, transfer to a warmed dish and serve.

Energy 648kcal/2723kJ; Fat 3.1g; Saturated fat 0.7g; Carbohydrate 91g; Fibre 0.2g.

Energy 331kcal/1378kJ Fat 9.4g Saturated fat 1.4g Carbohydrate 54.1g Fibre 2g.

Pea & Mushroom Pilau

Tiny white mushrooms and petits pois, or baby peas, look great in this delectable rice dish.

Serves 6

450g/1lb/2¼ cups basmati rice
15ml/1 tbsp oil
2.5ml/½ tsp cumin seeds
2 black cardamom pods
2 cinnamon sticks
3 garlic cloves, sliced

5ml/1 tsp salt
1 medium tomato, sliced
50g/2oz/⅔ cup button (white) mushrooms
75g/3oz/¾ cup petits pois (baby peas)
750ml/1¼ pints/3 cups water

1 Wash the rice well and leave it to soak in water for 30 minutes.

2 In a medium, heavy pan, heat the oil and add the cumin seeds, cardamom, cinnamon sticks, garlic and salt.

3 Add the tomato and mushrooms and stir-fry for 2–3 minutes.

4 Tip the rice into a colander and drain it thoroughly. Add it to the pan with the peas. Stir gently, making sure that you do not break up the grains of rice.

5 Add the water and bring to the boil. Lower the heat, cover and continue to cook for 15–20 minutes. Just before serving, remove the lid from the pan and fluff up the rice with a fork. Spoon into a dish and serve immediately.

> **Cook's Tip**
> *Petits pois are small green peas, picked when very young. The tender, sweet peas inside the immature pods are ideal for this delicately flavoured rice dish. However, if you can't find petits pois, garden peas can be used instead.*

Rice with Seeds & Spices

Toasted sunflower and sesame seeds impart a rich, nutty flavour to rice spiced with turmeric, cardamom and coriander, for this delicious change from plain boiled rice, and a colourful accompaniment to serve with spicy curries. Basmati rice gives the best texture and flavour, but you can use ordinary long grain rice instead, if you prefer.

Serves 4

5ml/1 tsp sunflower oil
2.5ml/½ tsp ground turmeric
6 cardamom pods, lightly crushed
5ml/1 tsp coriander seeds, lightly crushed

1 garlic clove, crushed
200g/7oz/1 cup basmati rice
400ml/14fl oz/1⅔ cups vegetable stock
115g/4oz/½ cup natural (plain) yogurt
15ml/1 tbsp toasted sunflower seeds
15ml/1 tbsp toasted sesame seeds
salt and ground black pepper
coriander (cilantro) leaves, to garnish

1 Heat the oil in a non-stick frying pan and fry the turmeric, cardamom pods, coriander seeds and garlic for about 1 minute, stirring constantly.

2 Add the rice and stock, bring to the boil, then cover and simmer for 15 minutes, or until just tender.

3 Stir in the yogurt and the toasted sunflower and sesame seeds. Season with salt and pepper and serve hot, garnished with coriander leaves.

> **Cook's Tip**
> *Seeds are particularly rich in minerals, so they are a good addition to all kinds of dishes. Light toasting will improve their fine flavour.*

Energy 423kcal/1768kJ; Fat 3.8g; Saturated fat 0.39g; Carbohydrate 92.9g; Fibre 1.3g.

Energy 248kcal/1036kJ; Fat 5.4g; Saturated fat 0.7g; Carbohydrate 42.8g; Fibre 0.5g.

Saffron Rice

The saffron crocus is a perennial bulb that flowers for only two weeks of the year, and each stigma has to be removed by hand and dried with care. Consequently, saffron is said to be worth its weight in gold. Kashmir in the northern region of India is a major producer, so it isn't surprising that the subcontinent has some wonderful recipes for this beautifully fragrant spice.

Serves 6
450g/1lb/2⅓ cups basmati
  rice
750ml/1¼ pints/3 cups water
3 green cardamom pods
2 cloves
5ml/1 tsp salt
45ml/3 tbsp semi-skimmed
  (low-fat) milk
2.5ml/½ tsp saffron threads,
  crushed

1 Wash the rice, put it in a bowl and pour over water to cover. Leave to soak for 20 minutes.

2 Drain the basmati rice and put it in a large pan with the measured water. Add the cardamoms, cloves and salt. Stir, then bring to the boil. Lower the heat, cover the pan tightly, and simmer for 5 minutes.

3 Meanwhile, place the milk in a small pan. Add the saffron threads and heat through gently.

4 Pour the saffron milk over the rice and stir. Cover again and continue cooking over a low heat for 5–6 minutes.

5 Remove the pan from the heat without lifting the lid. Leave the rice to stand for about 5 minutes, then fork through just before serving.

Cook's Tip
Washing and soaking the rice before cooking makes it fluffier.

Energy 273kcal/1141kJ Fat 0.5g Saturated fat 0.1g Carbohydrate 60.2g Fibre 0g.

Jasmine Fried Rice

This substantial and tasty dish is based on coconut-flavoured jasmine rice. Diced chicken, red pepper and corn add colour and extra flavour.

Serves 4
475ml/16fl oz/2 cups water
50g/2oz/½ cup coconut
  milk powder
350g/12oz/1¾ cups jasmine
  rice, rinsed
30ml/2 tbsp groundnut
  (peanut) oil
2 garlic cloves, chopped
1 small onion, finely chopped
2.5cm/1in piece fresh root
  ginger, grated
225g/8oz skinned chicken breast
  fillets, cut into 1cm/½in dice
1 red (bell) pepper, seeded
  and sliced
115g/4oz/1 cup drained
  canned corn
5ml/1 tsp chilli oil
5ml/1 tsp hot curry powder
2 eggs, beaten
salt
spring onion (scallion) shreds,
  to garnish

1 Pour the water into a pan and whisk in the coconut milk powder. Add the rice and bring to the boil. Reduce the heat, cover and cook for 12 minutes, or until the rice is tender and the liquid has been absorbed. Spread the rice on a baking sheet and leave until completely cold.

2 Heat the oil in a wok, add the garlic, onion and ginger, and stir-fry over a medium heat for 2 minutes.

3 Push the onion mixture to the sides of the wok, add the chicken to the centre and stir-fry for 2 minutes. Add the rice and toss well. Stir-fry over a high heat for about 3 minutes more, until the chicken is cooked through.

4 Stir in the sliced red pepper, corn, chilli oil and curry powder, with salt to taste. Toss over the heat for 1 minute. Stir in the beaten eggs and cook for 1 minute more. Garnish with the spring onion shreds and serve.

Energy 524kcal/2193kJ; Fat 10.7g; Saturated fat 1.8g; Carbohydrate 82.1g; Fibre 1.3g.

Caramelized Basmati Rice

This dish is the traditional accompaniment to a dhansak curry. Sugar is caramelized in hot oil before the rice is added, along with whole spices.

Serves 4

225g/8oz/generous 1 cup
  basmati rice
45ml/3 tbsp vegetable oil
20ml/4 tsp sugar
4 or 5 green cardamom
  pods, bruised
2.5cm/1in piece cinnamon stick
4 cloves
1 bay leaf, crumpled
2.5ml/½ tsp salt
475ml/16fl oz/2 cups hot water

1 Wash the rice, put it in a bowl and pour over water to cover. Leave to soak for 20 minutes.

2 Drain the rice in a colander, shaking it a little as you do so. Run the washed grains through your fingers to check that there is no excess water trapped between them. Set aside.

3 In a large pan, heat the vegetable oil over a medium heat. When the oil is hot, sprinkle the sugar over the surface and wait until it has caramelized. Do not stir.

4 Reduce the heat to low and add the spices and bay leaf. Allow to sizzle for 15–20 seconds, then add the rice and salt. Fry gently, stirring, for 2–3 minutes.

5 Pour in the water and bring to the boil. Let it boil steadily for 2 minutes then reduce the heat to very low. Cover the pan and cook for 8 minutes.

6 Remove the rice from the heat and leave to stand for 6–8 minutes. Fluff up the rice with a fork and serve.

> **Cook's Tip**
> *Watch the sugar carefully so that it does not burn.*

Basmati Rice with Vegetables

Serve this delectable dish with roast chicken, lamb cutlets or pan-fried fish. Add the vegetables near the end of cooking so that they retain their crispness and colour.

Serves 4

1 onion
2 garlic cloves
350g/12oz/1¾ cups basmati
  rice
45ml/3 tbsp vegetable oil
750ml/1¼ pints/3 cups water
  or vegetable stock
115g/4oz/⅔ cup fresh or
  drained canned corn
1 red or green (bell) pepper,
  seeded and chopped
1 large carrot, grated
fresh chervil sprigs, to garnish

1 Chop the onion and crush the garlic cloves.

2 Wash the rice in a sieve (strainer), and then soak in cold water for 20 minutes. Drain very thoroughly.

3 Heat the oil in a large pan and fry the onion for a few minutes over a medium heat until it starts to soften.

4 Add the rice to the pan and fry for about 10 minutes, stirring constantly to prevent the rice from sticking to the base of the pan. Stir in the crushed garlic.

5 Pour in the water or stock and stir into the rice well. Bring to the boil, then lower the heat. Cover the pan and simmer for 10 minutes.

6 Sprinkle the corn over the rice, spread the chopped pepper on top and sprinkle over the grated carrot.

7 Cover tightly and steam over a low heat until the rice is tender, then mix with a fork.

8 Pile the vegetables and rice on to a serving plate and garnish with chervil sprigs.

Energy 454kcal/1897kJ Fat 9.7g Saturated fat 1.2g Carbohydrate 82.7g Fibre 2.3g.

Energy 276kcal/1150kJ Fat 8.5g Saturated fat 1g Carbohydrate 44.9g Fibre 0g.

Tarka Dhal

Probably the most popular Indian lentil dish found today, Tarka Dhal is served in most Indian and Pakistani restaurants.

Serves 4
115g/4oz/½ cup masoor dhal (red split lentils)
50g/2oz/¼ cup mung dhal or yellow split peas
600ml/1 pint/2½ cups water
5ml/1 tsp grated fresh root ginger
5ml/1 tsp crushed garlic
1.5ml/¼ tsp ground turmeric
2 fresh green chillies, chopped
7.5ml/1½ tsp salt

For the tarka
30ml/2 tbsp oil
1 onion, sliced
1.5ml/¼ tsp mixed mustard and onion seeds
4 dried red chillies
1 tomato, sliced

For the garnish
15ml/1 tbsp chopped fresh coriander (cilantro)
1 or 2 fresh green chillies, seeded and sliced
15ml/1 tbsp chopped fresh mint

1 Boil all the masoor dhal and mung dhal or yellow split peas in the water with the ginger and garlic, turmeric and chopped green chillies for 15–20 minutes, or until soft.

2 Pound the mixture with a rolling pin or mash with a fork until it has the consistency of a creamy chicken soup.

3 If the lentil mixture looks too dry, add a little more water. Season with the salt. To prepare the tarka, heat the oil in a heavy pan and fry the onion with the mustard and onion seeds, dried red chillies and tomato for 2 minutes.

4 Spoon the mashed lentils into a serving dish and pour the tarka over. Garnish with fresh coriander, green chillies and mint, and serve immediately.

> **Cook's Tip**
> Use 1 or 2 red chillies if you want a milder tarka for the dhal.

Lentils Seasoned with Fried Spices

A simple supper dish for family or friends using traditional Indian lentils and peas.

Serves 4–6
115g/4oz/½ cup red gram (pigeon peas)
50g/2oz/¼ cup Bengal gram
4 fresh green chillies
5ml/1 tsp ground turmeric
1 large onion, sliced
400g/14oz can chopped tomatoes

60ml/4 tbsp vegetable oil
2.5ml/½ tsp mustard seeds
2.5ml/½ tsp cumin seeds
1 garlic clove, crushed
6 curry leaves
2 dried red chillies
salt
deep-fried onions and fresh coriander (cilantro), to garnish

1 Place the red gram and bengal gram in a heavy pan and pour in 350ml/12fl oz/1½ cups water. Add the chillies, turmeric and onion slices and bring to the boil. Simmer, covered, until the lentils are soft and the water has evaporated.

2 Mash the lentils with the back of a spoon. When nearly smooth, add the tomatoes and salt to taste, and mix well. If necessary, thin with a little hot water.

3 Heat the oil in a frying pan. Fry the remaining ingredients until the garlic browns. Pour the oil and spices over the lentils and cover. After 5 minutes, mix well, garnish, and serve.

> **Cook's Tips**
> • Red gram, or pigeon peas, are the fruit of a small shrub but are used as a vegetable. They form a staple food in India as well as Africa and the Caribbean, and you will find them in Asian and Caribbean stores and markets.
> • Bengal gram, or channa, is a small variety of chickpea, which is commonly used in Indian cuisine.

Courgettes with Split Lentils & Tomatoes

The nutty flavour of lentils goes particularly well with courgettes and tomatoes, perked up with a selection of aromatic spices. Serve with rice or bread for a filling and tasty supper.

Serves 4–6
225g/8oz courgettes (zucchini)
1 large onion, finely sliced
2 garlic cloves, crushed
2 fresh green chillies, chopped
175g/6oz/²⁄₃ cup mung dhal or yellow split peas
2.5ml/¹⁄₂ tsp ground turmeric
60ml/4 tbsp vegetable oil
2.5ml/¹⁄₂ tsp mustard seeds
2.5ml/¹⁄₂ tsp cumin seeds
1.5ml/¹⁄₄ tsp asafoetida
a few fresh coriander (cilantro) and mint leaves, chopped
6–8 curry leaves
2.5ml/¹⁄₂ tsp sugar
200g/7oz can chopped tomatoes
60ml/4 tbsp lemon juice
salt

1 Cut the courgettes into wedges. Finely slice the onion and crush the garlic. Chop the green chillies.

2 In a pan, simmer the lentils and turmeric in 300ml/¹⁄₂ pint/ 1¹⁄₄ cups water, until cooked but not mushy. Drain the cooked lentils, retaining the cooking liquid, and set aside while you cook the vegetables.

3 Heat the oil in a frying pan and add the courgette wedges, sliced onion, crushed garlic and chopped chillies. Add the mustard and cumin seeds, asafoetida, fresh coriander and mint, and stir in the curry leaves and sugar. Fry the ingredients together, stirring occasionally, and then add the chopped tomatoes. Mix well and add salt to taste.

4 Cover and cook until the courgettes are nearly tender but still crunchy.

5 Fold in the drained lentils and the lemon juice. If the dish is too dry, add some of the reserved cooking water. Reheat thoroughly and serve immediately.

Green Lentils & Rice

Also known as continental lentils, green lentils retain their shape and colour when cooked. They are an important source of protein and add a robust flavour to dishes such as this. Chillies, ginger, cardamoms and cinnamon make this a lively main-course rice, excellent served with a vegetable curry or a simple salad.

Serves 4–6
350g/12oz/1³⁄₄ cups patna rice
175g/6oz/³⁄₄ cup green lentils
50g/2oz/¹⁄₄ cup ghee
1 onion, finely chopped
2 garlic cloves, crushed
2.5cm/1in piece fresh root ginger, shredded
4 fresh green chillies, chopped
4 cloves
2.5cm/1in piece cinnamon stick
4 green cardamom pods
5ml/1 tsp ground turmeric
600ml/1 pint/2¹⁄₂ cups water
salt

1 Wash the rice and lentils, then soak them in a bowl of cold water for 20 minutes.

2 Gently heat the ghee in a large, heavy pan with a tight-fitting cover and fry the onion, garlic, ginger, chillies, cloves, cinnamon, cardamoms, turmeric and salt to taste until the onion is soft and translucent.

3 Drain the rice and lentils and add them to the spices in the pan. Sauté for 2–3 minutes. Add the water and bring the mixture to the boil.

4 Reduce the heat, cover and cook for about 20–25 minutes, or until all the water has been absorbed.

5 Take the pan off the heat and leave to rest with the lid on for 5 minutes.

6 Just before serving, gently toss the rice and lentils with a flat spatula, taking care not to break the delicate grains.

Energy 669kcal/2793kJ Fat 23.5g Saturated fat 15g Carbohydrate 97.4g Fibre 2.7g.

Energy 278kcal/1165kJ Fat 12g Saturated fat 1.5g Carbohydrate 31.9g Fibre 3.9g.

Creamy Black Lentils

Black lentils, or urad dhal, are available whole, split, and skinned and split.

Serves 4–6

175g/6oz/¾ cup black lentils, soaked
50g/2oz/¼ cup red split lentils
120ml/4fl oz/½ cup double (heavy) cream, plus extra to serve
120ml/4fl oz/½ cup natural (plain) yogurt
5ml/1 tsp cornflour (cornstarch)
40g/1½oz/3 tbsp ghee or vegetable oil
1 onion, finely chopped
5cm/2in piece fresh root ginger, crushed
4 fresh green chillies, chopped
1 tomato, chopped
2.5ml/½ tsp chilli powder
2.5ml/½ tsp ground turmeric
2.5ml/½ tsp ground cumin
2 garlic cloves, sliced
salt
coriander (cilantro) sprigs and sliced fresh red chilli, to garnish

1 Drain the black lentils and place in a large pan with the red lentils. Cover with water and bring to the boil. Reduce the heat, cover the pan and simmer until tender. Mash with a spoon, and cool.

2 In a bowl, mix together the cream, yogurt and cornflour, and stir into the lentils in the pan.

3 Heat 15g/½oz/1 tbsp of the ghee or oil in a karahi, wok or large pan, and fry the onion, ginger, half the green chillies and the tomato until the onion is soft.

4 Add the ground spices and salt, and fry for a further 2 minutes. Stir into the lentil mixture and mix well. Reheat, transfer to a heatproof serving dish and keep warm.

5 Heat the remaining ghee or oil in a frying pan over a low heat and fry the garlic slices and remaining chillies until the garlic slices are golden brown.

6 Pour over the lentils, and fold in the garlic and chilli just before serving. Garnish and serve with extra cream so that diners can add more as they eat, if they wish.

Energy 431kcal/1800kJ Fat 26.5g Saturated fat 16.2g Carbohydrate 35g Fibre 2.9g.

Lentils Seasoned with Garlic Oil

This dish is popular in southern India, where there are numerous variations. A single vegetable can be added to the lentils, or a combination of two or more. It is traditionally served with steamed rice dumplings or stuffed rice pancakes. The garlic-flavoured lentils are also extremely satisfying with plain boiled rice.

Serves 4–6
120ml/4fl oz/½ cup vegetable oil
2.5ml/½ tsp mustard seeds
2.5ml/½ tsp cumin seeds
2 dried red chillies
1.5ml/¼ tsp asafoetida
6–8 curry leaves
2 garlic cloves, crushed, plus 2 sliced
30ml/2 tbsp desiccated (dry unsweetened shredded) coconut
225g/8oz/1 cup red lentils, washed and drained
10ml/2 tsp sambhar masala or other curry powder
2.5ml/½ tsp ground turmeric
450ml/¾ pint/scant 2 cups water
450g/1lb mixed vegetables, such as okra, courgettes (zucchini), aubergine (eggplant), cauliflower, shallots and (bell) peppers, chopped
60ml/4 tbsp tamarind juice
4 firm tomatoes, quartered
a few coriander (cilantro) leaves, chopped

1 Heat half the oil in a karahi, wok, or large pan, and stir-fry the next seven ingredients until the coconut begins to brown.

2 Stir in the prepared red lentils with the masala and turmeric. Stir-fry for 2–3 minutes and add the water. Bring to the boil and reduce the heat to low.

3 Cover the pan and leave to simmer for 25–30 minutes, or until the lentils are mushy. Add the chopped mixed vegetables, tamarind juice and tomato quarters. Cook until the vegetables are just tender.

4 Heat the remaining oil in a small pan over a low heat, and fry the garlic slices until golden. Stir in the fresh coriander leaves, then pour over the lentils and vegetables. Mix together at the table before serving.

Energy 477kcal/1994kJ Fat 28.7g Saturated fat 7.1g Carbohydrate 38.6g Fibre 6.8g.

Lentils & Rice

Here, lentils are cooked with whole and ground spices, potato, rice and onion to produce a tasty and nutritious meal.

Serves 4

150g/5oz/¾ cup tuvar dhal or
   red split lentils

115g/4oz/½ cup basmati rice
1 large potato
1 large onion
30ml/2 tbsp oil
4 whole cloves
1.5ml/¼ tsp cumin seeds
1.5ml/¼ tsp ground turmeric
10ml/2 tsp salt
300ml/½ pint/1¼ cups water

1 Wash the tuvar dhal or red split lentils and rice in several changes of cold water. Put into a bowl and cover with water. Leave to soak for 15 minutes, then transfer to a strainer and drain well.

2 Peel the potato, then cut it into 2.5cm/1in chunks. Using a sharp knife, thinly slice the onion and set aside for later.

3 Heat the oil in a heavy pan and fry the cloves and cumin seeds for 2 minutes until the seeds are beginning to splutter.

4 Add the onion and potato chunks and fry for 5 minutes. Add the lentils, rice, turmeric and salt and fry for a further 3 minutes.

5 Add the water. Bring to the boil, cover and simmer gently for 15–20 minutes until all the water has been absorbed and the potato chunks are tender. Leave to stand, covered, for about 10 minutes before serving.

> **Cook's Tip**
> *Red split lentils are widely available in most supermarkets. Before cooking they are salmon-coloured and they turn a pale, dull yellow during cooking. They have a mild, pleasant, nutty flavour. Soaking them in water speeds up the cooking process but isn't strictly necessary.*

Spinach Dhal

Many different types of dhal are eaten in India and each region has its own speciality. This is a delicious, lightly spiced dish with a mild nutty flavour from the yellow lentils, which combine well with the spinach.

Serves 4

175g/6oz/1 cup chana dhal
   or yellow split peas
175ml/6fl oz/¾ cup water
15ml/1 tbsp oil
1.5ml/¼ tsp black mustard
   seeds

1 onion, thinly sliced
2 garlic cloves, crushed
2.5cm/1in piece fresh root
   ginger, grated
1 fresh red chilli, finely chopped
275g/10oz frozen spinach,
   thawed
1.5ml/¼ tsp chilli powder
2.5ml/½ tsp ground coriander
2.5ml/½ tsp garam masala
2.5ml/½ tsp salt

1 Wash the chana dhal or split peas in several changes of cold water. Put into a bowl and cover with plenty of water. Leave to soak for 30 minutes.

2 Drain the pulses and put them in a large pan with the water. Bring to the boil, cover and simmer for 20–25 minutes, or until they are soft.

3 Meanwhile, heat the oil in a large, heavy pan and fry the mustard seeds for 2 minutes until they begin to splutter.

4 Add the onion, garlic, ginger and chilli and fry for 5–6 minutes until softened but not coloured.

5 Add the spinach and cook for 10 minutes or until the spinach is dry and the liquid has been absorbed. Stir in the remaining spices and salt, and cook for 2–3 minutes.

6 Drain the split peas, add them to the spinach mixture and cook for about 5 minutes. Transfer to a warmed serving dish and serve immediately.

Energy 332kcal/1396kJ; Fat 6.7g; Saturated fat 0.76g; Carbohydrate 58.6g; Fibre 3.4g.

Energy 183kcal/778kJ Fat 2g Saturated fat 0.44g Carbohydrate 30.3g Fibre 4.9g.

Spiced Aubergine

Chunks of aubergine are coated in a rich sauce and sprinkled with sesame seeds to make an unusual side dish that is quick to cook. This straightforward yet versatile vegetarian dish can be served hot, warm or cold, as the occasion demands.

Serves 4–6
2 aubergines, total weight about 600g/1lb 6oz, cut into large chunks
15ml/1 tbsp salt
5ml/1 tsp chilli powder, or to taste
75–90ml/5–6 tbsp sunflower oil
15ml/1 tbsp rice wine or medium-dry sherry
100ml/3½fl oz/scant ½ cup water
75ml/5 tbsp chilli bean sauce (see Cook's Tip)
salt and ground black pepper
a few toasted sesame seeds, to garnish

1 Place the aubergine chunks on a plate, sprinkle them with the salt and leave to stand for 15–20 minutes. Rinse well, drain and dry thoroughly on kitchen paper. Toss the aubergine cubes in the chilli powder.

2 Heat a wok and add the oil. When the oil is hot, add the aubergine chunks, with the rice wine or sherry. Stir constantly until the aubergine chunks start to turn a little brown. Stir in the water, cover the wok and steam for 2–3 minutes. Add the chilli bean sauce and cook for 2 minutes. Season to taste, then spoon on to a serving dish, sprinkle with sesame seeds and serve.

Cook's Tip
If you can't get hold of chilli bean sauce, use 15–30ml/ 1–2 tbsp chilli paste mixed with 2 crushed garlic cloves, 15ml/1 tbsp each dark soy sauce and rice vinegar, and 10ml/2 tsp light soy sauce.

Carrot & Cauliflower Stir-fry

Slicing the carrots into thin batons helps them cook quickly. This dish has a crunchy texture and uses only a few whole spices.

Serves 4
2 large carrots
1 small cauliflower
15ml/1 tbsp oil
1 bay leaf
2 cloves
1 small cinnamon stick
2 cardamom pods
3 black peppercorns
5ml/1 tsp salt
50g/2oz/½ cup frozen peas, thawed
10ml/2 tsp lemon juice
15ml/1 tbsp chopped fresh coriander (cilantro), plus fresh leaves to garnish

1 Cut the carrots into thin batons about 2.5cm/1in long. Separate the cauliflower into small florets.

2 Heat the oil in a karahi, wok or heavy pan and add the bay leaf, cloves, cinnamon stick, cardamom pods and peppercorns. Quickly stir-fry over a medium heat for 30–35 seconds, then add the salt.

3 Next add the carrot batons and cauliflower florets and continue to stir-fry for 3–5 minutes.

4 Add the peas, lemon juice and chopped coriander and cook for a further 4–5 minutes. Serve garnished with the whole coriander leaves.

Variation
Substitute broccoli or sliced courgette (zucchini) for the cauliflower, if you like.

Cook's Tip
As both carrots and cauliflower can be eaten raw, they need only minimal cooking or they will lose their crunchy texture.

Energy 193kcal/798kJ; Fat 17.1g; Saturated fat 2.1g; Carbohydrate 8.7g; Fibre 3.2g.

Energy 84kcal/349kJ; Fat 3.75g; Saturated fat 0.6g; Carbohydrate 9.05g; Fibre 3.67g.

Spicy Potatoes & Cauliflower

This dish is simplicity itself to make and can be eaten as a main meal with Indian breads or rice, a raita such as cucumber and yogurt, and a fresh mint relish.

Serves 2
225g/8oz potatoes
75ml/5 tbsp groundnut
   (peanut) oil
5ml/1 tsp ground cumin
5ml/1 tsp ground coriander
1.5ml/¼ tsp ground turmeric
1.5ml/¼ tsp cayenne pepper
1 fresh green chilli, seeded
   and finely chopped
1 medium cauliflower, broken
   into small florets
5ml/1 tsp cumin seeds
2 garlic cloves, cut into
   shreds
15–30ml/1–2 tbsp fresh
   coriander (cilantro),
   finely chopped
salt

1 Cook the potatoes in their skins in boiling salted water for about 20 minutes, until just tender. Drain and leave to cool. When cool enough to handle, peel and cut into 2.5cm/1in cubes.

2 Heat 45ml/3 tbsp of the oil in a frying pan or wok. When hot, add the ground cumin, coriander, turmeric, cayenne pepper and chilli. Let the spices sizzle for a few seconds.

3 Add the cauliflower and about 60ml/4 tbsp water. Cook over medium heat, stirring continuously, for 6–8 minutes. Add the potatoes and stir-fry for 2–3 minutes. Season with salt, then remove from the heat.

4 Heat the remaining oil in a small frying pan. When hot, add the cumin seeds and garlic, and cook until lightly browned. Pour the mixture over the vegetables. Sprinkle with the chopped coriander and serve at once.

Cook's Tip
Divide the cauliflower into small florets so that it will cook evenly and quickly.

Cauliflower & Potato Curry

Potatoes and cauliflower make a wonderful combination for a curry, and a substantial side dish. Here they are combined with the mild flavours of cumin, coriander and turmeric with just enough chilli to give the dish that little extra punch.

5ml/1 tsp ground coriander
5ml/1 tsp ground cumin
1.5ml/¼ tsp chilli powder
2.5ml/½ tsp ground turmeric
2.5ml/½ tsp salt
chopped fresh coriander (cilantro),
   to garnish
tomato and onion salad and
   pickle, to serve

Serves 4
450g/1lb potatoes, cut into
   2.5cm/1in chunks
30ml/2 tbsp oil
5ml/1 tsp cumin seeds
1 fresh green chilli, finely chopped
450g/1lb cauliflower, broken
   into florets

1 Par-cook the potatoes in a large pan of boiling water for about 10 minutes. Drain well and set aside.

2 Heat the oil in a large, heavy pan. Add the cumin seeds and fry them for 2 minutes until they begin to splutter. Add the chilli and fry for a further 1 minute.

3 Add the cauliflower florets and fry, stirring, for 5 minutes.

4 Add the potatoes and the ground spices and salt and cook for a further 7–10 minutes, or until both the vegetables are tender. Garnish with fresh coriander and serve with tomato and onion salad and pickle.

Variation
Use sweet potatoes instead of ordinary potatoes for a curry with a sweeter flavour.

Energy 189kcal/791kJ; Fat 7.4g; Saturated fat 0.77g; Carbohydrate 24.6g; Fibre 3.5g.

Energy 409kcal/1698kJ; Fat 29.7g; Saturated fat 3.8g; Carbohydrate 26.6g; Fibre 5.4g.

Potatoes in Tomato Sauce

This delicious curry makes an excellent accompaniment to almost any other savoury dish, but goes particularly well with Balti dishes. Served with rice, it makes a great vegetarian main course.

Serves 4

10ml/2 tsp oil
1.5ml/¼ tsp onion seeds
4 curry leaves
2 medium onions, diced
400g/14oz can tomatoes
5ml/1 tsp ground cumin
7.5ml/1½ tsp ground coriander
5ml/1 tsp chilli powder
5ml/1 tsp grated fresh root ginger
5ml/1 tsp crushed garlic
1.5ml/¼ tsp ground turmeric
5ml/1 tsp salt
15ml/1 tbsp lemon juice
15ml/1 tbsp chopped fresh
    coriander (cilantro)
2 medium potatoes, diced

1 Heat the oil in a karahi, wok or heavy pan and add the onion seeds, curry leaves and diced onions. Fry over a medium heat for a few minutes, stirring occasionally and being careful not to burn the onions.

2 Meanwhile, place the canned tomatoes in a bowl and add the ground cumin and coriander, chilli powder, ginger, garlic, turmeric, salt, lemon juice and fresh coriander. Mix the ingredients together until well blended.

3 Pour this mixture into the pan and stir for about 1 minute to mix thoroughly with the onions.

4 Finally, add the diced potatoes, cover the pan and cook gently for 7–10 minutes over low heat. Check that the potatoes are properly cooked through, then serve.

Variations
This curry is also delicious if you add a few cauliflower or broccoli florets with the potatoes, or if you substitute diced parsnips for the potatoes. To emphasize the tomato flavour, stir in 15ml/1 tbsp tomato purée (paste).

Potatoes in Red Sauce

This is a lightly spiced dish, perfect for children or those who like mild curries.

Serves 4–6

450g/1lb small new potatoes
7.5ml/1½ tsp coriander
    seeds
7.5ml/1½ tsp cumin seeds
4 garlic cloves
90ml/6 tbsp vegetable oil
45ml/3 tbsp thick tamarind
    juice (see Cook's Tip)
60ml/4 tbsp tomato purée
    (paste)
4 curry leaves
salt
5ml/1 tsp sugar
coriander (cilantro) sprig,
    to garnish

1 Boil the potatoes until they are fully cooked but still retain their shape. To test, insert a thin sharp knife into the potatoes. It should come out clean when the potatoes are fully cooked. Drain well.

2 Grind the coriander seeds with the cumin seeds and garlic to a coarse paste using a mortar and pestle or food processor.

3 Heat the oil in a karahi, wok or frying pan. Fry the paste, tamarind juice, tomato purée, curry leaves, salt and sugar until the oil separates.

4 Add the potatoes and stir to coat them in the spicy tomato mixture. Reduce the heat, cover the pan and simmer for about 5 minutes. Garnish and serve.

Cook's Tip
You can buy tamarind concentrate or break off a piece of tamarind slab equivalent to 15ml/1 tbsp. Soak in 150ml/ ¼ pint/⅔ cup hot water for 10 minutes. Mash the tamarind into a paste and pass it through a sieve (strainer). The fine pulp and juice will go through, leaving behind the fibrous husk. Strain the juice. Tamarind pods have a long shelf life and they require soaking to release their juice.

Energy 119kcal/502kJ; Fat 2.27g; Saturated fat 0.24g; Carbohydrate 22.91g; Fibre 2.88g.

Energy 231kcal/962kJ; Fat 16.8g; Saturated fat 2.1g; Carbohydrate 19.2g; Fibre 1.1g.

Spinach & Potatoes & Red Chillies

India is blessed with over 18 varieties of spinach. If you have access to an Indian or Chinese grocer, look out for some of the more unusual varieties.

Serves 4–6
225g/8oz potatoes
60ml/4 tbsp vegetable oil
2.5cm/1in piece fresh root
   ginger, crushed
4 garlic cloves, crushed
1 onion, chopped
2 fresh green chillies, chopped
2 dried red chillies, chopped
5ml/1 tsp cumin seeds
225g/8oz fresh spinach, trimmed,
   washed and chopped, or
   225g/8oz frozen spinach,
   thawed and drained
salt
2 firm tomatoes, roughly chopped,
   to garnish

1 Wash the potatoes and cut into quarters. If using small new potatoes, leave them whole. Heat the oil in a frying pan and fry the potatoes until brown on all sides. Remove and put aside.

2 Remove the excess oil, leaving about 15ml/1 tbsp in the pan. Fry the ginger, garlic, onion, green chillies, dried red chillies and cumin seeds until the onion is golden brown.

3 Add the potatoes and salt, and stir well. Cover the pan and cook over a medium heat, stirring occasionally, until the potatoes are tender when pierced with a sharp knife.

4 Add the spinach and stir well. Using two wooden spoons or spatulas, toss the mixture over the heat until the spinach is tender and all the excess fluid has evaporated.

5 Spoon into a heated serving dish or on to individual plates and garnish with the chopped tomatoes. Serve hot.

Variation
This recipe also tastes very good if you substitute sweet potatoes for ordinary potatoes. Slice them just before cooking, or they may discolour.

Energy 177kcal/734kJ; Fat 11.8g; Saturated fat 1.4g; Carbohydrate 15g; Fibre 2.9g.

Bombay Potatoes

This authentic dish belongs to the Gujarati, a totally vegetarian sect and the largest population group in the city of Mumbai.

Serves 4–6
2 onions
2 fresh green chillies
50g/2oz/2 cups fresh coriander
   (cilantro)
450g/1lb new potatoes
5ml/1 tsp turmeric
60ml/4 tbsp vegetable oil
2 dried red chillies
6–8 curry leaves
1.5ml/¼ tsp asafoetida
2.5ml/½ tsp each cumin,
   mustard, onion, fennel and
   nigella seeds
lemon juice, to taste
salt

1 Chop the onions and chillies finely, and coarsely chop the coriander.

2 Scrub the potatoes under cold running water and cut them into small pieces.

3 Boil the potatoes in water with a little salt and 2.5ml/½ tsp of the turmeric for 10–15 minutes, or until tender. Drain the potatoes well then mash them and set aside.

4 Heat the oil in a frying pan and fry the dried chillies and curry leaves until the chillies are nearly burnt.

5 Add the sliced onions, green chillies, fresh coriander and remaining turmeric to the pan, add the asafoetida, cumin, mustard, onion, fennel and nigella seeds. Cook, stirring occasionally, until the onions are soft.

6 Fold in the potatoes and add a few drops of water. Cook over a low heat for about 10 minutes, stirring well to ensure the spices are evenly mixed.

7 Add lemon juice to taste, and serve immediately.

Energy 207kcal/865kJ; Fat 11.6g; Saturated fat 1.4g; Carbohydrate 24.3g; Fibre 2.2g.

Fiery Spiced Potatoes

The quantity of red chillies used here may be too fiery for some palates. For a milder version, seed the chillies, use fewer, or substitute them with a roughly chopped sweet red pepper instead.

Serves 4

12–14 baby new potatoes, peeled and halved
15ml/1 tbsp oil
2.5ml/½ tsp crushed dried red chillies
2.5ml/½ tsp cumin seeds
2.5ml/½ tsp fennel seeds
2.5ml/½ tsp crushed coriander seeds
1 medium onion, sliced
3 or 4 fresh red chillies, chopped
15ml/1 tbsp chopped fresh coriander (cilantro)
salt

1 Boil the potatoes in a pan of salted water until just cooked but still firm. Remove from the heat and drain off the water.

2 In a karahi, wok or deep pan, heat the oil quickly over high heat, then turn down the heat to medium. Add the crushed chillies, cumin, fennel and coriander seeds and a little salt and quickly stir-fry for about 30–40 seconds.

3 Add the onion and fry gently until golden brown. Then add the new potatoes, fresh red chillies and fresh coriander.

4 Cover and cook for 5–7 minutes over a very low heat. Serve hot.

Cook's Tip
Baby new potatoes have a wonderful flavour and texture, which are absolutely perfect for this dish. If you want to try older potatoes, choose ones that retain their shape well and cut them into large chunks. Watch them carefully so that they do not overcook and fall apart.

Spiced Potatoes & Carrots Parisienne

Ready-prepared "parisienne" vegetables have recently become available in many supermarkets. These are simply root vegetables that have been peeled and cut into perfectly spherical shapes. This dish looks very fresh and appetizing and is delicious. If you can't locate "parisienne" vegetables, you can simply dice the potatoes and carrots yourself, or cut them into batons.

Serves 4

175g/6oz carrots parisienne
175g/6oz potatoes parisienne
115g/4oz green beans, sliced
75g/3oz/6 tbsp butter
15ml/1 tbsp vegetable oil
1.5ml/¼ tsp onion seeds
1.5ml/¼ tsp fenugreek seeds
4 dried red chillies
2.5ml/½ tsp mustard seeds
6 curry leaves
1 medium onion, sliced
5ml/1 tsp salt
4 garlic cloves, sliced
4 fresh red chillies
15ml/1 tbsp chopped fresh coriander (cilantro)
15ml/1 tbsp chopped fresh mint, plus 1 mint sprig to garnish

1 Drop the carrots, potatoes and green beans into a pan of boiling water, and cook for about 7 minutes, or until they are just tender but not overcooked. Drain in a colander, then refresh under cold water to arrest the cooking process. Drain again and set to one side.

2 Heat the butter and oil in a deep frying pan or a large karahi and add the onion seeds, fenugreek seeds, dried red chillies, mustard seeds and curry leaves. When these have sizzled for a few seconds, add the onion and fry for 3–5 minutes, stirring the mixture occasionally.

3 Add the salt, garlic and fresh chillies, followed by the cooked vegetables, and stir gently for about 5 minutes, over a medium heat.

4 Add the fresh coriander and mint, and serve hot, garnished with a sprig of mint.

Potatoes in Yogurt Sauce

It is nice to use tiny new potatoes with the skins on for this recipe. The yogurt adds a tangy flavour to this fairly spicy dish, which is delicious served with plain or wholemeal chapatis.

Serves 4
small bunch fresh coriander (cilantro)
12 new potatoes, halved

275g/10oz/1¼ cups natural (plain) low-fat yogurt
300ml/½ pint/1¼ cups water
1.5ml/¼ tsp ground turmeric
5ml/1 tsp chilli powder
5ml/1 tsp ground coriander
2.5ml/½ tsp ground cumin
5ml/1 tsp soft brown sugar
1.5ml/¼ tsp salt
15ml/1 tbsp oil
5ml/1 tsp cumin seeds
2 green chillies, sliced

1 Cut off the roots and any thick stalks from the coriander and chop the leaves finely. Set aside.

2 Boil the potatoes in salted water with their skins on until they are just tender, then drain and set aside.

3 Mix together the yogurt, water, turmeric, chilli powder, ground coriander, ground cumin, sugar and salt in a bowl. Set aside.

4 Heat the oil in a medium, heavy pan and stir in the cumin seeds. Fry for 1 minute.

5 Reduce the heat, stir in the spicy yogurt mixture and cook for about 3 minutes over medium heat.

6 Add the chopped fresh coriander, green chillies and cooked potatoes. Blend everything together and cook for a further 5–7 minutes, stirring from time to time. Serve hot.

Cook's Tip
If new potatoes are unavailable, use 450g/1lb ordinary waxy potatoes instead. Peel them and cut into large chunks, then cook as described above.

Masala Mashed Potatoes

This delightfully simple variation on the popular Western side dish can be used as an accompaniment to just about any main course dish, not just Indian food. There are easily obtainable alternatives to mango powder if you cannot get hold of any (see Cook's Tip).

Serves 4
3 medium potatoes
15ml/1 tbsp chopped fresh mint and coriander (cilantro), mixed
5ml/1 tsp mango powder (amchur)

5ml/1 tsp salt
5ml/1 tsp crushed black peppercorns
1 fresh red chilli, chopped
1 fresh green chilli, chopped
50g/2oz/¼ cup butter

1 Boil the potatoes until soft and then mash them down using a masher or potato ricer.

2 Stir the remaining ingredients together in a small bowl.

3 Stir the spice mixture into the mashed potatoes. Mix together thoroughly with a fork and serve warm as an accompaniment.

Cook's Tip
Mango powder, also known as amchur, is the unripe green fruit of the mango tree ground to a powder. The sour mangoes are sliced and dried in the sun, turning a light brown, before they are ground. Mango powder adds a fruity sharpness and a slightly resinous bouquet to a dish. It is widely used with vegetables and is usually added towards the end of the cooking time. If mango powder is unavailable, the nearest substitute is lemon or lime juice, in double or treble quantity.

Energy 100kcal/416kJ; Fat 5.3g; Saturated fat 1.25g; Carbohydrate 11.4g; Fibre 0.8g.

Energy 169kcal/712kJ; Fat 4.3g; Saturated fat 0.78g; Carbohydrate 27.6g; Fibre 1.2g.

Potatoes in Chilli Tamarind Sauce

In this favourite potato dish from the state of Karnataka, the combination of chilli and tamarind awakens the taste buds immediately. This version adapts the traditional recipe slightly, to reduce the customary pungency and enhance the fiery appearance of this delicious combination.

Serves 4–6
450g/1lb small new potatoes, washed and dried
25g/1oz whole dried red chillies, preferably Kashmiri
7.5ml/1 1/2 tsp cumin seeds
4 garlic cloves, chopped
90ml/6 tbsp vegetable oil
60ml/4 tbsp thick tamarind juice
30ml/2 tbsp tomato purée (paste)
4 curry leaves
5ml/1 tsp sugar
1.5ml/1/4 tsp asafoetida
salt
coriander (cilantro) sprigs and lemon wedges, to garnish

1 Boil the new potatoes until they are fully cooked, ensuring they do not break. To test, insert a thin sharp knife into the potatoes. It should come out clean when they are fully cooked. Drain and cool the potatoes in iced water to prevent them from cooking further.

2 Soak the chillies for 5 minutes in warm water. Drain and grind with the cumin seeds and garlic to a coarse paste, either using a mortar and pestle or in a food processor.

3 Heat the oil and fry the paste, tamarind juice, tomato purée, curry leaves, sugar, asafoetida and salt until the oil can be seen to have separated from the spice paste.

4 Add the potatoes and stir to coat. Reduce the heat, cover and simmer for 5 minutes. Garnish and serve.

> **Variation**
> Chunks of large potatoes can be used as an alternative to new potatoes. Alternatively, try this dish with sweet potatoes. The spicy sweet-and-sour taste works very well in this variation.

Energy 227kcal/945kJ; Fat 16.8g; Saturated fat 2.1g; Carbohydrate 18.1g; Fibre 1.1g.

Potatoes with Roasted Poppy Seeds

Poppy seeds are used in Indian cooking as thickening agents, and to lend a nutty taste to sauces.

Serves 4
45ml/3 tbsp white poppy seeds
45–60ml/3–4 tbsp vegetable oil
675g/1 1/2lb potatoes, peeled and cut into 1cm/1/2in cubes
2.5ml/1/2 tsp black mustard seeds
2.5ml/1/2 tsp onion seeds
2.5ml/1/2 tsp cumin seeds
2.5ml/1/2 tsp fennel seeds
1 or 2 dried red chillies, chopped or broken into small pieces
2.5ml/1/2 tsp ground turmeric
2.5ml/1/2 tsp salt
150ml/1/4 pint/2/3 cup warm water
fresh coriander (cilantro) sprigs, to garnish
pooris and natural (plain) yogurt, to serve

1 Preheat a karahi, wok or large pan over a medium setting. When the pan is hot, reduce the heat slightly and add the poppy seeds. Stir them around in the pan until they are just a shade darker. Remove from the pan and leave to cool.

2 In the pan, heat the vegetable oil over a medium heat and fry the cubes of potato until they are light brown. Remove them with a slotted spoon and drain on kitchen paper.

3 To the same oil, add the mustard seeds. As soon as they begin to pop, add the onion, cumin and fennel seeds and the chillies. Let the chillies blacken, but remove them from the pan before they burn.

4 Stir in the turmeric and follow quickly with the fried potatoes and salt. Stir well and add the warm water. Cover the pan with the lid and reduce the heat to low. Cook for 8–10 minutes, or until the potatoes are tender.

5 Grind the cooled poppy seeds in a mortar and pestle or spice grinder. Stir the ground seeds into the potatoes. It should form a thick paste which should cling to the potatoes. If there is too much liquid, continue to stir over a medium heat until you have the right consistency. Transfer to a serving dish. Garnish with coriander and serve with pooris and natural yogurt.

Energy 201kcal/842kJ; Fat 13.5g; Saturated fat 1.6g; Carbohydrate 29g; Fibre 2.2g.

Spiced Coconut Mushrooms

Here is a simple and delicious way to cook mushrooms. They can be served with almost any Indian meal as well as with traditional Western grilled or roasted meats and poultry.

Serves 4

30ml/2 tbsp groundnut (peanut) oil
2 garlic cloves, finely chopped
2 fresh red chillies, seeded and sliced into rings
3 shallots, finely chopped
225g/8oz/3 cups brown cap (cremini) mushrooms, thickly sliced
150ml/¼ pint/⅔ cup coconut milk
30ml/2 tbsp chopped fresh coriander (cilantro)
salt and ground black pepper

1 Heat a karahi, wok or shallow pan until hot, add the oil and swirl it around. Add the garlic and chillies, then stir-fry for a few seconds.

2 Add the shallots and stir-fry them for 2–3 minutes until softened. Add the mushrooms and stir-fry for 3 minutes.

3 Pour in the coconut milk and bring to the boil. Boil rapidly over a high heat until the liquid has reduced by about half and coats the mushrooms. Season to taste with salt and pepper.

4 Sprinkle over the chopped coriander and toss the mushrooms gently to mix. Serve immediately.

Variations
• Use chopped fresh chives instead of chopped fresh coriander (cilantro), if you wish.
• White (button) mushrooms or field (portabello) mushrooms would also work well instead of brown cap (cremini) mushrooms.
• Sprinkle some chopped toasted cashew nuts over the mushrooms before serving, if you like.

Spinach with Mushrooms

A tasty vegetable that is often overlooked, spinach is highly nutritious. Cooked in this way it tastes wonderful. Serve with chapatis.

Serves 4

450g/1lb fresh or frozen spinach, thawed
30ml/2 tbsp oil
2 medium onions, diced
6–8 curry leaves
1.5ml/¼ tsp onion seeds
5ml/1 tsp crushed garlic
5ml/1 tsp grated fresh root ginger
5ml/1 tsp chilli powder
5ml/1 tsp salt
7.5ml/1½ tsp ground coriander
1 large red (bell) pepper, seeded and sliced
115g/4oz/1½ cups mushrooms, roughly chopped
225g/8oz/1 cup low-fat fromage frais or ricotta cheese
30ml/2 tbsp fresh coriander (cilantro) leaves

1 If using fresh spinach, blanch it briefly in boiling water and drain thoroughly. If using frozen spinach, drain well. Set aside.

2 Heat the oil in a karahi, wok or heavy pan and fry the onions with the curry leaves and the onion seeds for 1–2 minutes. Add the garlic, ginger, chilli powder, salt and ground coriander. Stir-fry for a further 2–3 minutes.

3 Add half the red pepper slices and all the mushrooms and continue to stir-fry for 2–3 minutes.

4 Add the spinach and stir-fry for 4–6 minutes, then add the fromage frais or ricotta and half the fresh coriander, followed by the remaining red pepper slices. Stir-fry for a further 2–3 minutes before serving, garnished with the remaining coriander.

Cook's Tip
Whether you use fresh or frozen spinach, make sure it is well drained, otherwise the stir-fried mixture will be too wet when you add the fromage frais or ricotta. Tip the spinach into a colander, and press it against the sides of the colander with a wooden spoon to extract as much liquid as possible.

Energy 67kcal/280kJ; Fat 5.9g; Saturated fat 1.2g; Carbohydrate 2.4g; Fibre 0.8g.

Energy 188kcal/778kJ; Fat 11.57g; Saturated fat 5.99g; Carbohydrate 14.71g; Fibre 4.68g.

Courgettes with Mushrooms in a Yogurt Sauce

The slightly tart flavour of yogurt makes a creamy sauce which is delicious with cooked mushrooms and courgettes.

Serves 4

15ml/1 tbsp oil
1 medium onion, roughly chopped
5ml/1 tsp ground coriander
5ml/1 tsp ground cumin
5ml/1 tsp salt
2.5ml/½ tsp chilli powder

225g/8oz/3 cups mushrooms, sliced
2 courgettes (zucchini), sliced
45ml/3 tbsp natural (plain) low-fat yogurt
15ml/1 tbsp chopped fresh coriander (cilantro)

1 Heat the oil in a heavy pan and fry the onion until golden brown. Lower the heat to medium, add the ground coriander, cumin, salt and chilli powder and stir together well.

2 Once the onion and the spices are well blended, add the mushrooms and courgettes, and stir-fry gently for about 5 minutes until soft. If the mixture is too dry, add just a little water to loosen.

3 Finally, add the yogurt and mix it well into the vegetables.

4 Sprinkle with chopped fresh coriander and serve immediately.

> **Cook's Tip**
> *Yogurt has a great affinity with stir-fried vegetables and this lovely combination of sliced courgettes (zucchini) and mushrooms would make a tasty accompaniment to serve with poultry or lamb dishes. If you prefer, you could use aubergines (eggplants) or mushrooms instead.*

Stuffed Okra

A delicious accompaniment to any dish, this can also be served on a bed of strained yogurt which gives an excellent contrast in flavour.

Serves 4–6

225g/8oz large okra
15ml/1 tbsp mango powder (amchur)

2.5ml/½ tsp ground ginger
2.5ml/½ tsp ground cumin
2.5ml/½ tsp chilli powder (optional)
2.5ml/½ tsp turmeric
a few drops of vegetable oil
30ml/2 tbsp cornflour (cornstarch), placed in a plastic bag
vegetable oil, for frying
salt

1 Wash the okra and dry on kitchen paper. Carefully trim off the tops without making a hole. Using a sharp knife, make a slit lengthways in the centre of each okra but do not cut all the way through.

2 In a bowl, mix the mango powder, ginger, cumin, chilli if using, turmeric and salt with a few drops of oil. Leave the mixture to rest for 1–2 hours.

3 Using your fingers, part the slit of each okra carefully and fill each with as much of the spice filling as possible.

4 Put all the okra into the plastic bag with the cornflour and shake the bag carefully to coat the okra evenly.

5 Fill a frying pan with enough oil to sit 2.5cm/1in deep, heat it and fry the okra in small batches for about 5–8 minutes, or until they are brown and slightly crisp. Serve hot.

> **Cook's Tip / Variation**
> *Dusting the okra in cornflour before frying helps to ensure that none of the sticky liquid escapes and keeps the pods perfectly crisp.*

Energy 64kcal/265kJ; Fat 3.70g; Saturated fat 0.58g; Carbohydrate 4.80g; Fibre 1.40g.

Energy 176kcal/734kJ; Fat 12.4g; Saturated fat 1.6g; Carbohydrate 15.5g; Fibre 2.3g.

Masala Okra

Okra, or "lady's fingers", are a very popular Indian vegetable. Here the pods are stir-fried with a dry masala mixture to make a tasty side dish.

Serves 4

450g/1lb okra
2.5ml/½ tsp ground turmeric
5ml/1 tsp chilli powder
15ml/1 tbsp ground cumin
15ml/1 tbsp ground coriander
1.5ml/¼ tsp salt
1.5ml/¼ tsp sugar
15ml/1 tbsp lemon juice
30ml/2 tbsp chopped fresh
  coriander (cilantro)
15ml/1 tbsp oil
2.5ml/½ tsp cumin seeds
2.5ml/½ tsp black mustard
  seeds
chopped fresh tomatoes,
  to garnish
poppadums, to serve

1 Wash, dry and trim the stalks away from the top of the okra, being careful not to pierce the pod itself, otherwise the sticky juices will be released and will affect the final dish. Set the okra aside. In a bowl, mix together the turmeric, chilli powder, cumin, ground coriander, salt, sugar, lemon juice and fresh coriander.

2 Heat the oil in a large, heavy pan. Add the cumin seeds and mustard seeds, and fry for about 2 minutes or until they start to splutter.

3 Scrape in the spice mixture and continue to fry for 2 minutes.

4 Add the okra, cover and cook over a low heat for 10 minutes, or until tender. Garnish with chopped fresh tomatoes and serve with poppadums.

> **Cook's Tip**
> *When buying okra, choose firm, brightly coloured pods that are less than 10cm/4in long; larger ones can be stringy.*

Okra in Yogurt

This tangy vegetable dish can be served as an accompaniment, but it also makes an excellent vegetarian meal if served with tarka dhal and warm, freshly made chapatis.

Serves 4

450g/1lb okra
15ml/1 tbsp oil
2.5ml/½ tsp onion seeds
3 medium fresh green
  chillies, chopped
1 medium onion, sliced
1.5ml/¼ tsp ground
  turmeric
2.5ml/½ tsp salt
15ml/1 tbsp natural (plain)
  low-fat yogurt
2 medium tomatoes, sliced
15ml/1 tbsp chopped fresh
  coriander (cilantro)
chapatis, to serve

1 Wash and trim the okra, cut into 1cm/½in pieces and place in a bowl. Set aside.

2 Heat the oil in a medium, heavy pan, add the onion seeds, green chillies and onion, and fry for about 5 minutes until the onion has turned golden brown.

3 Reduce the heat. Add the ground turmeric and salt to the onions and fry for about 1 minute.

4 Next, add the prepared okra, turn the heat to medium-high and quickly stir-fry the okra until they are lightly golden.

5 Stir in the yogurt, tomatoes and, finally, the coriander. Cook for a further 2 minutes.

6 Transfer the okra to a serving dish and serve immediately with freshly made chapatis.

> **Cook's Tip**
> *It is always wise to wear plastic or rubber gloves when preparing chillies as they contain a strong irritant that will sting open cuts or eyes if it comes into contact with them.*

Energy 82kcal/342kJ; Fat 4.2g; Saturated fat 0.41g; Carbohydrate 7.6g; Fibre 5.3g.

Energy 102kcal/424kJ; Fat 5.4g; Saturated fat 0.4g; Carbohydrate 8.6g; Fibre 4.7g.

Green Beans with Corn

Frozen green beans are useful for this dish, as they are quick to cook. It makes an excellent vegetable accompaniment.

Serves 4

15ml/1 tbsp oil
1.5ml/¼ tsp mustard seeds
1 medium red onion, diced
50g/2oz/⅓ cup frozen corn
50g/2oz/¼ cup canned red
   kidney beans, drained
175g/6oz frozen green beans
1 fresh red chilli, seeded
   and diced
1 garlic clove, chopped

2.5cm/1in piece fresh root ginger,
   finely chopped
15ml/1 tbsp chopped fresh
   coriander (cilantro)
5ml/1 tsp salt
1 medium tomato, seeded and
   diced, to garnish

1 Heat the oil in a karahi, wok or heavy pan for about 30 seconds, then add the mustard seeds and onion. Stir-fry for 2–3 minutes.

2 Add the corn, red kidney beans and green beans. Stir-fry for 3–5 minutes.

3 Add the red chilli, chopped garlic and ginger, coriander and salt, and stir-fry for 2–3 minutes.

4 Remove the pan from the heat. Transfer the vegetables to a serving dish and garnish with the diced tomato.

Cook's Tip

This is a good stand-by dish as it uses frozen and canned ingredients. To make sure you have always got a chilli available for making this dish, or others like it, you can freeze whole fresh chillies, washed but not blanched.

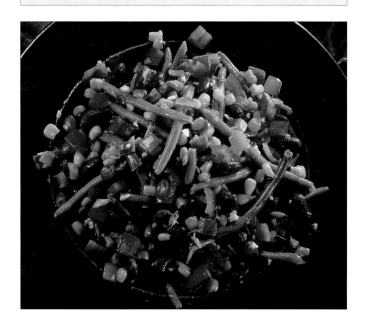

Vegetables & Beans with Curry Leaves

Bright, shiny green curry leaves look like small bay leaves, although they are not as tough. A popular seasoning ingredient in Indian cooking, curry leaves add a spicy flavour to dishes such as this dry vegetable and bean curry.

Serves 4

3 fresh green chillies
1 medium carrot
50g/2oz green beans
1 medium red (bell) pepper

15ml/1 tbsp oil
6 curry leaves
3 garlic cloves, sliced
3 dried red chillies
1.5ml/¼ tsp onion seeds
1.5ml/¼ tsp fenugreek
   seeds
115g/4oz/½ cup drained
   canned red kidney beans
5ml/1 tsp salt
30ml/2 tbsp lemon juice

1 Cut the chillies in half lengthways. Remove the membranes and seeds and chop the flesh.

2 Cut the carrot into strips and slice the green beans diagonally. Remove the seeds and stalk from the pepper and cut the flesh into strips.

3 Heat the oil in a karahi, wok or deep heavy pan. Add the curry leaves, sliced garlic cloves, dried chillies, and onion and fenugreek seeds.

4 When these ingredients turn a shade darker, add the chillies, kidney beans, carrot strips, green beans and pepper strips, stirring constantly.

5 Stir in the salt and the lemon juice. Lower the heat, cover and cook for about 5 minutes.

6 Transfer the hot curry to a serving dish and serve immediately.

Energy 84kcal/349kJ; Fat 3.44g; Saturated fat 0.5g; Carbohydrate 11.13g; Fibre 2.7g.

Energy 79kcal/331kJ; Fat 3.3g; Saturated fat 0.37g; Carbohydrate 9.7g; Fibre 2.6g.

Kidney Bean Curry

This is a popular Punjabi-style dish using red kidney beans. You can replace the dried beans with a 400g/14oz can if you prefer. Other pulses also work well in this dish.

Serves 4

225g/8oz/scant 1 cup dried
  red kidney beans
30ml/2 tbsp oil
2.5ml/½ tsp cumin seeds
1 onion, thinly sliced
1 fresh green chilli, finely chopped

2 garlic cloves, crushed
2.5cm/1in piece fresh root
  ginger, grated
30ml/2 tbsp curry paste
5ml/1 tsp ground cumin
5ml/1 tsp ground coriander
2.5ml/½ tsp chilli powder
2.5ml/½ tsp salt
400g/14oz can chopped
  tomatoes
30ml/2 tbsp chopped fresh
  coriander (cilantro)

1 Leave the kidney beans to soak overnight in a bowl of cold water.

2 Drain the beans and put in a large pan with double the volume of water. Boil vigorously for 10 minutes. Skim off any scum. Cover and cook for 1–1½ hours or until the beans are soft. If you want to reduce the cooking time, cook the beans in a pressure cooker for 20–25 minutes. Alternatively, replace the dried beans with canned beans. Use a 400g/14oz can and drain it very thoroughly.

3 Meanwhile, heat the oil in a large, heavy frying pan and fry the cumin seeds for 2 minutes until they begin to splutter. Add the onion, chilli, garlic and ginger, and fry for 5 minutes. Stir in the curry paste, cumin, ground coriander, chilli powder and salt, and cook for 5 minutes.

4 Add the tomatoes and simmer for 5 minutes. Drain the beans and stir them in with the fresh coriander, reserving a little of the herb for the garnish. Cover and cook for 15 minutes, adding a little water if necessary. Serve garnished with the reserved fresh coriander.

Mung Beans with Potatoes

Small mung beans are one of the quicker-cooking pulses. They do not require soaking and are easy and convenient to use. In this recipe they are cooked with potatoes and Indian spices to give a tasty and nutritious dish.

Serves 4

175g/6oz/1 cup mung beans
750ml/1¼ pints/3 cups water
225g/8oz potatoes, cut into
  2cm/¾in chunks
30ml/2 tbsp oil
2.5ml/½ tsp cumin seeds

1 fresh green chilli, finely
  chopped
1 garlic clove, crushed
2.5cm/1in piece fresh root
  ginger, finely chopped
1.5ml/¼ tsp ground turmeric
2.5ml/½ tsp chilli powder
5ml/1 tsp salt
5ml/1 tsp sugar
4 curry leaves
5 tomatoes, peeled and finely
  chopped
15ml/1 tbsp tomato purée
  (paste)
curry leaves, to garnish
plain rice, to serve

1 Wash the beans. Pour the water into a pan, add the beans and bring to the boil. Boil hard for 15 minutes, then reduce the heat, cover the pan and simmer until soft, about 30 minutes cooking time. Drain.

2 In a separate pan, par-boil the potatoes in boiling water for 10 minutes, then drain well.

3 Heat the oil in a heavy pan and fry the cumin seeds until they splutter. Add the chilli, garlic and ginger, and fry for 3–4 minutes.

4 Add the turmeric, chilli powder, salt and sugar, and cook for 2 minutes, stirring to prevent the mixture from sticking to the pan.

5 Add the 4 curry leaves, chopped tomatoes and tomato purée, and simmer for about 5 minutes until the sauce thickens. Mix the tomato sauce and the potatoes with the mung beans and heat through. Garnish with the extra curry leaves and serve with plain boiled rice.

Energy 258kcal/1087kJ; Fat 7.8g; Saturated fat 0.86g; Carbohydrate 33.7g; Fibre 11.7g.

Energy 254kcal/1070kJ; Fat 6.8g; Saturated fat 0.89g; Carbohydrate 36.9g; Fibre 6.3g.

Yogurt Salad

If this salad looks and tastes familiar, it isn't surprising. It is very similar to coleslaw, except that yogurt is used instead of mayonnaise, and cashew nuts are added.

Serves 4
115g/4oz cabbage
350ml/12fl oz/1½ cups natural (plain) low-fat yogurt
10ml/2 tsp clear honey
2 medium carrots, thickly sliced
2 spring onions (scallions), roughly chopped
50g/2oz/⅓ cup sultanas (golden raisins)
50g/2oz/½ cup cashew nuts (optional)
16 white grapes, halved
2.5ml/½ tsp salt
5ml/1 tsp chopped fresh mint

1 Use a mandolin, if you have one, to shred the cabbage finely. Alternatively, use a sharp knife to slice through the layers of the cabbage.

2 Using a fork, beat the yogurt in a bowl with the honey.

3 In a separate bowl, which will be suitable for serving the salad, mix together the carrots, spring onions, cabbage, sultanas, cashew nuts (if you are using them), grapes, salt and the chopped fresh mint.

4 Pour the sweetened yogurt mixture over the salad, mix well and serve.

Variation
For Squash and Yogurt Salad, mix together 2.5ml/½ tsp dry mustard, 2.5ml/½ tsp ground cumin, 2.5ml/½ tsp salt, 5ml/ 1 tsp grated fresh root ginger and 150ml/¼ pint/⅔ cup natural yogurt. Chop half a green (bell) pepper and add to the spicy yogurt. Peel 250g/9oz butternut squash, then slice it and boil or steam until tender. Add to the yogurt mixture and stir well.

Energy 119kcal/503kJ; Fat 0.9g; Saturated fat 0.49g; Carbohydrate 23.4g; Fibre 1.8g.

Nutty Salad

The smooth creamy dressing is perfect with the crunchy nuts.

Serves 4
150g/5oz can red kidney beans
1 medium onion, cut into 12 rings
1 medium green courgette (zucchini), sliced
1 medium yellow courgette (zucchini), sliced
50g/2oz/⅔ cup pasta shells, cooked
50g/2oz/½ cup cashew nuts
25g/1oz/¼ cup peanuts
fresh coriander (cilantro) and lime wedges, to garnish

For the dressing
115g/4oz/½ cup low-fat fromage frais or ricotta cheese
30ml/2 tbsp natural (plain) low-fat yogurt
1 fresh green chilli, chopped
15ml/1 tbsp chopped fresh coriander (cilantro)
salt and ground black pepper
2.5ml/½ tsp crushed dried red chillies
15ml/1 tbsp lemon juice

1 Drain the kidney beans. Arrange them with the onion rings, courgette slices and pasta in a salad dish and sprinkle the cashew nuts and peanuts over the top.

2 In a separate bowl, mix together the fromage frais or ricotta cheese, yogurt, green chilli, fresh coriander and salt and pepper to taste. Beat well using a fork until all the ingredients are thoroughly combined. You may find it easier to add the coriander leaves a few at a time and mix in, to allow their flavour to permeate the mixture and ensure the resulting dressing is smooth in texture.

3 Sprinkle the crushed red chillies and lemon juice over the dressing. Garnish the salad with fresh coriander and lime wedges, and serve with the dressing.

Cook's Tip
Make the dressing just before serving the salad, so that the flavour of the coriander will be at its most intense.

Energy 199kcal/829kJ; Fat 11.6g; Saturated fat 2.63g; Carbohydrate 15.2g; Fibre 2.9g.

Spinach & Mushroom Salad

This salad is especially good served with glazed garlic prawns or any other seafood curry.

Serves 4
10 baby corn cobs
115g/4oz/3 cups mushrooms
2 medium tomatoes
20 small spinach leaves
8–10 onion rings

salt and ground black pepper
fresh coriander (cilantro) sprigs and lime slices, to garnish (optional)

1 Halve the baby corn cobs and slice the mushrooms and tomatoes.

2 Arrange all the salad ingredients in a large serving bowl. Season with salt and pepper and garnish with fresh coriander and lime slices, if you like.

Tofu & Cucumber Salad

This is a nutritious and refreshing salad with a hot, sweet-and-sour dressing. It is ideal for a buffet.

Serves 4–6
1 small cucumber
oil, for frying
1 square fresh or 115g/4oz long-life tofu
115g/4oz beansprouts, trimmed and rinsed
salt

For the dressing
1 small onion, grated
2 garlic cloves, crushed
2.5ml/½ tsp chilli powder
30–45ml/2–3 tbsp dark soy sauce
15–30ml/1–2 tbsp rice wine vinegar
10ml/2 tsp dark brown sugar
salt
celery leaves, to garnish

1 Trim the ends from the cucumber and then cut it into neat cubes.

2 Sprinkle the trimmed cucumber with salt and set aside while you prepare the remaining ingredients.

3 Heat a little oil in a pan and fry the tofu on both sides until golden brown. Drain well on absorbent kitchen paper and cut into cubes.

4 Prepare the dressing by blending together the onion, garlic and chilli powder. Stir in the soy sauce, vinegar, sugar and salt to taste. You can do this in a screw-topped glass jar.

5 Just before serving, rinse the cucumber under cold running water. Drain and dry thoroughly.

6 Toss the cucumber, tofu and beansprouts together in a serving bowl and pour over the dressing. Garnish with the celery leaves and serve immediately.

Baby Vegetable Salad with a Chilli Dressing

Warm salads make a pleasant change, and the flavours of the dressing are enhanced. Take the opportunity in spring to use the new season's baby vegetables for this mouthwatering combination, which makes an excellent accompaniment to spicy meals or to grilled meat or fish.

Serves 6
10 baby potatoes, halved
15 baby carrots

10 baby courgettes (zucchini)
115g/4oz/1½ cups button (white) mushrooms

For the dressing
45ml/3 tbsp lemon juice
25ml/1½ tbsp oil
15ml/1 tbsp chopped fresh coriander (cilantro)
5ml/1 tsp salt
2 fresh green chillies, finely sliced

1 Boil the potatoes, carrots and courgettes in water until tender. Drain them and place in a serving dish with the mushrooms.

2 Make the dressing in a separate bowl. Mix together the lemon juice, oil, fresh coriander, salt and chillies.

3 Toss the vegetables thoroughly in the chilli dressing and transfer to a serving bowl.

Variation
For a mild version of this dish replace the green chillies with finely chopped green (bell) pepper.

Cook's Tip
As well as looking extremely attractive, the tiny baby vegetables give this salad a lovely flavour. Other baby vegetables, such as leeks, baby corn or cauliflower florets, can be used just as well.

Top: Energy 25kcal/103kJ; Fat 0.6g; Saturated fat 0.09g; Carbohydrate 2.8g; Fibre 1.8g.
Above: Energy 65kcal/269kJ; Fat 4.6g; Saturated fat 0.6g; Carbohydrate 3.7g; Fibre 0.5g.

Energy 73kcal/308kJ; Fat 3.1g; Saturated fat 0.39g; Carbohydrate 10.1g; Fibre 1.5g.

Mango, Tomato & Red Onion Salad

This salad makes a delicious appetizer. The under-ripe mango blends well with the tomato.

Serves 4

1 firm under-ripe mango
2 large tomatoes or 1 beefsteak
   tomato, sliced
½ red onion, sliced into
   rings
½ cucumber, peeled and thinly
   sliced
chopped chives, to garnish

For the dressing

30ml/2 tbsp vegetable oil
15ml/1 tbsp lemon juice
1 garlic clove, crushed
2.5ml/½ tsp hot pepper sauce
salt and ground black pepper

1 Using a sharp knife or peeler, remove the skin from the mango, then cut and slice the flesh into bite-size pieces.

2 Arrange the mango, tomatoes, onion and cucumber on a large serving plate.

3 Make the dressing. Blend the oil, lemon juice, garlic, pepper sauce and seasoning in a blender or food processor, or shake vigorously in a small screw-top jar.

4 Spoon the dressing over the salad. Garnish with the chopped chives and serve.

> **Cook's Tip**
> *When cutting a mango, first peel the skin off with a sharp knife or peeler. Next, cut the fleshy cheeks from each side. Trim carefully around the fruit, following the curvature of the stone (pit), to remove all the flesh. You will end up with the stone, two cheeks and two thinner strips of fruit, which can then be sliced.*

Peppery Bean Salad

This pretty salad uses canned beans for speed and convenience.

Serves 4–6

425g/15oz can red kidney beans
425g/15oz can black-eyed beans
   (peas)
425g/15oz can chickpeas
¼ red (bell) pepper
¼ green (bell) pepper
6 radishes
15ml/1 tbsp chopped spring onion
   (scallion), plus extra to garnish

For the dressing

5ml/1 tsp ground cumin
15ml/1 tbsp tomato ketchup
30ml/2 tbsp olive oil
15ml/1 tbsp white wine
   vinegar
1 garlic clove, crushed
2.5ml/½ tsp hot pepper
   sauce

1 Drain the red kidney beans, black-eyed beans and chickpeas, and rinse under cold running water. Shake off the excess water and tip them into a large bowl.

2 Core, seed and chop the red and green peppers. Trim the radishes and slice thinly. Add the peppers, radishes and spring onion to the bowl.

3 To make the dressing, mix together the cumin, tomato ketchup, oil, white wine vinegar and crushed garlic in a small bowl. Add a little salt and hot pepper sauce to taste, and stir again thoroughly to combine.

4 Pour the dressing over the salad and mix. Cover the salad and chill for at least 1 hour before serving, garnished with the sliced spring onion.

> **Cook's Tip**
> *Look out for cans of mixed beans at the supermarket. These contain a colourful medley and would be perfect for this salad.*

Energy 89kcal/370kJ; Fat 5.8g; Saturated fat 0.7g; Carbohydrate 8.6g; Fibre 1.9g.

Energy 430kcal/1814kJ; Fat 9.3g; Saturated fat 1.3g; Carbohydrate 64.8g; Fibre 19.8g.

Spicy Potato Salad

This tasty salad is quick to prepare, and makes a satisfying accompaniment to grilled or barbecued meat or fish.

Serves 6
900g/2lb potatoes
2 red (bell) peppers
2 celery sticks
1 shallot
2 or 3 spring onions (scallions)
1 fresh green chilli
1 garlic clove, crushed

10ml/2 tsp finely chopped
    fresh chives
10ml/2 tsp finely chopped
    fresh basil
15ml/1 tbsp finely chopped
    fresh parsley
30ml/2 tbsp single (light) cream
45ml/3 tbsp mayonnaise
5ml/1 tsp prepared mild mustard
7.5ml/1½ tsp sugar
salt
chopped fresh chives, to garnish

1 Peel the potatoes. Boil in salted water for 10–12 minutes, until tender. Drain and cool, then cut into cubes and place in a large mixing bowl.

2 Halve the peppers, cut away and discard the core and seeds and cut the flesh into small pieces. Finely chop the celery, shallot and spring onions and slice the chilli very thinly, discarding the seeds. Add the vegetables to the potatoes together with the garlic and herbs.

3 Mix the cream, mayonnaise, mustard and sugar in a small bowl, stirring until the mixture is well combined.

4 Pour the dressing over the salad and stir gently to coat evenly. Serve, garnished with the chopped chives.

> **Cook's Tip**
> New potatoes would also work deliciously well in this recipe. Scrub them lightly to remove any earth and, unless they are very small, halve them. Cook them until just tender; test them with a knife.

Sweet Potato & Carrot Salad

This warm salad has a piquant flavour. As a main course, it will serve two.

Serves 4
1 medium sweet potato
2 carrots, cut into thick
    diagonal slices
3 medium tomatoes
8–10 iceberg lettuce leaves
75g/3oz/½ cup drained canned
    chickpeas

For the dressing
15ml/1 tbsp clear honey
90ml/6 tbsp natural (plain)
    low-fat yogurt
2.5ml/½ tsp salt
5ml/1 tsp coarsely ground
    black pepper

For the garnish
15ml/1 tbsp walnuts
15ml/1 tbsp sultanas
    (golden raisins)
1 small onion, cut into rings

1 Peel and dice the sweet potato. Cook in boiling water until soft but not mushy, remove from the heat, cover the pan and set aside.

2 Cook the carrots in a pan of boiling water for just a few minutes, making sure that they remain crunchy. Add the carrots to the sweet potatoes.

3 Drain the water from the sweet potatoes and carrots and mix them together in a bowl.

4 Slice the tops off the tomatoes, then scoop out and discard the seeds. Roughly chop the flesh.

5 Line a glass bowl with the lettuce leaves. Add the carrots, chickpeas and tomatoes to the potatoes and carrots. Mix lightly, then spoon the mixture into the lettuce-lined bowl.

6 Put all the dressing ingredients in a screw-top jar and shake well to combine, or put in a bowl and beat using a fork.

7 Garnish the salad with the walnuts, sultanas and onion rings. Pour the dressing over the salad or serve it in a separate bowl.

Energy 127kcal/532kJ; Fat 3.7g; Saturated fat 0.47g; Carbohydrate 20.6g; Fibre 3.1g.

Energy 185kcal/777kJ; Fat 6.7g; Saturated fat 1.3g; Carbohydrate 29.3g; Fibre 2.6g.

Grape & Walnut Raita

Refreshing raitas are served to cool the effect of hot curries. Cucumber and mint raita is the best known combination. Here is a refreshing fruit and nut version, which is particularly good with beef curries.

2 firm bananas
5ml/1 tsp sugar
salt
5ml/1 tsp freshly ground
  cumin seeds
1.5ml/¼ tsp freshly roasted
  cumin seeds, chilli powder
  or paprika, to garnish

Serves 4
350ml/12fl oz/1½ cups
  natural (plain) yogurt
75g/3oz seedless grapes
50g/2oz/½ cup shelled
  walnuts

1 Place the yogurt in a chilled bowl and add the grapes and walnuts.

2 Slice the bananas directly into the bowl and fold in gently before they turn brown.

3 Add the sugar, salt and ground cumin, and gently mix together.

4 Chill, and just before serving, sprinkle on the cumin seeds, chilli powder or paprika.

Variations
• Instead of grapes, try kiwi fruit, peaches or nectarines.
• Almonds or hazelnuts can be used instead of or as well as the walnuts.
• For Coconut and Raisin Raita, coarsely grate half a fresh coconut by hand or using a food processor. Mix in a bowl with 225g/8oz natural (plain) yogurt and 2.5ml/½ tsp sugar. Stir in 25g/1oz chopped fresh coriander (cilantro) or mint, and add salt to taste. Transfer to a serving bowl.

Spiced Yogurt

Yogurt is always a welcome accompaniment to hot curries. Here, it is topped with a hot spice mixture to provide a contrast in both taste and temperature.

**Makes 450ml/¾ pint/
scant 2 cups**
450ml/¾ pint/scant 2 cups
  natural (plain) yogurt

2.5ml/½ tsp freshly ground
  fennel seeds
salt
2.5ml/½ tsp sugar
60ml/4 tbsp vegetable oil
1 dried red chilli
1.5ml/¼ tsp mustard seeds
1.5ml/¼ tsp cumin seeds
4–6 curry leaves
a pinch each of asafoetida and
  ground turmeric

1 In a heatproof serving dish, mix together the yogurt, fennel seeds, salt and sugar. Cover and chill until you are nearly ready to serve.

2 Heat the oil in a frying pan and fry the dried chilli, mustard and cumin seeds, curry leaves, asafoetida and turmeric.

3 When the chilli turns dark, pour the oil and spices over the yogurt. Fold the yogurt together with the spices at the table just before serving.

Variation
Asafoetida is quite bitter. Leave it out if you prefer.

Cook's Tip
You must keep asafoetida in an airtight container because its sulphurous odour will affect other foods and spices. It is most commonly available as a powder or granules, and is also sold in lumps that need to be crushed before using. It is a very powerful spice and should therefore be used in minute quantities. Even in its ground state, asafoetida lasts well over a year if stored properly, away from light and air.

Energy 36kcal/149kJ; Fat 2.6g; Saturated fat 0.4g; Carbohydrate 1.8g; Fibre 0g.

Energy 184kcal/771kJ; Fat 9.6g; Saturated fat 1.2g; Carbohydrate 19.2g; Fibre 1g.

Sweet-&-sour Raita

This raita teams honey with mint sauce, chilli and fresh coriander to make a soothing mixture with underlying warmth. It goes well with biryanis.

Serves 4
475ml/16fl oz/2 cups natural
   (plain) low-fat yogurt
5ml/1 tsp salt
5ml/1 tsp sugar
30ml/2 tbsp clear honey
7.5ml/1½ tsp mint sauce
30ml/2 tbsp roughly chopped
   fresh coriander (cilantro)
1 fresh green chilli, seeded and
   finely chopped
1 medium onion, diced
50ml/2fl oz/¼ cup water

1 Pour the yogurt into a bowl and whisk it well. Add the salt, sugar, honey and mint sauce.

2 Taste to check the sweetness and add more honey, if desired.

3 Reserve a little chopped coriander for the garnish and add the rest to the yogurt mixture, with the chilli, onion and water.

4 Whisk once again and pour into a serving bowl. Garnish with the reserved coriander and place in the refrigerator until ready to serve.

Variation
For Spinach Raita, finely chop 225g/8oz cooked spinach. Add to 450ml/¾ pint/scant 2 cups natural (plain) yogurt and mix in 2 chopped green chillies, 1.5ml/¼ tsp sugar, and salt and pepper to taste.

Cook's Tip
A 5–10cm/2–4in piece of peeled, seeded and grated cucumber can also be added to raita. Drain the cucumber in a colander, pressing it against the sides to extract excess liquid, which would dilute the raita.

Energy 128kcal/541kJ; Fat 1.18g; Saturated fat 0.64g; Carbohydrate 24.40g; Fibre 0.53g.

Sweet-&-sour Tomato & Onion Relish

This delicious relish can be served with any savoury meal. Choose vine-ripened tomatoes, if you can, as they have a superior flavour.

Serves 4
2 medium firm tomatoes
1 medium onion
1 fresh green chilli
15ml/1 tbsp fresh mint leaves
15ml/1 tbsp fresh coriander
   (cilantro) leaves
2.5ml/½ tsp Tabasco sauce
15ml/1 tbsp clear honey
2.5ml/½ tsp salt
30ml/2 tbsp lime juice
15ml/1 tbsp natural (plain)
   low-fat yogurt

1 Place the tomatoes in hot water for a few seconds. Lift each tomato out in turn, using a slotted spoon. The skins should have split, making it easy to remove them. Peel off carefully.

2 Cut the tomatoes in half, and squeeze out the seeds. Chop the flesh roughly. Set them aside while you prepare the other ingredients.

3 Using a sharp knife, roughly chop the onion, green chilli, mint and fresh coriander.

4 Place the herb mixture in a food processor with the Tabasco sauce, honey, salt and lime juice. Add the tomatoes to this and grind everything together for a few seconds.

5 Pour into a small serving bowl. Stir in the yogurt just before you serve the relish.

Cook's Tip
This relish will keep for up to 1 week in the refrigerator: prepare up to the end of step 4 but do not add the yogurt until just before you want to serve it.

Energy 43kcal/180kJ; Fat 0.29g; Saturated fat 0.06g; Carbohydrate 9.43g; Fibre 0.96g.

Fresh Coriander Relish

Delicious as an accompaniment to kebabs, samosas and bhajias, this relish can also be used as a spread for cucumber or tomato sandwiches.

Makes about 450g/1lb/ 2 cups

30ml/2 tbsp vegetable oil
1 dried red chilli
1.5ml/¼ tsp each cumin, fennel
    and onion seeds
1.5ml/¼ tsp asafoetida
4 curry leaves
115g/4oz/1⅓ cups desiccated
    (dry unsweetened shredded)
    coconut
10ml/2 tsp sugar
salt
3 fresh green chillies, chopped
175–225g/6–8oz fresh coriander
    (cilantro), chopped
60ml/4 tbsp mint sauce
juice of 3 lemons

1 Heat the oil in a frying pan and add the dried chilli, the cumin, fennel and onion seeds, the asafoetida, curry leaves, desiccated coconut, sugar and salt. Fry, stirring often, until the coconut turns golden brown. Tip into a bowl and leave to cool.

2 Grind the spice mixture with the green chillies, fresh coriander and mint sauce. Moisten with lemon juice. Scrape into a bowl and chill before serving.

> **Cook's Tip**
> This may seem like a lot of coriander, but it is compacted when ground with the spices.

> **Variation**
> For Coriander and Walnut Relish, put 90ml/6 tbsp fresh coriander leaves, 2 garlic cloves, 50g/2oz chopped onion and 60ml/4 tbsp sugar into a food processor and grind until thick. Add 50g/2oz/½ cup chopped walnuts and mix well. Add salt and ground black pepper to taste.

Tomato Relish

This is a simple relish that can be served with most meals. It provides a contrast to hot curries, with its crunchy texture and refreshing ingredients.

Serves 4–6

2 small fresh green chillies
2 limes
2.5ml/½ tsp sugar,
    or to taste
2 onions, finely chopped
4 firm tomatoes, finely chopped
½ cucumber, finely chopped
a few fresh coriander (cilantro)
    leaves, chopped
salt and ground black pepper
a few fresh mint leaves,
    to garnish

1 Using a sharp knife, cut both chillies in half. Scrape out the seeds, then chop the chillies finely and place them in a small bowl.

2 Squeeze the limes. Pour the juice into a glass bowl and add the sugar, with salt and pepper to taste. Set the bowl aside until the sugar and salt have dissolved, stirring the mixture occasionally.

3 Add the chopped chillies to the bowl, with the chopped onions, tomatoes, cucumber, chilli and fresh coriander leaves. Mix well.

4 Cover the bowl with clear film (plastic wrap) and place in the refrigerator for at least 3 hours, so that the flavours blend. Just before serving, taste the relish and add more salt, pepper or sugar if needed. Garnish with mint and serve.

> **Cook's Tip**
> For a milder flavour, use just one chilli, or dispense with the chilli altogether and substitute with a green (bell) pepper.

Energy 51kcal/211kJ; Fat 5.2g; Saturated fat 3.5g; Carbohydrate 0.8g; Fibre 0.9g.

Energy 47kcal/198kJ; Fat 0.5g; Saturated fat 0.1g; Carbohydrate 9.4g; Fibre 2.3g.

Fried Sesame Seed Chutney

This versatile chutney doubles as a dip, and also a sandwich filling with thin slices of cucumber.

Serves 4
175g/6oz/³⁄₄ cup sesame seeds
5ml/1 tsp salt
120–150ml/4–5fl oz/¹⁄₂–²⁄₃ cup water
2 fresh green chillies, seeded and diced
60ml/4 tbsp chopped fresh coriander (cilantro)
15ml/1 tbsp chopped fresh mint
15ml/1 tbsp tamarind paste
30ml/2 tbsp sugar
5ml/1 tsp oil
1.5ml/¹⁄₄ tsp onion seeds
4 curry leaves
onion rings, sliced chillies and fresh coriander leaves, to garnish

1 Dry-roast the sesame seeds by putting them into a pan without adding any oil. Cook over medium to high heat, tossing them occasionally so that they brown evenly all over. Watch them carefully as they will burn if left. Leave the seeds to cool and then grind them in a coffee grinder until they become a grainy powder.

2 Transfer the sesame powder to a bowl. Add the salt, water, diced chillies, coriander, mint, tamarind paste and sugar, and use a fork to mix everything together.

3 Taste and adjust the seasoning, if necessary; the mixture should have a sweet-and-sour flavour. Add a little more tamarind paste if it needs to be more sour, or sugar to sweeten, if required.

4 Heat the oil in a heavy pan and fry the onion seeds and curry leaves together.

5 Tip the sesame seed paste into the pan and stir-fry for about 45 seconds. Transfer the chutney to a serving dish and leave to cool completely.

6 Garnish with onion rings, sliced green and red chillies and fresh coriander leaves and serve with your chosen curry.

Apricot Chutney

Chutneys can add zest to most meals, and in India you will usually find a selection of different kinds served in tiny bowls for people to choose from. Dried apricots are readily available from supermarkets and health food shops.

Makes about 450g/1lb/ 2 cups
450g/1lb/2 cups dried apricots, finely diced
5ml/1 tsp garam masala
275g/10oz/1¹⁄₄ cups soft light brown sugar
450ml/³⁄₄ pint/scant 2 cups malt vinegar
5ml/1 tsp grated fresh root ginger
5ml/1 tsp salt
75g/3oz/¹⁄₂ cup sultanas (golden raisins)
450ml/³⁄₄ pint/scant 2 cups water

1 Put the dried apricots and garam masala into a medium pan and add the light brown sugar, malt vinegar, ginger, salt, sultanas and water. Mix thoroughly with a spoon.

2 Bring to the boil, then reduce the heat and simmer for 30–35 minutes, stirring occasionally.

3 When the chutney has thickened to a fairly stiff consistency, spoon it into 2–3 clean jam jars and leave to cool. This chutney should be stored in the refrigerator.

Variation
For Orchard Fruit Chutney, put 675g/1¹⁄₂lb peeled, cored and chopped cooking apples into a large pan with 115g/4oz/¹⁄₄ cup each dried peaches and apricots and 50g/2oz/scant ¹⁄₂ cup raisins. Chop 5 garlic cloves and grate a 5cm/2in piece of fresh root ginger and add them to the pan. Add 350g/12oz soft light brown sugar, 400ml/14fl oz/1²⁄₃ cups malt vinegar, 10ml/2 tsp salt and 5ml/1 tsp cayenne pepper. Bring the mixture to the boil and simmer for 30 minutes, stirring frequently.

Energy 347kcal/1438kJ; Fat 28.31g; Saturated fat 4.03g; Carbohydrate 25.31g; Fibre 3.63g.

Energy 118kcal/506kJ; Fat 0.2g; Saturated fat 0g; Carbohydrate 29.7g; Fibre 2g.

Fresh Tomato & Onion Chutney

Chutneys are served with most meat dishes in Indian cuisine. This one is lightly spiced and perfect to accompany a heavily spiced meal.

Serves 4
8 tomatoes
1 medium onion, chopped
45ml/3 tbsp light muscovado (brown) sugar
5ml/1 tsp garam masala
5ml/1 tsp ground ginger
175ml/6fl oz/¾ cup malt vinegar
5ml/1 tsp salt
15ml/1 tbsp clear honey
natural (plain) yogurt, sliced green chilli and fresh mint leaves, to garnish

1 Wash the tomatoes and cut them into quarters.

2 Place them with the onion in a heavy pan, and add the sugar, garam masala, ginger, vinegar, salt and honey.

3 Half-cover the pan with a lid and cook over a low heat for about 20 minutes.

4 Mash the tomatoes with a fork to break them up, then continue to cook them on a slightly higher heat until the chutney thickens.

5 Spoon the chutney into a bowl and leave to cool, then cover and place in the refrigerator until needed.

6 Serve chilled, garnished with yogurt, sliced chilli and mint leaves.

Cook's Tips
• *This chutney will keep for about 2 weeks in a covered container in the refrigerator. Add the garnish when ready to serve.*
• *Malt vinegar is generally used for chutneys that require a rich flavour as it has a fuller flavour than white wine vinegar.*
• *The sugar and vinegar give the chutney its flavour as well as its keeping qualities.*

Energy 118kcal/503kJ; Fat 0.66g; Saturated fat 0.18g; Carbohydrate 43.9g; Fibre 2.34g.

Tomato Chutney with Cinnamon & Nigella

This delicious relish is especially suited to lentil dishes. If kept in a covered bowl in the refrigerator, it will keep for a week.

Makes 450–500g/1–1¼lb/ 2–2¼ cups
90ml/6 tbsp vegetable oil
5cm/2in piece cinnamon stick
4 cloves
5ml/1 tsp freshly roasted cumin seeds
5ml/1 tsp nigella seeds
4 bay leaves
5ml/1 tsp mustard seeds, crushed
4 garlic cloves
800g/1¾lb canned, chopped tomatoes
5cm/2in piece fresh root ginger, crushed
5ml/1 tsp chilli powder
5ml/1 tsp ground turmeric
60ml/4 tbsp brown sugar

1 Pour the oil into a frying pan, karahi or wok and place over a medium heat. When the oil is hot, fry the cinnamon, cloves, cumin and nigella seeds, bay leaves and mustard seeds for about 5 minutes.

2 Crush the garlic cloves and add them to the spice mixture. Fry until golden. Meanwhile, drain the tomatoes, reserving the juices.

3 Add the ginger, chilli powder, turmeric, sugar and the reserved tomato juices. Simmer until reduced, add the tomatoes and cook for 15–20 minutes. Cool and serve.

Cook's Tip
Nigella seeds, or kalonji, are frequently used in Indian cooking. They are small black oval-shaped seeds that have a delicate, slightly peppery flavour a little like oregano. They are most often seen sprinkled over naan breads. They have a strong flavour so should be used sparingly in cooking. They add depth to the flavour of this chutney but can be omitted if you are unable to find them.

Energy 53kcal/224kJ; Fat 3.8g; Saturated fat 0.5g; Carbohydrate 4.8g; Fibre 0.4g.

Mint & Coconut Chutney

Makes about 350ml/
12fl oz/1½ cups
50g/2oz fresh mint leaves
90ml/6 tbsp desiccated (dry
unsweetened shredded)
coconut

15ml/1 tbsp sesame seeds
1.5ml/¼ tsp salt
175ml/6fl oz/¾ cup natural
(plain) yogurt

1 Finely chop the fresh mint leaves, using a sharp kitchen knife.

2 Put the mint with the desiccated coconut, sesame seeds, salt and yogurt into a food processor or blender and process until smooth. Transfer the chutney to a sterilized jar, cover and chill until needed.

Tomato & Fresh Chilli Chutney

Makes about 475ml/
16fl oz/2 cups
1 red (bell) pepper
4 tomatoes, chopped
2 fresh green chillies, chopped
1 garlic clove, crushed
1.5ml/¼ tsp salt

2.5ml/½ tsp sugar
5ml/1 tsp chilli powder
45ml/3 tbsp tomato purée
(paste)
15ml/1 tbsp chopped fresh
coriander (cilantro)

1 Halve the red pepper and remove the core and seeds. Roughly chop the red pepper halves.

2 Process the pepper with the tomatoes, chillies, garlic, salt, sugar, chilli powder, tomato purée and coriander with 30ml/ 2 tbsp water in a food processor until smooth. Transfer to a sterilized jar, cover and chill until needed.

> **Cook's Tip**
> *This chutney can be stored in the refrigerator for up to 5 days.*

Mango Chutney

Chutneys are usually served as an accompaniment to curry but this one is particularly nice served in a cheese sandwich or as a dip with poppadums.

Makes 450g/1lb/2 cups
60ml/4 tbsp malt vinegar
2.5ml/½ tsp crushed dried
chillies
6 cloves
6 peppercorns
5ml/1 tsp roasted cumin seeds

2.5ml/½ tsp onion seeds
salt
175g/6oz/scant 1 cup sugar
450g/1lb green (unripe)
mangoes
5cm/2in piece fresh root ginger,
thinly sliced
2 garlic cloves, crushed
thin rind of 1 orange or lemon
(optional)

1 Use a sharp knife to cut two thick slices from either side of the large flat stone (pit) of the mango. Make criss-cross cuts in the flesh on each slice and then turn inside out. The cubes of flesh will stand proud of the skin. Cut these off close to the skin. Cut the remaining flesh from around the stone.

2 Pour the vinegar into a pan, and add the chillies, cloves, peppercorns, cumin and onion seeds, salt and sugar. Place over a low heat and simmer to infuse (steep) the spices in the vinegar – about 15 minutes.

3 Add the mango, ginger, garlic and peel, if using. Simmer until the mango is mushy and most of the vinegar has evaporated. When cool, pour into sterilized bottles. Cover and leave for a few days before serving.

> **Cook's Tip**
> *Fresh root ginger freezes very well, which can be handy if you find it difficult to get fresh ginger locally. It can be sliced or grated straight from the freezer and will thaw on contact with hot food.*

Energy 52kcal/224kJ; Fat 0g; Saturated fat 0g; Carbohydrate 13.7g; Fibre 0.7g.

Top: Energy 753kcal/3117kJ; Fat 66.6g; Saturated fat 50.2g; Carbohydrate 21.7g; Fibre 13.5g.
Above: Energy 187kcal/794kJ; Fat 2.5g; Saturated fat 0.5g; Carbohydrate 33.2g; Fibre 7.5g.

English Pickled Onions

The English love of pickled onions is famous, and at the time of the Raj the popular pickle was introduced into India. They should be stored in a cool, dark place for at least 6 weeks before being eaten.

Makes 3 or 4 450g/1lb jars
1kg/2¼lb pickling onions
115g/4oz/½ cup salt

750ml/1¼ pints/3 cups malt vinegar
15ml/1 tbsp sugar
2 or 3 dried red chillies
5ml/1 tsp brown mustard seeds
15ml/1 tbsp coriander seeds
5ml/1 tsp allspice berries
5ml/1 tsp black peppercorns
5cm/2in piece fresh root ginger, sliced
2 or 3 blades of mace
2 or 3 fresh bay leaves

1 Trim off the root end of each onion, but leave the onion layers attached. Cut a thin slice off the top (neck) end of each onion. Place the onions in a bowl, then cover with boiling water. Leave to stand for about 4 minutes, then drain. Peel off the skin from each onion with a small, sharp knife.

2 Place the peeled onions in a bowl and cover with cold water, then drain the water off and pour it into a large pan. Add the salt and heat slightly to dissolve it, then cool before pouring the brine over the onions. Cover the bowl with a plate and weigh it down slightly so that all the onions are submerged in the brine. Leave the onions to stand in the salted water for 24 hours.

3 Pour the vinegar into a large pan. Wrap all the remaining ingredients, except the bay leaves, in a piece of muslin (cheesecloth) or sew them into a coffee filter paper. Add to the vinegar with the bay leaves. Bring to the boil, simmer for 5 minutes, then remove from the heat. Leave to infuse (steep) overnight.

4 Drain the onions, rinse and pat dry. Pack them into sterilized jars. Add some or all of the spice from the vinegar, but not the ginger slices. The pickle will get hotter if you add the chillies. Pour the vinegar over the onions to cover and add the bay leaves. Cover the jars with non-metallic lids.

Energy 120kcal/500kJ; Fat 0.7g; Saturated fat 0g; Carbohydrate 26.3g; Fibre 4.7g.

Fresh Coconut Chutney with Onion & Chilli

Serve a bowl of this tasty fresh chutney as an accompaniment for any Indian-style main course.

Serves 4–6
200g/7oz fresh coconut, grated
3 or 4 fresh green chillies, seeded and chopped
20g/¾oz fresh coriander (cilantro), chopped, plus 2 or 3 sprigs to garnish
30ml/2 tbsp chopped fresh mint

30–45ml/2–3 tbsp lime juice
about 2.5ml/½ tsp salt
about 2.5ml/½ tsp caster (superfine) sugar
15–30ml/1–2 tbsp coconut milk (optional)
30ml/2 tbsp groundnut (peanut) oil
5ml/1 tsp nigella seeds
1 small onion, very finely chopped

1 Place the coconut, chillies, coriander and mint in a food processor. Add 30ml/2 tbsp of the lime juice, then process until thoroughly chopped.

2 Scrape the mixture into a bowl and add more lime juice to taste. Add salt and sugar to taste. If the mixture is dry, stir in 15–30ml/1–2 tbsp coconut milk.

3 Heat the oil in a small pan and fry the nigella seeds until they begin to pop, then reduce the heat and add the onion. Fry, stirring frequently, for 4–5 minutes, until the onion is soft.

4 Stir the onion mixture into the coconut mixture and leave to cool. Garnish with coriander before serving.

Cook's Tip
Nigella seeds, sometimes called black onion seeds or black cumin, can be found in Asian grocery stores, usually sold under the name kalonji.

Energy 168kcal/693kJ; Fat 17.2g; Saturated fat 11.1g; Carbohydrate 2.4g; Fibre 2.8g.

Red Onion, Garlic & Lemon Relish

This powerful relish is flavoured with spices and punchy preserved lemons. It reached India by way of Spain, being introduced by Jewish refugees forced to leave that country in the 15th century.

Serves 6

45ml/3 tbsp olive oil

3 large red onions, sliced

2 heads of garlic, separated into cloves and peeled

10ml/2 tsp coriander seeds, crushed but not finely ground

10ml/2 tsp light muscovado sugar, plus a little extra

pinch of saffron threads

5cm/2in piece cinnamon stick

2 or 3 small whole dried red chillies (optional)

2 fresh bay leaves

30–45ml/2–3 tbsp sherry vinegar

juice of ½ small orange

30ml/2 tbsp chopped preserved lemon

salt and ground black pepper

1 Heat the oil in a heavy pan. Add the onions and stir, then cover and reduce the heat to the lowest setting. Cook for 10–15 minutes, stirring occasionally, until the onions are soft and pale gold in colour.

2 Add the whole peeled garlic cloves and the crushed coriander seeds. Cover and cook for 5–8 minutes until the garlic is soft.

3 Add a pinch of salt, lots of pepper and the sugar. Stir, then cook, uncovered, for 5 minutes. Soak the saffron in about 45ml/3 tbsp warm water for 5 minutes, then add it to the onions, with the soaking water. Add the cinnamon stick, dried chillies, if using, and bay leaves. Stir in 30ml/2 tbsp of the sherry vinegar and the orange juice.

4 Cook over a low heat, uncovered, until the onions are very soft and most of the liquid has evaporated. Stir in the preserved lemon and cook gently for a further 5 minutes. Taste and adjust the seasoning, adding more salt, sugar and/or vinegar to taste. Serve warm or at room temperature. The relish tastes best if it is left to stand for 24 hours.

Onion, Mango & Peanut Chaat

Chaats are spiced relishes of vegetables and nuts, delicious with many savoury Indian dishes.

Serves 4

90g/3½oz/scant 1 cup unsalted peanuts

15ml/1 tbsp peanut oil

1 onion, chopped

½ cucumber, seeded and diced

1 mango, peeled, stoned (pitted) and diced

1 fresh green chilli, seeded and chopped

30ml/2 tbsp chopped fresh coriander (cilantro)

15ml/1 tbsp chopped fresh mint

15ml/1 tbsp lime juice

pinch of light muscovado (brown) sugar

For the chaat masala

10ml/2 tsp ground toasted cumin seeds

2.5ml/½ tsp cayenne pepper

5ml/1 tsp mango powder (amchur)

2.5ml/½ tsp garam masala

a pinch of ground asafoetida

salt and ground black pepper

1 To make the chaat masala, grind all the spices together, then season with 2.5ml/½ tsp each salt and pepper.

2 Fry the peanuts in the oil until lightly browned, then drain on kitchen paper until cool.

3 Mix the onion, cucumber, mango, chilli, fresh coriander and mint in a bowl. Sprinkle in 5ml/1 tsp of the chaat masala. Stir in the peanuts and then add lime juice and/or sugar to taste. Set the mixture aside for 20–30 minutes for the flavours to mature.

4 Spoon the mixture into a serving bowl, sprinkle another 5ml/1 tsp of the chaat masala over and serve.

> **Cook's Tip**
> Any remaining chaat masala will keep in a sealed jar for 4–6 weeks.

Energy 107kcal/442kJ; Fat 5.8g; Saturated fat 0.8g; Carbohydrate 12g; Fibre 2.2g.

Energy 187kcal/776kJ; Fat 13.3g; Saturated fat 2.5g; Carbohydrate 11.1g; Fibre 2.9g.

Hot Lime Pickle

A good lime pickle is not only delicious served with any meal, but it also increases the appetite and aids digestion.

Makes 450g/1lb/2 cups
25 limes
225g/8oz/1 cup salt
50g/2oz/½ cup fenugreek powder
50g/2oz/½ cup mustard powder
150g/5oz/½ cup chilli powder
15g/½oz/2 tbsp ground turmeric
600ml/1 pint/2½ cups mustard oil
5ml/1 tsp asafoetida
30ml/2 tbsp yellow mustard seeds, crushed

1 Cut each lime into 8 pieces and remove the seeds, if you like. Put the limes in a large sterilized jar or glass bowl.

2 Add the salt and toss with the limes. Cover and leave in a warm place for 1–2 weeks, until they become soft and dull brown in colour.

3 Mix together the fenugreek powder, mustard powder, chilli powder and turmeric, and add to the limes. Cover and leave to rest in a warm place for a further 2 or 3 days.

4 Heat the mustard oil in a frying pan and fry the asafoetida and mustard seeds. When the oil reaches smoking point, pour it over the limes.

5 Mix well, cover with a clean cloth and leave in a warm place for about 1 week before serving or bottling.

Cook's Tips
• You will need to plan far ahead to make this pickle, as it requires at least three weeks to mature at various different stages of preparation before it can be eaten. This long process is essential for the flavours to develop fully, making a strong-tasting traditional pickle.
• To sterilize jars for bottling, boil in water for 10 minutes.

Energy 82kcal/336kJ; Fat 8.9g; Saturated fat 1.1g; Carbohydrate 0g; Fibre 0g.

Green Chilli Pickle

Southern India is the source of some of the hottest curries and pickles. You might imagine that eating them would be a case of going for the burn, but they actually cool the body.

Makes 450–550g/1–1¼lb/ 2–2½ cups
50g/2oz/4 tbsp yellow mustard seeds, crushed
50g/2oz/4 tbsp freshly ground cumin seeds
25g/1oz/¼ cup ground turmeric
50g/2oz garlic cloves, crushed, plus 20 small garlic cloves, peeled but left whole
150ml/¼ pint/⅔ cup white vinegar
75g/3oz/6 tbsp sugar
10ml/2 tsp salt
150ml/¼ pint/⅔ cup mustard oil
450g/1lb small fresh green chillies

1 Mix the mustard and cumin seeds, the turmeric, crushed garlic, vinegar, sugar and salt together in a sterilized glass bowl.

2 Cover with a cloth and leave to rest for 24 hours. This enables the spices to infuse and the sugar and salt to melt.

3 Heat the mustard oil in a frying pan and gently fry the spice mixture for about 5 minutes. (Keep a window open while cooking with mustard oil as it is pungent and the smoke may irritate the eyes.)

4 Add the whole, peeled garlic cloves and fry for a further 5 minutes.

5 Halve each fresh green chilli, washing your hands carefully afterwards. Add the chillies and cook gently until tender but still green in colour. This will take about 30 minutes over low heat.

6 Cool thoroughly, then pour into sterilized jars, ensuring that the oil is evenly distributed if you are using more than one jar. Leave to rest for a week before serving.

Energy 54kcal/226kJ; Fat 5.7g; Saturated fat 0.6g; Carbohydrate 0.1g; Fibre 0g.

Bombay Duck Pickle

Boil (or bombil) is the name of a fish that is found off the west coast of India during the monsoon season. It is salted and dried in the sun and is characterized by a distinctive strong smell. How this fish acquired the name Bombay duck in the Western world is unknown. Bombay duck can be served hot or cold, and is usually eaten with Indian breads and vegetable dishes.

Serves 4–6

6–8 pieces boil (Bombay duck)
60ml/4 tbsp vegetable oil
2 fresh red chillies, chopped
15ml/1 tbsp sugar
450g/1lb cherry tomatoes, halved
115g/4oz deep-fried onions
red onion rings, to garnish (optional)

1 Soak the fish in water for 5 minutes and then pat it dry using kitchen paper.

2 Heat the oil in a frying pan and fry the fish pieces for about 30–45 seconds on both sides until crisp. Be careful not to burn them or they will taste bitter. Drain well.

3 Transfer the drained fish pieces to a plate and leave to cool, and then break them into small pieces.

4 Cook the remaining ingredients until the tomatoes become pulpy and the onions are blended into a sauce. Fold in the Bombay duck and mix well.

5 Leave to cool, then garnish and serve. Alternatively, ladle into a hot sterilized jar, cover and leave to cool.

> **Cook's Tip**
> *As an alternative to boil, try using skinned mackerel fillets, but don't fry them. You will need only 30ml/2 tbsp vegetable oil to make the sauce.*

Energy 233kcal/973kJ; Fat 15.3g; Saturated fat 1.8g; Carbohydrate 11.5g; Fibre 2g.

Sweet-&-sour Pineapple

This may sound like a Chinese recipe, but it is a traditional Bengali dish known as *tok*. The predominant flavour is ginger, and the pieces of golden pineapple, dotted with plump, juicy raisins, have plenty of visual appeal with taste to match. It is equally delicious if made with mangoes instead of the pineapple.

2.5ml/½ tsp cumin seeds
2.5ml/½ tsp onion seeds
10ml/2 tsp grated fresh root ginger
5ml/1 tsp crushed dried chillies
50g/2oz/⅓ cup seedless raisins
115g/4oz/½ cup sugar
7.5ml/1½ tsp salt

Serves 4

800g/1¾lb canned pineapple rings or chunks in natural juice
15ml/1 tbsp vegetable oil
2.5ml/½ tsp black mustard seeds

1 Drain the pineapple in a colander and reserve the juice. Chop the pineapple rings or chunks finely (you should have approximately 500g/1¼lb).

2 Heat the vegetable oil in a karahi, wok or large pan over a medium heat and immediately add the mustard seeds. As soon as they pop, add the cumin seeds, then the onion seeds. Add the ginger and chillies, and stir-fry the spices briskly for 30 seconds until they release their flavours.

3 Add the pineapple, raisins, sugar and salt. Add 300ml/½ pint/1¼ cups of the juice (made up with cold water if necessary) and stir into the pineapple mixture.

4 Bring the mixture to the boil, reduce the heat to medium and cook, uncovered, for 20–25 minutes.

Energy 264kcal/1124kJ; Fat 3.2g; Saturated fat 0.3g; Carbohydrate 61.5g; Fibre 2.7g.

BREADS

Naan

Probably the most popular bread enjoyed with an Indian curry is naan, which was introduced from Persia. In Persian, the word "naan" means bread. Traditionally, naan is not rolled, but patted and stretched until the teardrop shape is achieved. You can, of course, roll it out to a circle, then gently pull the lower end, which will give you the traditional shape.

Makes 3

225g/8oz/2 cups unbleached
  strong white bread flour
2.5ml/½ tsp salt
15g/½oz fresh yeast
60ml/4 tbsp lukewarm milk
15ml/1 tbsp vegetable oil
30ml/2 tbsp natural (plain)
  yogurt
1 egg
30–45ml/2–3 tbsp melted ghee
  or butter, for brushing

1 Sift the flour and salt together into a large bowl. In a smaller bowl, cream the yeast with the milk. Set aside for 15 minutes. Add the yeast and milk mixture, vegetable oil, yogurt and egg to the flour. Combine the mixture using your hands until it forms a soft dough. Add a little more of the lukewarm water if the dough is too dry.

2 Turn the dough out on to a lightly floured surface and knead for about 10 minutes, or until it feels smooth. Return the dough to the bowl, cover and leave in a warm place for about 1 hour, or until it has doubled in size. Preheat the oven to its highest setting – it should not be any lower than 230°C/450°F/Gas 8.

3 Turn out the dough back on to the floured surface and knead for a further 2 minutes. Divide into three equal pieces, shape into balls and roll out into teardrop shapes 25cm/10in long, 13cm/5in wide and 5mm–8mm/¼–⅓in thick.

4 Preheat the grill (broiler) to its highest setting. Meanwhile, place the naan on preheated baking sheets and bake for 3–4 minutes, or until puffed up. Remove from the oven and place under the hot grill for a few seconds until the tops brown slightly. Brush with ghee or butter and serve warm.

Garlic & Coriander Naan

Traditionally cooked in a very hot clay oven known as a tandoor, naan are usually eaten with dry meat or vegetable dishes.

Makes 3

275g/10oz/2½ cups unbleached
  strong white bread flour
5ml/1 tsp salt

5ml/1 tsp dried yeast
60ml/4 tbsp natural (plain) yogurt
15ml/1 tbsp melted butter or
  ghee, plus 30–45ml/2–3 tbsp
  for brushing
1 garlic clove, finely chopped
5ml/1 tsp black onion seeds
15ml/1 tbsp fresh coriander
  (cilantro)
10ml/2 tsp clear honey

1 Sift the flour and salt together into a large bowl. In a smaller bowl, cream the yeast with the yogurt. Set aside for 15 minutes. Add the yeast mixture to the flour with the smaller quantity of melted butter or ghee, and add the chopped garlic, black onion seeds and chopped coriander, mixing to a soft dough.

2 Tip out the dough on to a lightly floured surface and knead for about 10 minutes until smooth and elastic. Place in a lightly oiled bowl, cover with lightly oiled clear film (plastic wrap) and leave to rise in a warm place for 45 minutes, or until the dough has doubled in bulk.

3 Preheat the oven to 230°C/450°F/Gas 8. Place three heavy baking sheets in the oven to heat. Turn the dough out on to a lightly floured surface and knock back (punch down). Divide into three equal pieces and shape each into a ball.

4 Cover two of the balls of dough with oiled clear film and roll out the third into a teardrop shape about 25cm/10in long, 13cm/5in wide and about 5mm–8mm/¼–⅓in thick. Preheat the grill (broiler) to its highest setting. Place the single naan on the hot baking sheets and bake for 3–4 minutes, or until puffy.

5 Remove the naan from the oven and place under the hot grill for a few seconds or until browned slightly. Wrap in a dish towel to keep warm while you roll out and cook the remaining naan. Brush with melted butter or ghee and serve warm.

Energy 197kcal/830kJ; Fat 8.2g; Saturated fat 5g; Carbohydrate 29.2g; Fibre 1.2g.

Energy 326kcal/1378kJ; Fat 6.8g; Saturated fat 1.3g; Carbohydrate 59.7g; Fibre 2.3g.

Chapatis

A chapati is an unleavened bread made from chapati flour, a ground wholemeal flour known as *atta*, which is finer than the Western equivalent. An equal quantity of standard wholemeal flour and plain flour will also produce satisfactory results, although chapati flour is available from Indian grocers. This is the everyday bread of the Indian home.

Makes 8–10
225g/8oz/2 cups chapati flour or wholemeal (whole-wheat) flour
2.5ml/½ tsp salt
175ml/6fl oz/¾ cup water

1 Sift the flour and salt into a mixing bowl. Make a well in the centre and gradually stir in the water, mixing well with your fingers.

2 Form a supple dough and knead for 7–10 minutes. Ideally, cover with clear film (plastic wrap) and leave to one side for 15–20 minutes to rest.

3 Divide the dough into 8–10 equal portions. Roll out each piece to a circle on a well-floured surface.

4 Place a tava (chapati griddle) or heavy frying pan over a high heat. When steam rises from it, lower the heat to medium and add the first chapati to the pan.

5 When the chapati begins to bubble, turn it over. Press down with a clean dish towel or a flat spoon and turn once again.

6 Remove the cooked chapati from the pan and keep warm in a piece of foil lined with kitchen paper while you cook the other chapatis.

7 Repeat the process until all the breads are cooked. Serve hot.

Spiced Naan

Another excellent recipe for naan bread, this time with fennel seeds, onion seeds and cumin seeds.

Makes 6
450g/1lb/4 cups strong white bread flour
5ml/1 tsp baking powder
2.5ml/½ tsp salt
1 sachet easy-blend (rapid-rise) dried yeast
5ml/1 tsp caster (superfine) sugar
5ml/1 tsp fennel seeds
10ml/2 tsp onion seeds
5ml/1 tsp cumin seeds
150ml/¼ pint/⅔ cup hand-hot milk
30ml/2 tbsp oil, plus extra for brushing
150ml/¼ pint/⅔ cup natural (plain) yogurt
1 egg, beaten

1 Sift the flour, baking powder and salt into a mixing bowl. Stir in the yeast, sugar, fennel seeds, onion seeds and cumin seeds. Make a well in the centre. Stir the hand-hot milk into the flour mixture, then add the oil, yogurt and beaten egg. Mix to form a ball of dough.

2 Tip the dough out on to a lightly floured surface and knead it for 10 minutes until smooth. Return to the clean, lightly oiled bowl and roll the dough to coat it with oil. Cover the bowl with clear film (plastic wrap) and set aside in a warm place until the dough has doubled in bulk.

3 Put a heavy baking sheet in the oven and preheat the oven to 240°C/475°F/Gas 9. Also preheat the grill (broiler). Knead the dough again lightly and divide it into six pieces. Keep five pieces covered while working with the sixth. Quickly roll the piece of dough out to a teardrop shape, brush lightly with oil and slap the naan on to the hot baking sheet. Repeat with the remaining dough.

4 Bake the naan in the oven for 3 minutes until puffed up, then place the baking sheets under the grill for about 30 seconds or until the naan are lightly browned. Serve hot or warm as an accompaniment to an Indian curry.

Energy 294kcal/1248kJ; Fat 2.6g; Saturated fat 0.8g; Carbohydrate 61.3g; Fibre 2.3g.

Energy 96kcal/408kJ; Fat 0.4g; Saturated fat 0.1g; Carbohydrate 21.9g; Fibre 0.9g.

Red Lentil Pancakes

This is a type of *dosa*, which is essentially a pancake from southern India, but used in the similar fashion to north Indian bread.

Makes 6
150g/5oz/¾ cup long grain rice
50g/2oz/¼ cup red lentils
250ml/8fl oz/1 cup warm water

5ml/1 tsp salt
2.5ml/½ tsp ground
 turmeric
2.5ml/½ tsp ground black
 pepper
30ml/2 tbsp chopped fresh
 coriander (cilantro)
oil, for frying and drizzling

1 Place the rice and lentils in a large bowl, cover with the warm water, cover and soak for at least 8 hours or overnight.

2 Drain off the water and reserve. Place the rice and lentils in a food processor and blend until smooth. Blend in the reserved water. Scrape into a bowl, cover with clear film (plastic wrap) and leave in a warm place to ferment for about 24 hours.

3 Stir in the salt, turmeric, pepper and coriander. Heat a heavy frying pan over a medium heat for a few minutes until hot. Smear with oil and add about 30–45ml/2–3 tbsp batter.

4 Using the rounded base of a soup spoon, gently spread the batter out, using a circular motion, to make a pancake that is about 15cm/6in in diameter.

5 Cook in the pan for 1½–2 minutes, or until set. Drizzle a little oil over the pancake and around the edges. Turn over and cook for about 1 minute, or until golden brown. Keep the cooked pancakes warm in a low oven or on a plate over simmering water while cooking the remaining pancakes. Serve warm.

> **Variation**
> *Add 60ml/4 tbsp grated coconut to the batter just before cooking for a richer flavour.*

Energy 190kcal/798kJ; Fat 8.5g; Saturated fat 1.1g; Carbohydrate 26.1g; Fibre 0.5g.

Parathas

Making a paratha is similar to making flaky pastry. The difference lies in the handling of the dough; this can be handled freely, unlike that for a flaky pastry.

50g/2oz/½ cup plain
 (all-purpose) flour
5ml/1 tsp salt
40g/1½oz/3 tbsp ghee or
 unsalted (sweet) butter
water, to mix

Makes 12–15
350g/12oz/3 cups chapati flour
 or an equal quantity of
 wholemeal (whole-wheat) flour
 and plain (all-purpose) flour,
 plus 50g/2oz/½ cup for dusting

1 Sift the flours and salt into a bowl. Make a well in the centre and add 10ml/2 tsp melted ghee or butter. Fold it into the flour to make a crumbly texture.

2 Gradually add water to make a soft, pliable dough. Knead until smooth. Cover and leave to rest for 30 minutes.

3 Melt the remaining ghee or butter over a low heat. Divide the dough into 12–15 equal portions and keep covered. Take one portion at a time and roll out on a lightly floured surface to about 10cm/4in in diameter.

4 Brush the dough with a little of the melted ghee or sweet butter and sprinkle with flour.

5 With a sharp knife, make a straight cut from the centre to the edge of the dough, then lift a cut edge and roll the dough into a cone shape. Lift it and flatten it again into a ball. Roll the dough out again on a lightly floured surface until it is 18cm/7in wide.

6 Heat a griddle and cook one paratha at a time, placing a little of the remaining ghee along the edges. Cook on each side until golden brown. Serve hot.

Energy 123kcal/521kJ; Fat 2.8g; Saturated fat 1.4g; Carbohydrate 21.9g; Fibre 2.8g.

Missi Rotis

This is a speciality from the Punjab. Gram flour, also known as besan, is used instead of the usual chapati flour. In the Punjab, *missi rotis* are very popular with a glass of lassi, a refreshing yogurt drink.

Makes 4
115g/4oz/1 cup gram flour
115g/4oz/1 cup wholemeal
    (whole-wheat) flour
1 fresh green chilli, seeded
    and chopped
1/2 onion, finely chopped
15ml/1 tbsp chopped fresh
    coriander (cilantro)
2.5ml/1/2 tsp ground
    turmeric
2.5ml/1/2 tsp salt
15ml/1 tbsp vegetable oil
120–150ml/4–5fl oz/1/2–2/3 cup
    lukewarm water
30–45ml/2–3 tbsp melted
    unsalted (sweet) ghee or butter

1 Mix the two types of flour, the chilli, onion, coriander, turmeric and salt together in a large bowl. Stir in the oil.

2 Mix in sufficient water to make a pliable soft dough. Transfer the dough on to a lightly floured surface and knead until smooth.

3 Place the dough in a lightly oiled bowl, cover with lightly oiled clear film (plastic wrap) and leave to rest for 30 minutes.

4 Place the dough on to a lightly floured surface. Divide into four equal pieces and shape into balls in the palms of your hands. Roll out each ball into a thick round about 15–18cm/ 6–7in in diameter.

5 Heat a griddle or heavy frying pan over a medium heat for a few minutes until hot.

6 Brush both sides of one roti with a little melted ghee or butter. Add it to the griddle or frying pan and cook for about 2 minutes, turning after 1 minute. Brush the cooked roti lightly with melted ghee or butter again, slide it on to a plate and keep warm in a low oven while cooking the remaining rotis in the same way. Serve the rotis warm.

Energy 226kcal/958kJ; Fat 3.5g; Saturated fat 0.5g; Carbohydrate 45.9g; Fibre 2g.

Tandoori Rotis

Roti means bread and is the most common food eaten in central and northern India. *Tandoori roti* is traditionally baked in a tandoor, or clay oven, but it can also be made successfully in an electric or gas oven at the highest setting.

5ml/1 tsp salt
250ml/8fl oz/1 cup water
30–45ml/2–3 tbsp melted ghee
    or unsalted (sweet) butter

Makes 6
350g/12oz/3 cups chapati
    flour or wholemeal
    (whole-wheat) flour

1 Sift the flour and salt into a large mixing bowl. Add the water and mix to a soft, pliable dough.

2 Knead on a lightly floured surface for 3–4 minutes until smooth. Place the dough in a lightly oiled bowl, cover with lightly oiled clear film (plastic wrap) and leave to rest for about 1 hour.

3 Tip out the dough on to a lightly floured surface. Divide the dough into six pieces and shape each into a ball. Press out into a larger round with the palm of your hand, cover with lightly oiled clear film and leave to rest for about 10 minutes.

4 Meanwhile, preheat the oven to 230°C/450°F/Gas 8. Place three baking sheets in the oven to heat. Roll the rotis into 15cm/ 6in rounds, place two on each baking sheet and bake for 8–10 minutes. Brush with melted ghee or butter and serve warm.

> **Cook's Tip**
> *Chapati flour, known as* atta, *is a fine wholemeal flour used in Indian breads.*

Energy 181kcal/769kJ; Fat 1.3g; Saturated fat 0.2g; Carbohydrate 37.3g; Fibre 5.3g.

Bhaturas

These leavened and deep-fried breads are from the Punjab, where the local people enjoy them with a bowl of spicy chickpea curry. The combination has become a classic over the years and is known as *choley bhature*. Bhaturas must be eaten hot and cannot be reheated.

Makes 10

15g/½oz fresh yeast
5ml/1 tsp sugar
120ml/4fl oz/½ cup lukewarm water
200g/7oz/1¾ cups strong white bread flour
50g/2oz/⅓ cup semolina
2.5ml/½ tsp salt
15g/½oz/1 tbsp ghee or butter
30ml/2 tbsp natural (plain) yogurt
oil, for frying

1 Mix the yeast with the sugar and water in a jug (pitcher).

2 Sift the flour into a large bowl and stir in the semolina and salt. Rub in the butter or ghee.

3 Add the yeast mixture and yogurt, and mix to a dough. Turn out on to a lightly floured surface and knead for 10 minutes, or until smooth and elastic.

4 Place the dough in an oiled bowl, cover with oiled clear film (plastic wrap) and leave to rise in a warm place for about 1 hour, or until doubled in bulk.

5 Turn the dough out on to a lightly floured surface and knock back (punch down). Divide into ten equal pieces and shape each into a ball. Flatten into discs with the palm of your hand. Roll out on a lightly floured surface into 13cm/5in rounds.

6 Pour oil to a depth of 1cm/½in into a deep frying pan. Heat, and slide one bhatura into the oil. Fry for about 1 minute, turning over after 30 seconds.

7 Drain the bhatura well on kitchen paper. Keep each bhatura warm in a low oven while frying the remaining bhaturas. Serve immediately, while hot.

Pooris

These delicious little deep-fried breads, shaped into discs, make it temptingly easy to overindulge. In most areas, they are made of wholemeal flour, but in the east and north-east of India, they are made from plain refined flour, and are known as *loochis*.

Makes 12

115g/4oz/1 cup unbleached plain (all-purpose) flour
115g/4oz/1 cup wholemeal (whole-wheat) flour
2.5ml/½ tsp salt
2.5ml/½ tsp chilli powder
30ml/2 tbsp vegetable oil
100–120ml/3½–4fl oz/7–8 tbsp water
oil, for frying

1 Sift the flours, salt and chilli powder, if using, into a large mixing bowl. Add the vegetable oil then add sufficient water to mix to a dough.

2 Tip the dough out on to a lightly floured surface and knead for 8–10 minutes until smooth.

3 Place in an oiled bowl and cover with oiled clear film (plastic wrap). Leave for 30 minutes.

4 Place the dough on the floured surface. Divide into 12 pieces. Keeping the rest of the dough covered, roll one piece into a 13cm/5in round. Repeat with the remaining dough. Stack the pooris, layered between clear film, to keep them moist.

5 Pour the oil for frying to a depth of 2.5cm/1in in a deep frying pan and heat it to 180°C/350°F. Using a metal spatula, lift one poori and slide it into the oil; it will sink but then return to the surface and begin to sizzle. Gently press the poori into the oil. It will puff up. Turn the poori over after a few seconds and allow it to cook for a further 20–30 seconds.

6 Remove the poori from the pan and pat dry with kitchen paper. Place the cooked poori on a large baking tray and keep warm in a low oven while you cook the remaining pooris. Serve warm.

Energy 144kcal/605kJ; Fat 6.6g; Saturated fat 1.4g; Carbohydrate 19.7g; Fibre 0.7g.

Energy 79kcal/333kJ; Fat 2.2g; Saturated fat 0.3g; Carbohydrate 13.6g; Fibre 1.2g.

Ensaimadas

These sweet bread rolls are a popular snack and can be served with various different fillings.

Makes 10–12

30ml/2 tbsp caster (superfine) sugar, plus extra for sprinkling
150ml/¼ pint/⅔ cup warm water
15ml/1 tbsp active dried yeast
450g/1lb/4 cups strong white bread flour
5ml/1 tsp salt
115g/4oz/½ cup butter, softened, plus 30ml/2 tbsp melted butter for the filling
4 egg yolks
90–120ml/6–8 tbsp warm milk
115g/4oz/1 cup grated Cheddar cheese (or similar well-flavoured hard cheese)

1 Dissolve 5ml/1 tsp of the sugar in the warm water, then sprinkle in the dried yeast. Stir, then set aside for 10 minutes or until frothy. Sift the flour and salt into a large bowl.

2 Cream the softened butter with the remaining sugar in a large bowl. When it is fluffy, beat in the egg yolks and a little of the sifted flour. Gradually stir in the remaining flour with the yeast mixture and enough milk to form a soft but not sticky dough. Transfer to an oiled plastic bag. Close the bag loosely, leaving plenty of room for the dough to rise. Leave in a warm place for about 1 hour, until the dough doubles in bulk.

3 On a lightly floured surface, knock back (punch down) the dough, then roll it out into a large rectangle. Brush the surface with half the melted butter, sprinkle with the cheese, then roll up from a long side like a Swiss (jelly) roll. Knead the dough thoroughly, then divide into 10–12 pieces.

4 Roll each piece of dough into a thin rope, 38cm/15in long. On greased baking sheets, coil each rope into a loose spiral. Leave to rise for about 45 minutes or until doubled in size. Preheat the oven to 220°C/425°F/Gas 7. Bake the ensaimadas for 15–20 minutes, until golden. Remove from the oven, then brush with the remaining melted butter and sprinkle with caster sugar. Serve warm.

Sugar Bread Rolls

These delicious sweet rolls make an unusual end to a meal.

Makes 10

350g/12oz/3 cups strong white bread flour
5ml/1 tsp salt
15ml/1 tbsp caster (superfine) sugar
5ml/1 tsp dried yeast
150ml/¼ pint/⅔ cup hand-hot water
3 egg yolks
50g/2oz/¼ cup unsalted (sweet) butter, softened, plus 25g/1oz/ 2 tbsp extra
75g/3oz Cheddar cheese or Monterey Jack, grated
50g/2oz/¼ cup sugar

1 Sift the flour, salt and caster sugar into a food processor fitted with a dough blade or the bowl of an electric mixer fitted with a dough hook. Make a well in the centre. Dissolve the yeast in the hand-hot water and pour into the well. Add the egg yolks and leave for a few minutes until bubbles appear on the surface of the liquid.

2 Mix the ingredients for 30–45 seconds to form a firm dough. Add the softened butter and knead for 2–3 minutes in a food processor, or for 4–5 minutes with an electric mixer, until smooth. Transfer the dough out to a floured bowl, cover and leave in a warm place to rise until doubled in bulk.

3 Transfer the dough to a lightly floured surface and divide it into 10 pieces. Spread the grated cheese over the surface. Roll each of the dough pieces into a 13cm/5in length, incorporating the cheese as you do so. Coil into snail shapes and place on a lightly greased high-sided tray measuring 30 × 20cm/12 × 8in.

4 Cover the rolls with clear film (plastic wrap) and leave in a warm place for 45 minutes or until doubled in bulk.

5 Preheat the oven to 190°C/375°F/Gas 5 and then bake the rolls for 20–25 minutes. Melt the remaining butter, brush it over the rolls, sprinkle with the sugar and allow to cool. Separate the rolls before serving.

Energy 327kcal/1372kJ; Fat 16.2g; Saturated fat 9.3g; Carbohydrate 38.6g; Fibre 1.4g.

Energy 235kcal/986kJ; Fat 9.5g; Saturated fat 5.9g; Carbohydrate 33.7g; Fibre 1.1g.

Pears in Spiced Wine

Familiar Indian spices, infused in a red wine syrup, give pears a lovely warm flavour. The colour is beautiful, too.

Serves 4
1 bottle full-bodied red wine
1 cinnamon stick
4 cloves
2.5ml/ ½ tsp freshly grated
  nutmeg
2.5ml/ ½ tsp ground
  ginger
8 peppercorns
175g/6oz/scant 1 cup
  caster (superfine) sugar
thinly pared rind of ½ orange
thinly pared rind of ½ lemon
8 firm ripe pears

1 Pour the wine into a heavy pan into which the pears will fit snugly when standing upright.

2 Stir the cinnamon stick, cloves, nutmeg, ginger, peppercorns, caster sugar and citrus rinds into the wine.

3 Peel the pears, leaving the stalks intact, and stand them in the pan. The wine should only just cover the pears.

4 Bring the liquid to the boil, lower the heat, cover and simmer very gently for 30 minutes, or until the pears are tender. Using a slotted spoon, transfer the pears to a bowl.

5 Boil the poaching liquid until it has reduced by half and is thick and syrupy.

6 Strain the syrup over and around the pears and serve the dessert hot or cold.

> **Cook's Tip**
> Serve the pears with a mascarpone cream, made by combining equal quantities of mascarpone cheese and double (heavy) cream, and adding a little vanilla extract for flavour. They also taste good with yogurt or ice cream.

Melon & Strawberry Salad

A beautiful and colourful fruit salad, this is suitable to serve as a refreshing appetizer or to round off a rich and spicy meal. Don't be tempted to chill the salad; it tastes best at room temperature.

Serves 4
1 Galia or Ogen melon
1 honeydew melon or other
  melon of your choice
  (see Cook's Tip)
½ watermelon
225g/8oz/2 cups
  strawberries
15ml/1 tbsp lemon juice
15ml/1 tbsp clear honey
15ml/1 tbsp chopped
  fresh mint

1 Prepare the melons by cutting them in half and discarding the seeds by scraping them out with a spoon.

2 Use a melon baller to scoop out the flesh into balls or a knife to cut it into cubes. Place these in a fruit bowl.

3 Rinse and take the stems off the strawberries, twisting them so that they remove the hull at the same time. If the hull remains inside, use a fine, sharp knife to cut it out. Cut the fruit in half and add them to the bowl.

4 Mix together the lemon juice and honey and add 15ml/ 1 tbsp water to make this easier to pour over the fruit. Mix into the fruit gently.

5 Sprinkle the chopped mint over the top of the fruit and serve.

> **Cook's Tip**
> Use whichever melons are available: replace Galia or Ogen with cantaloupe melon, or replace watermelon with charentais, for example. Try to choose three melons with a variation in colour for an attractive effect.

Energy 191kcal/806kJ; Fat 0.3g; Saturated fat 0g; Carbohydrate 43.1g; Fibre 6.6g.

Energy 114kcal/482kJ; Fat 0.7g; Saturated fat 0g; Carbohydrate 26.5g; Fibre 1.6g.

Citrus Fruit Salad

This is a very appetizing and refreshing salad, with a typically Indian combination of citrus fruits seasoned with salt and pepper. It will provide the perfect ending to a heavy meal.

Serves 6

2 navel oranges
I honeydew melon
1/2 watermelon
I fresh mango
I15g/4oz seedless green and
   black grapes

225g/8oz canned mandarin
   segments, drained
225g/8oz canned grapefruit
   segments, drained
juice of I lemon
salt and ground black pepper
2.5ml/1/2 tsp sugar
1.5ml/1/4 tsp freshly ground
   cumin seeds

I Using a sharp knife, cut a thin slice of peel and pith from each end of an orange. Place cut side down on a plate and cut off the peel and pith in strips. Remove any remaining pith. Cut out each segment leaving the membrane behind. Squeeze the remaining juice from the membrane. Repeat with the other orange.

2 Cut the honeydew melon in half and scrape out the seeds using a spoon. Remove the seeds from the watermelon in the same way. Use a melon baller to scoop out the flesh into balls or a knife to cut it into cubes.

3 Using a sharp knife take two thick slices from either side of the large flat stone (pit) of the mango without peeling the fruit. Make slices into the flesh and then turn the skin inside out. The slices of flesh will stand proud of the skin and can be easily cut off.

4 Place all the fruit in a large serving bowl and add the lemon juice. Toss gently to prevent damaging the fruit.

5 Mix together the remaining ingredients and sprinkle over the fruit. Gently toss, chill thoroughly and serve.

Energy 167kcal/710kJ; Fat 0.8g; Saturated fat 0.2g; Carbohydrate 39.5g; Fibre 3.1g.

Spiced Fruit Salad

Exotic fruits are becoming commonplace in supermarkets these days and it is fun to experiment with the different varieties. Look out in particular for physalis, star fruit, papaya and passion fruit.

Serves 4–6

75g/3oz/6 tbsp sugar
300ml/1/2 pint/1 1/4 cups
   water
30ml/2 tbsp syrup from a jar
   of preserved stem ginger

2 pieces star anise
2.5cm/1in cinnamon
   stick
I clove
juice of 1/2 lemon
2 fresh mint sprigs
I mango
2 bananas, sliced
8 fresh or drained canned
   lychees
225g/8oz/2 cups strawberries,
   hulled and halved
2 pieces preserved stem ginger,
   cut into sticks
I medium pineapple

I Put the sugar, water, ginger syrup, star anise, cinnamon, clove, lemon juice and mint into a pan. Bring to the boil, then simmer for 3 minutes. Strain into a bowl and set aside to cool.

2 Remove the top and bottom from the mango and cut off the outer skin. Stand the mango on one end and remove the flesh in two pieces either side of the flat stone (pit). Slice evenly.

3 Add the mango slices to the syrup with the bananas, lychees, strawberries and stem ginger. Mix in well, making sure the fruits are well coated in the sugary liquid.

4 Cut the pineapple in half by slicing down the centre, using a very sharp knife. Loosen the flesh with a smaller, serrated knife, and remove the flesh by cutting around the rim and scooping it out. The pineapple halves will resemble two boat shapes. Do not discard the pineapple flesh, but cut it into chunks and add to the fruity syrup.

5 Spoon some of the fruit salad into the pineapple halves and serve on a large dish. There will be sufficient fruit salad in the bowl to refill the pineapple halves at least once.

Energy 110kcal/468kJ; Fat 0.3g; Saturated fat 0.1g; Carbohydrate 27.1g; Fibre 2.4g.

Mangoes with Sticky Rice

Sticky rice is just as good in desserts as in savoury dishes, and mangoes, with their delicate fragrance and velvety flesh, complement it especially well. You need to start preparing this dish the day before you intend to serve it.

Serves 4
175ml/6fl oz/ ¾ cup thick
   coconut milk
115g/4oz/ ⅔ cup white
   glutinous rice
45ml/3 tbsp sugar
pinch of salt
2 ripe mangoes
strips of pared lime rind, to decorate

1 Pour the coconut milk into a bowl and leave to stand until the cream rises to the top.

2 Rinse the glutinous rice thoroughly in several changes of cold water until it runs clear, then leave to soak overnight in a bowl of fresh cold water.

3 Drain the rice well and spread it out evenly in a steamer lined with muslin (cheesecloth). Cover and steam over a double boiler or a pan of simmering water for about 20 minutes, or until the rice is tender.

4 Reserve 45ml/3 tbsp of the cream from the top of the coconut milk. Pour the remainder into a pan and add the sugar and salt. Heat, stirring constantly, until the sugar has dissolved, then bring to the boil. Remove the pan from the heat, pour the coconut milk into a bowl and leave to cool.

5 Tip the cooked rice into a bowl and pour over the cooled coconut milk mixture. Stir well, then leave the rice mixture to stand for 10–15 minutes.

6 Meanwhile, peel the mangoes, cut the flesh away from the central stones (pits) and cut into slices.

7 Spoon the rice on to individual serving plates. Arrange the mango slices on one side, then drizzle with the reserved coconut cream. Decorate with strips of lime rind and serve.

Energy 200kcal/846kJ; Fat 0.8g; Saturated fat 0.2g; Carbohydrate 46g; Fibre 2g.

Papayas in Jasmine Flower Syrup

The fragrant flower syrup can be prepared in advance, using fresh jasmine flowers from a houseplant or the garden. It tastes fabulous with papayas, but it is also good with all sorts of desserts. Try it with ice cream or spooned over lychees or mangoes.

Serves 2
105ml/7 tbsp water
45ml/3 tbsp palm sugar or
   light muscovado (brown)
   sugar
20–30 jasmine flowers, plus
   a few extra to decorate
   (optional)
2 ripe papayas
juice of 1 lime

1 Place the water and sugar in a small pan. Heat gently, stirring occasionally, until the sugar has dissolved, then simmer, without stirring, over a low heat for 4 minutes.

2 Pour into a bowl, leave to cool slightly, then add the jasmine flowers. Leave to infuse (steep) for at least 20 minutes.

3 Peel the papayas and slice in half lengthways. Scoop out and discard the seeds. Place the papayas on serving plates and squeeze over the lime.

4 Strain the syrup into a clean bowl, discarding the flowers. Spoon the syrup over the papayas. If you like, decorate with a few fresh jasmine flowers.

Variation
Slices of mango would work well in this recipe in place of papayas.

Cook's Tip
Although scented white jasmine flowers are perfectly safe to eat, it is important to be sure that they have not been sprayed with pesticides or other harmful chemicals. Washing them may not remove all the residue.

Energy 233kcal/990kJ; Fat 0.4g; Saturated fat 0g; Carbohydrate 58.7g; Fibre 8.8g.

Mango & Coconut Stir-fry

Choose a ripe mango for this recipe. If you buy one that is a little underripe, leave it in a warm place for a day or two before using.

Serves 4

¼ coconut
1 large, ripe mango
juice and finely grated rind
     of 2 limes
15ml/1 tbsp sunflower oil
15g/½oz/1 tbsp butter
30ml/2 tbsp clear honey
crème fraîche or ice cream,
     to serve

1 Prepare the coconut if necessary. Drain the milk and remove the flesh. Peel with a vegetable peeler so that it forms flakes.

2 Peel the mango. Cut the stone (pit) out of the middle of the fruit. Cut each half of the mango into slices. Place the mango slices in a bowl and pour over the lime juice and rind. Set aside.

3 Meanwhile heat a karahi or wok, then add 10ml/2 tsp of the oil. When the oil is hot, add the butter. Once the butter has melted, stir in the coconut flakes and stir-fry for 1–2 minutes until the coconut is golden brown. Remove and drain on kitchen paper. Wipe out the pan. Strain the mango slices, reserving the juice.

4 Heat the pan again and add the remaining oil. When the oil is hot, add the mango and stir-fry for 1–2 minutes, then add the juice and leave to bubble and reduce for 1 minute.

5 Stir in the honey. When it has dissolved, spoon the mango and its juices into one large serving bowl or individual dishes. Sprinkle on the stir-fried coconut flakes and serve with crème fraîche or ice cream.

> **Variation**
> *Nectarine or peach slices can be used instead of the mango.*

Kheer

Both Muslim and Hindu communities prepare kheer, which is traditionally served in mosques and temples.

Serves 4–6

15g/½oz/1 tbsp ghee
5cm/2in piece cinnamon stick
175g/6oz/¾ cup soft
     brown sugar
115g/4oz/1 cup coarsely
     ground rice
1.2 litres/2 pints/5 cups
     full cream (whole) milk
5ml/1 tsp ground cardamom
50g/2oz/⅓ cup sultanas
     (golden raisins)
25g/1oz/¼ cup flaked
     (sliced) almonds
2.5ml/½ tsp freshly grated
     nutmeg, to serve

1 In a heavy pan, melt the ghee and fry the cinnamon stick and soft brown sugar. Watch carefully while frying and when the sugar begins to caramelize reduce the heat immediately, or remove the pan from the heat, as sugar can burn very quickly.

2 Return the pan to the heat and add the rice and half the milk. Bring to the boil, stirring constantly to avoid the milk boiling over. Reduce the heat and simmer until the rice is cooked, stirring regularly.

3 Stir in the remaining milk, with the ground cardamom, sultanas and almonds. Leave to simmer until the mixture thickens, stirring constantly to prevent the kheer from sticking to the base of the pan, about 1½ hours.

4 When the mixture is thick and creamy, spoon it into a serving dish or individual dishes. Serve the kheer hot or cold, sprinkled with the freshly grated nutmeg. Decorate with tinfoil, if you like.

> **Cook's Tip**
> *Kheer is traditionally cooked twice: once until the rice grains disintegrate and then with the spices and flavourings. This recipe uses ground rice and so it will take less time to cook.*

Energy 357kcal/1478kJ; Fat 32.7g; Saturated fat 24.1g; Carbohydrate 13.8g; Fibre 7g.

Energy 588kcal/2463kJ; Fat 20.6g; Saturated fat 11.1g; Carbohydrate 90.6g; Fibre 0.7g.

Ground Rice Pudding

This delicious and light ground rice pudding is the perfect end to a spicy meal. It can be served either hot or cold.

Serves 4–6

50g/2oz/½ cup coarsely
 ground rice
4 green cardamom pods, crushed
900ml/1½ pints/3¾ cups
 semi-skimmed (low-fat) milk
90ml/6 tbsp sugar
15ml/1 tbsp rose water
15ml/1 tbsp crushed pistachio
 nuts, to garnish

1 Place the ground rice in a pan with the cardamom pods.

2 Add 600ml/1 pint/2½ cups of the milk and bring to the boil over a medium heat, stirring occasionally.

3 Add the remaining milk and stir over a medium heat for about 10 minutes, or until the rice mixture thickens to the consistency of a creamy chicken soup.

4 Stir in the sugar and rose water and continue to cook for a further 2 minutes.

5 Garnish with the pistachio nuts and serve.

Variation
For an even richer version of this pudding, you could add 40g/1½oz ground almonds to the rice at step 1.

Cook's Tip
Rose water is a distillation of scented rose petals which has the intense fragrance and flavour of roses. It is a popular flavouring in Indian cooking. Use it cautiously, adding just enough to suit your taste.

Black Rice Pudding

This unusual rice pudding, flavoured with fresh root ginger, is quite delicious. When cooked, black rice still retains its husk and has a nutty texture. Serve in small bowls, with a little coconut milk or cream poured over each helping.

1cm/½in piece fresh root
 ginger, bruised
50g/2oz/¼ cup soft dark
 brown sugar
50g/2oz/¼ cup sugar
300ml/½ pint/1¼ cups coconut
 milk or cream, to serve

Serves 6

115g/4oz/generous ½ cup black
 glutinous rice
475ml/16fl oz/2 cups water

1 Put the black glutinous rice in a sieve (strainer) and rinse well under cold running water.

2 Drain and put in a large pan, with the water. Bring to the boil and stir to prevent the rice from settling on the base of the pan. Cover and cook for about 30 minutes.

3 Add the ginger and both the brown and white sugar.

4 Cook for a further 15 minutes, adding a little more water if necessary, until the rice is cooked and porridge-like.

5 Remove the ginger and serve warm, in bowls, topped with coconut milk or cream.

Cook's Tip
Although black glutinous rice looks similar to wild rice, which is the seed of a rush plant, it is in fact a true rice. It has a particularly nutty flavour that is ideal for puddings and cakes. Long cooking makes the pudding thick and creamy, as the rice is naturally sticky.

Energy 260kcal/1102kJ; Fat 5.8g; Saturated fat 2.53g; Carbohydrate 46g; Fibre 0.3g.

Energy 146kcal/616kJ; Fat 0.5g; Saturated fat 0.1g; Carbohydrate 34.2g; Fibre 0g.

Baked Rice Pudding

Black glutinous rice, also known as black sticky rice, has long dark grains and a nutty taste reminiscent of wild rice. This baked pudding has a distinct character and flavour all of its own, as well as an intriguing appearance.

Serves 4–6

175g/6oz/scant 1 cup white or black glutinous rice
30ml/2 tbsp soft light brown sugar
475ml/16fl oz/2 cups coconut milk
250ml/8fl oz/1 cup water
3 eggs
30ml/2 tbsp sugar

1 Combine the glutinous rice and brown sugar in a pan. Pour in half the coconut milk and the water.

2 Bring to the boil, reduce the heat to low and simmer, stirring occasionally, for 15–20 minutes, or until the rice has absorbed most of the liquid. Preheat the oven to 150°C/300°F/Gas 2.

3 Spoon the rice mixture into a single, large ovenproof dish or divide it among individual ramekins. Beat the eggs with the remaining coconut milk and sugar in a bowl.

4 Strain the egg mixture into a jug (pitcher), then pour it evenly over the par-cooked rice in the dish or ramekins.

5 Place the dish or individual ramekins in a roasting pan. Carefully pour in enough hot water to come halfway up the sides of the dish or ramekins.

6 Cover with foil and bake for about 35–60 minutes, or until the custard has set. Serve warm or cold.

> **Cook's Tip**
> *Throughout South-east Asia, black glutinous rice is usually used for sweet dishes, whereas its white counterpart is more often used in savoury recipes.*

Traditional Indian Vermicelli

Indian vermicelli, made from wheat, is much finer than Italian vermicelli and has a good texture in desserts. It is available from Asian stores.

15ml/1 tbsp flaked (sliced) almonds
15ml/1 tbsp chopped pistachio nuts
15ml/1 tbsp sugar

Serves 4

115g/4oz/1 cup Indian vermicelli
1.2 litres/2 pints/5 cups water
2.5ml/½ tsp saffron threads
15ml/1 tbsp sugar
60ml/4 tbsp low-fat fromage frais or Greek (US strained plain) yogurt, to serve

To decorate

15ml/1 tbsp shredded fresh or desiccated (dry unsweetened shredded) coconut

1 Crush the vermicelli in your hands and place it in a pan. Pour in the water, add the saffron and bring to the boil. Boil for about 5 minutes.

2 Stir in the sugar and continue cooking until the water has evaporated. Press through a sieve (strainer), if necessary, to remove any excess liquid.

3 Place the vermicelli in a serving dish and decorate with the coconut, almonds, pistachio nuts and sugar. Serve with fromage frais or yogurt.

> **Cook's Tip**
> *You can use a variety of fruits instead of nuts to garnish this dessert. Try a few soft fruits such as blackberries, raspberries or strawberries, or add some chopped dried apricots or sultanas.*

Energy 298kcal/1252kJ; Fat 5.2g; Saturated fat 1.4g; Carbohydrate 54.3g; Fibre 0g.

Energy 196kcal/822kJ; Fat 6.6g; Saturated fat 2.27g; Carbohydrate 31.8g; Fibre 0.8g.

Kulfi with Cardamom

The delicious, traditional Indian ice cream, kulfi, is always made with sweetened full cream milk and is a lovely refreshing way to end an Indian meal. Making kulfi is easy if you use yogurt pots or dariole moulds.

Serves 6
2 litres/3 ½ pints/9 cups creamy milk
12 cardamoms
175g/6oz/scant 1 cup caster (superfine) sugar
25g/1oz/¼ cup blanched almonds, chopped
toasted flaked (sliced) almonds and cardamoms, to decorate

1 Place the milk and cardamom pods in a large, heavy pan. Bring to the boil then simmer vigorously until reduced by one-third.

2 Strain the milk into a bowl, discarding the cardamoms, then stir in the caster sugar and chopped almonds until the sugar is dissolved. Leave to cool.

3 Pour the mixture into a freezerproof container, cover and freeze until almost firm, stirring every 30 minutes.

4 When almost solid, pack the ice cream into six kulfi moulds or clean yogurt pots. Return to the freezer until required, removing the pots about 10 minutes before serving and turning out the individual ices. Decorate with toasted almonds and cardamoms before serving.

Variation
Rose water is also a traditional flavouring for kulfi. Add 15ml/ 1 tbsp to the recipe, if you like.

Cook's Tip
Use a large pan for reducing the milk as there needs to be plenty of room for it to bubble up.

Energy 401kcal/1686kJ; Fat 19.3g; Saturated fat 11.2g; Carbohydrate 46.8g; Fibre 0.3g.

Leche Flan

Serve this delicious dessert hot or cold with whipped cream or crème fraîche.

Serves 8
5 large eggs
30ml/2 tbsp caster (superfine) sugar
few drops vanilla extract
400g/14oz can evaporated (unsweetened condensed) milk

300ml/½ pint/1¼ cups milk
5ml/1 tsp finely grated lime rind
strips of lime rind, to decorate

For the caramel
225g/8oz/generous 1 cup sugar
120ml/4fl oz/½ cup water

1 To make the caramel, put the sugar and water in a heavy pan. Stir to dissolve the sugar, then boil without stirring until the caramel is golden.

2 Quickly pour into eight individual ramekins, rotating them to coat the sides. Leave to one side to set.

3 Preheat the oven to 150°C/300°F/Gas 2. Beat the eggs, sugar and vanilla extract in a bowl.

4 Mix the evaporated milk and fresh milk in a pan. Heat to just below boiling point, then pour on to the egg mixture, stirring all the time. Strain the custard mixture into a jug (pitcher) and add the grated lime rind. Leave the custard to cool. Pour into the caramel-coated ramekins.

5 Place the ramekins in a roasting pan and pour in enough warm water to come halfway up the sides of the dishes.

6 Transfer the roasting pan to the oven and cook the custards for 35–45 minutes or until just set. They will just shimmer when the ramekins are gently shaken.

7 Serve the custards in their ramekin dishes. Alternatively, invert them on to serving plates. Break up the caramel into smaller pieces and use to decorate the custards. The custards can be served warm or cold, decorated with strips of lime rind.

Energy 229kcal/967kJ; Fat 6.2g; Saturated fat 2.7g; Carbohydrate 36.4g; Fibre 0g.

Tapioca Pudding

This pudding, made from large pearl tapioca and coconut milk and served warm, is much lighter than the Western-style version. You can adjust the sweetness to your taste. Serve with lychees, or you could try the smaller, similar-tasting logans.

Serves 4

115g/4oz/⅔ cup tapioca
475ml/16fl oz/2 cups water
175g/6oz/¾ cup sugar
pinch of salt
250ml/8fl oz/1 cup coconut milk
250g/9oz prepared tropical
   fruits
finely shredded rind of 1 lime,
   to decorate

1 Soak the tapioca in warm water for 1 hour so that the grains swell. Drain.

2 Put the measured water in a pan and bring to the boil. Stir in the sugar and salt.

3 Add the tapioca and coconut milk and simmer for 10 minutes or until the tapioca turns transparent.

4 Serve warm with some tropical fruits and decorate with the finely shredded lime rind.

Cook's Tip
Sliced kiwi fruits, mangoes and strawberries would make a bright and tasty selection to serve with this pudding. Or you could try sliced bananas, nectarines and raspberries.

Variation
Serve this tapioca pudding with a refreshing peach salad for a change. Peel, stone (pit) and very thinly slice 8 peaches and put them in a serving bowl. Add 30ml/2 tbsp rose water, 20ml/ 4 tsp sugar, the juice of 1 lemon and 50ml/2fl oz/¼ cup freshly squeezed orange juice. Chill well before serving.

Energy 327kcal/1388kJ; Fat 0.6g; Saturated fat 0.2g; Carbohydrate 80.6g; Fibre 2.2g.

Steamed Custard in Nectarines

Steaming nectarines or peaches brings out their natural colour and sweetness, so this is a good way of making the most of underripe or less flavourful fruit.

Serves 4–6

6 nectarines
1 large (US extra large) egg
45ml/3 tbsp palm sugar or light
   muscovado (brown) sugar
30ml/2 tbsp coconut milk

1 Cut the nectarines in half. Using a teaspoon, scoop out the stones (pits) and a little of the surrounding flesh.

2 Lightly beat the egg, then add the sugar and the coconut milk. Beat until the sugar has dissolved.

3 Transfer the nectarines to a steamer and carefully fill the cavities three-quarters full with the custard mixture. Steam over a pan of simmering water for 5–10 minutes.

4 Remove from the heat and leave to cool completely before transferring to plates and serving.

Variations
• This recipe would also work well with peaches or pears. The pears might need a little longer to cook.
• A soft berry coulis would make a delicious accompaniment to the nectarines. Cook 350g/12oz/2 cups raspberries in a pan with 30ml/2 tbsp sugar and 15ml/1 tbsp water for about 10 minutes, or until the juices run. Press the raspberries through a fine sieve (strainer) to remove the seeds. Put a spoonful of coulis on to each plate beside the nectarines.

Cook's Tip
Palm sugar, also known as jaggery, is made from the sap of certain Asian palm trees, such as coconut and palmyrah. If you buy it as a cake or large lump, grate it before use.

Energy 154kcal/658kJ; Fat 1.6g; Saturated fat 0.4g; Carbohydrate 32.4g; Fibre 2.7g.

Caramel Custard with Fresh Fruit

A creamy caramel dessert is a wonderful way to end a meal. It is light and delicious, and this recipe is very simple to make. Fresh fruit is the perfect accompaniment.

Serves 6

30ml/2 tbsp sugar
30ml/2 tbsp water

For the custard

6 eggs
4 drops vanilla extract
115g/4oz/generous ½ cup sugar
*750ml/1¼ pints/3 cups
    semi-skimmed (low-fat) milk*
*fresh fruit, such as strawberries,
    blueberries, orange and
    banana slices, and raspberries,
    to serve*

1 To make the caramel, place the sugar and water in a heavy pan and heat until the sugar has dissolved and the mixture is bubbling and pale gold in colour. Watch the sugar carefully, as it can quickly burn once it begins to caramelize. Pour carefully into a 1.2 litre/2 pint/5 cup soufflé dish. Leave the caramel to cool.

2 Preheat the oven to 180°C/350°F/Gas 4. To make the custard, break the eggs into a medium mixing bowl and whisk until frothy.

3 Stir the vanilla extract into the whisked eggs and gradually add the sugar. Add the milk in a steady stream, whisking constantly.

4 Pour the custard over the top of the caramel.

5 Cook the custard in the oven for 35–40 minutes. Remove from the oven and leave to cool for 30 minutes or until the mixture is set.

6 Loosen the custard from the sides of the dish with a knife. Place a serving dish upside-down on top of the soufflé dish and invert, giving a gentle shake if necessary to turn out the custard on to the serving dish.

7 Arrange any fresh fruit of your choice around the custard on the serving dish and serve immediately.

Energy 194kcal/823kJ; Fat 4.7g; Saturated fat 2.01g; Carbohydrate 32.9g; Fibre 0g.

Coconut Cream Diamonds

Although commercially ground rice can be used for this dish, grinding jasmine rice yourself – in a food processor – gives a much better result.

Serves 4–6

*75g/3oz/scant ½ cup jasmine
    rice, soaked overnight in
    175ml/6fl oz/¾ cup water*
*350ml/12fl oz/1½ cups
    coconut milk*
*150ml/¼ pint/⅔ cup single
    (light) cream*

*50g/2oz/¼ cup caster
    (superfine) sugar*
*raspberries and fresh mint leaves,
    to decorate*

For the coulis

*75g/3oz/¾ cup blackcurrants,
    stalks removed*
*30ml/2 tbsp caster
    (superfine) sugar*
*75g/3oz/½ cup fresh or
    frozen raspberries*

1 Put the rice and its soaking water into a food processor and process for a few minutes until the mixture is soupy. Heat the coconut milk and cream in a non-stick pan. When the mixture is on the point of boiling, stir in the rice mixture. Cook over a very gentle heat for 10 minutes, stirring constantly.

2 Stir the sugar into the coconut rice mixture and continue cooking for a further 10–15 minutes, or until the mixture is thick and creamy. Line a rectangular tin (pan) with baking parchment. Pour the coconut rice mixture into the pan, cool, then chill until the dessert is set and firm.

3 To make the coulis, put the blackcurrants in a bowl and sprinkle with the sugar. Set aside for 30 minutes. Transfer the blackcurrants and raspberries to a sieve (strainer) over a bowl. Using a spoon, press the fruit against the sieve so that the juices collect in the bowl. Taste the coulis and add more sugar if necessary.

4 Cut the coconut cream into diamonds. Spoon a little of the coulis on to each plate, arrange the diamonds on top and decorate with the raspberries and mint leaves.

Energy 248kcal/1043kJ; Fat 7.8g; Saturated fat 4.8g; Carbohydrate 42.2g; Fibre 1.2g.

Mango Sorbet with Sauce

After a heavy meal, this delightful sorbet makes a very refreshing dessert. Mango is said to be one of the oldest fruits cultivated in India, having been presented by Lord Shiva to his beautiful wife, Parvathi.

Serves 4–6
900g/2lb mango pulp
2.5ml/¹/₂ tsp lemon juice
grated rind of 1 orange and
  1 lemon

4 egg whites
50g/2oz/¹/₄ cup caster
  (superfine) sugar
120ml/4fl oz/¹/₂ cup double
  (heavy) cream
50g/2oz/¹/₂ cup icing
  (confectioners') sugar

1 In a large, chilled bowl, mix half of the mango pulp with the lemon juice and the grated rind.

2 Whisk the egg whites until peaks form, then gently fold them into the mango mixture, with the caster sugar. Cover with clear film (plastic wrap) and place in the freezer for at least 1 hour.

3 Remove from the freezer and beat again. Transfer to an ice cream container, and freeze until fully set.

4 In a bowl, whip the double cream with the icing sugar and the remaining mango pulp. Cover and chill the sauce for 24 hours.

5 Remove the sorbet 10 minutes before serving. Scoop out individual servings and cover with a generous helping of mango sauce. Serve immediately.

> ### Variation
> *Try this sorbet made with full-flavoured locally grown strawberries when in season for a delicious change.*

Energy 387kcal/1631kJ; Fat 16.6g; Saturated fat 10.3g; Carbohydrate 58.4g; Fibre 5.9g.

Indian Ice Cream

Kulfi-wallahs (ice-cream vendors) have always made kulfi, and continue to this day, without using modern freezers. Kulfi is packed into metal cones sealed with dough and then churned in clay pots until set. Try this method – it works extremely well in an ordinary freezer.

350g/12oz/3 cups icing
  (confectioners') sugar
5ml/1 tsp ground cardamom
15ml/1 tbsp rose water
175g/6oz/1¹/₂ cups pistachio
  nuts, chopped
75g/3oz/¹/₂ cup sultanas
  (golden raisins)
75g/3oz/³/₄ cup flaked
  (sliced) almonds
25g/1oz/3 tbsp glacé (candied)
  cherries, halved

Serves 4–6
3 × 400ml/14fl oz cans
  evaporated (unsweetened
  condensed) milk
3 egg whites

1 Remove the labels from the cans of evaporated milk and lay the cans down in a pan with a tight-fitting cover. Fill the pan with water to reach three-quarters up the cans. Bring to the boil, cover and simmer for 20 minutes. (Don't leave the cans of evaporated milk unattended. Top up the water if necessary; the pan must never boil dry.) When cool, remove the cans and chill in the refrigerator for 24 hours. Chill a large bowl too.

2 Whisk the egg whites in another large bowl until peaks form. Open the cans and empty the milk into the chilled bowl. Whisk until doubled in quantity, then fold in the whisked egg whites and icing sugar.

3 Gently fold in the remaining ingredients, cover the bowl with clear film (plastic wrap) and place in the freezer for 1 hour.

4 Remove the ice cream from the freezer and mix well with a fork. Transfer to a serving container and return to the freezer for a final setting. Remove from the freezer 10 minutes before serving.

Energy 1123kcal/4722kJ; Fat 47.3g; Saturated fat 10.3g; Carbohydrate 144.2g; Fibre 5.1g.

Watermelon Ice

After a hot and spicy meal, the only thing more refreshing than ice-cold watermelon is this cooling watermelon ice. Making it is simplicity itself.

4 kaffir lime leaves, torn into small pieces
500g/1lb watermelon

Serves 4–6
90ml/6 tbsp caster (superfine) sugar
105ml/7 tbsp water

1 Put the caster sugar, water and kaffir lime leaves in a pan. Heat gently until the sugar has dissolved. Pour into a large bowl and set aside to cool.

2 Cut the watermelon into wedges with a large knife. Cut the flesh from the rind, remove the seeds and chop the flesh.

3 Spoon the watermelon into a food processor. Process to a slush, then mix with the sugar syrup. Chill the mixture in the refrigerator for 3–4 hours.

4 Strain the mixture into a freezerproof container. Freeze for 2 hours, then remove from the freezer and beat with a fork to break up the ice crystals. Return the mixture to the freezer and freeze for 3 hours more, beating the mixture at half-hourly intervals. Freeze until firm.

5 Alternatively, use an ice-cream maker. Pour the chilled mixture into the machine and churn until it is firm enough to scoop. Serve immediately, or scrape into a freezerproof container and store in the freezer.

6 About 30 minutes before serving, transfer the watermelon ice to the refrigerator so that it softens slightly. This allows the full flavour of the watermelon to be apparent and makes the ice easier to scoop.

Spiced Lassi

Lassi, or buttermilk, is prepared by churning yogurt with water and then removing the fat. To make this refreshing drink without churning, use low-fat natural yogurt instead.

300ml/½ pint/1¼ cups water
2.5cm/1in piece fresh root ginger, finely crushed
2 fresh green chillies, finely chopped
2.5ml/½ tsp ground cumin salt and ground black pepper
a few fresh coriander (cilantro) leaves, chopped, to garnish

Serves 4
450ml/¾ pint/scant 2 cups natural (plain) yogurt

1 In a bowl, whisk the yogurt and water until well blended. The consistency should be that of full cream (whole) milk. Adjust by adding more water if necessary.

2 Add the ginger, chillies and ground cumin.

3 Season with the salt and black pepper, and mix well.

4 Pour into four serving glasses and chill. Garnish with chopped coriander before serving.

Cook's Tip
Lassi is often drunk with hot and spicy curries as it refreshes the palate well.

Variation
If you prefer an unspiced and cooler version, try Rose Water Lassi. Blend 300ml/½ pint/1¼ cups natural yogurt with 60ml/ 4 tbsp caster sugar, 400ml/14fl oz/1⅔ cups water and 15ml/ 1 tbsp rose water in a food processor or blender. Pour into individual glasses or a jug (pitcher) and add fresh mint leaves to decorate, if you like.

Energy 128kcal/545kJ; Fat 0.4g; Saturated fat 0.1g; Carbohydrate 32.4g; Fibre 0.1g.

Energy 63kcal/266kJ; Fat 1.1g; Saturated fat 0.6g; Carbohydrate 8.5g; Fibre 0g.

Pistachio Lassi

In India, lassi is not only made at home, but is also sold at roadside cafés, restaurants and hotels. There is no substitute for this drink, especially on a hot day. It is particularly good served with curries and similar hot dishes as it helps the body to digest spicy food.

Serves 4

300ml/½ pint/1¼ cups natural (plain) low-fat yogurt
5ml/1 tsp sugar, or to taste
300ml/½ pint/1¼ cups water
30ml/2 tbsp puréed fruit (optional)
15ml/1 tbsp crushed pistachio nuts, to decorate

1 Place the natural yogurt in a jug (pitcher) and whisk until frothy. Add the sugar.

2 Pour in the measured water and the puréed fruit, if using, and continue to whisk for 2 minutes.

3 Taste for sweetness and adjust as necessary. Pour the lassi into four serving glasses and serve chilled, decorated with crushed pistachio nuts.

> **Cook's Tips**
> • Refreshing, cooling drinks are the perfect accompaniment to spicy Indian dishes.
> • A variety of fruit juices are often served as well as water flavoured with freshly squeezed limes or lemons and sweetened with sugar. Fresh fragrant mint is usually used to decorate and flavour the drinks.

> **Variation**
> To make a simple savoury lassi, omit the sugar and fruit and add lemon juice, ground cumin and salt. Garnish with fresh mint leaves.

Tea & Fruit Punch

This delicious punch can be served hot or cold. White wine or brandy may be added to taste.

Makes 4

600ml/1 pint/2½ cups water
1 cinnamon stick
4 cloves
12.5ml/2½ tsp Earl Grey tea leaves
175g/6oz/scant 1 cup sugar
450ml/¾ pint/scant 2 cups tropical soft drink concentrate
1 lemon, sliced
1 small orange, sliced
½ cucumber, sliced

1 Bring the water to the boil in a pan with the cinnamon stick and cloves. Remove from the heat and add the tea leaves. Leave to brew for about 5 minutes. Stir and strain into a large bowl and chill in the refrigerator for 2–3 hours.

2 Add the sugar and the soft drink concentrate and allow to rest until the sugar has dissolved and the mixture cooled. Place the fruit and cucumber in a chilled punch bowl and pour over the tea mix. Chill for a further 24 hours before serving.

Almond Sherbet

Traditionally, this drink was always made in the month of Ramadan to break the Muslim fast. It should be served chilled.

Serves 4

50g/2oz/½ cup ground almonds
600ml/1 pint/2½ cups semi-skimmed (low-fat) milk
10ml/2 tsp sugar, or to taste

1 Put the ground almonds into a serving jug (pitcher).

2 Pour in the semi-skimmed milk and add the sugar; stir to mix.

3 Taste for sweetness and adjust as necessary. Serve very cold in long glasses. Chilling the glasses first helps to keep the drink cold and adds a sense of occasion.

Energy 70kcal/296kJ; Fat 2.6g; Saturated fat 0.63g; Carbohydrate 7.5g; Fibre 0g.

Top: Energy 1108kcal/4737kJ; Fat 0g; Saturated fat 0g; Carbohydrate 294.5g; Fibre 0g;
Above: Energy 155kcal/651kJ; Fat 9.4g; Saturated fat 2.04g; Carbohydrate 11g; Fibre 0.9g.

Index